FINE LINES: Summer 2019
Volume 28 Issue 2

Copyright © 2018, Fine Lines, Inc.
PO Box 241713
Omaha, NE 68124
www.finelines.org

ISBN: 978-1-09-349244-6

Fine Lines, Inc. is a 501 (c) 3 non-profit corporation.
EID: 47-0832351
All donations are tax-deductible.

Cover photo "Blades" by Tracy Ahrens, from her *Within* series. To learn more, visit tracyahrens.weebly.com.

Fine Lines logo designed by Kristy Stark Knapp, Knapp Studios
Book and cover design by Michael Campbell, MC Writing Services

Fine Lines

~ Summer 2019 ~

VOLUME 28 ISSUE 2

Edited by

David Martin

CONTENTS

F I N E   L I N E S

ABOUT FINE LINES

Fine Lines is published by Fine Lines, Inc., a 501 (c) 3 non-profit corporation. David Martin is the managing editor. In this quarterly publication, we share poetry and prose by writers of all ages in an attempt to add clarity and passion to our lives. Support is provided through donations, all of which are tax deductible. Join us in creating the lives we desire through the written word.

Composition is hard work. We celebrate its rewards in each issue. Share this publication with others who love creativity. We encourage authors and artists of all ages. Our national mailing list reaches every state. Increased literacy and effective, creative communication is critical for all.

Fine Lines editors believe writing of life's experiences brings order to chaos, beauty to existence, and celebration to the mysterious.

DONATIONS

Contributions are tax deductible. When you support *Fine Lines,* we send e-letters with *Fine Lines* news, upcoming events, the inside scoop on special issues, and provide copies to students who have no means to buy this publication. You will add to their literacy, too.

We offer two methods of payment for your *Fine Lines* donations:

- U.S. residents should make checks payable to *Fine Lines*. Please include your name, address, and email with your donation, and send to:

Fine Lines
PO Box 241713
Omaha, NE 68124

- We also accept credit card payments via PayPal.

SUBMISSIONS

- We accept submissions via email, file attachments, CDs formatted in MS Word for PCs, and laser-printed hard copies.
- Editors reply when writing is accepted for publication, and if a stamped, self-addressed envelope or email address is provided.
- Submissions must not include overt abuse, sexuality, profanity, drugs, alcohol, or violence.
- Do not send "class projects." Teachers may copy *Fine Lines* issues for their classes and submit student work for publication when they act as members and sponsors.
- Address changes and correspondence should be sent to the *Fine Lines* email address: fine-lines@cox.net

We encourage readers to respond to the ideas expressed by our authors. Letters to the editor may be printed in future issues after editing for length and clarity. Reader feedback is important to us. We support writers and artists with hope and direction. Write on.

Write On!

And those who were seen dancing
were thought to be insane
by those who could not
hear the music.

FRIEDRICH NIETZSCHE

DEDICATION

On the Joy of Writing on a Summer Afternoon

Something sighs contentedly. Perhaps it's
I, or else a pixie living in a tribe beneath
the shrubbery. Nothing weighs on me.
I feel so light that I'm surprised to find
myself still sitting on my rag of quilt upon
the grass instead of simply rising, chasing
birds, or playing tag with bees. But I am
earthen still, and glad of it, delighted to
be wrapped in humid air; it moves
sufficiently to cool my skin and curl my
hair. The ground is warm, a comfort, womb
of seed and tiny creature curled in sleep,
awaiting dusk.

— *Mary Campbell*

Fine Lines Word Cloud
Image by Anne Obradovich

WRITERS WRITE ANY
WAY THEY CAN

By no means am I a perfect writer, and I am nowhere near the quality that others have achieved. It is my will and drive that propels me through the rough patches and keeps me composed in times of chaos. My writing, no matter the subject or length, is symbolic of my personality, and within each sentence I produce, my soul is invested, entirely. However uncontrollable or unorthodox a soul may be, each one is singular. We cannot plagiarize a soul. In real life and my writing alike, if you want to know me, read my soul.

— Hunter Rud

"Ask questions from your heart, and you will be answered from the heart."

OMAHA TRIBE PROVERB

Justice

TESSA A. ADAMS

"And the day came when the risk to remain tight in a bud
was more painful than the risk it took to blossom."

UNKNOWN

LAINEY

Lainey loved to look at the river from above. On her runs, she took time to stop on the dock overlooking the sandbars and breathe in its thick, mossy scent. The power in its current taunted her, and if she was honest, terrified her. Her mother warned Lainey at a young age to never touch the river. "Don't even go close to the shoreline, Lainey. Even on the rocks, the river can whisk you away before you know it." When she was little, her mother's warning scared her enough to keep her on the octagon-shaped dock, but now, at the age of 17, in this small town where she knew she'd spend her foreseeable future, she invited thoughts of being swept away by the current. It had to be better than standing still.

She backed away from the edge and stretched her arms down to touch her running shoes. She acknowledged with gratitude the pull of her hamstrings and enjoyed this brief moment of pause. She pulled her long and lean body back up and tightened her high ponytail as she gazed out to the current one more time. Even tied up, her long, blonde hair touched the middle of her back. She turned her blue eyes from the river and glanced at her watch. Shoot. It was 4:25; she was late.

Lainey took off down the gravel road toward her small, three bedroom house in Justice, Nebraska. As she ran, she looked to the left away from the river. She noticed how the sunlight rested on the corn field. The wave of each stalk forced the other in the same direction. The dance they did for each other was breathtaking. Nature's choreography was unmatched, and the beauty in the belly of the country was something Lainey couldn't deny.

Some time ago, Nebraska had been deemed "fly over country," but if one took a second to come down and breathe in the fresh, natural air, feel the warm July breeze, and accept the embrace of nature, he or she could see what Lainey did. Nebraska, a blank canvas, gave permission for redefinition, for beginnings. For endings. Lainey knew this. Even in her short 17 years, she was thankful for the way these fields and hills raised her. However, lately, Nebraska felt as if it were closing in on her.

Lainey knew she had to be home by 4:30 in order to get there before her mother arrived. Lainey's summer responsibilities weren't all that different from those she maintained during the school year. Her mother worked two jobs to support them, and Lainey served as a young co-parent to 9-year-olds Madox and Zoey ever since her father set her family aside for Jack and Jim Beam. If she pushed herself, she could make it from the river to her house in under five minutes. She set the timer on her watch, smiled at the new physical challenge she had given herself, and picked up her pace. As she ran, she thought about how far her family had come since her father had walked out and since Mads was diagnosed.

As she felt the gravel beneath her shoes, Lainey thought with admiration about the connection Mads and Zoey had; they were twins, but their differences kept them together. Zoey was feisty, so feisty she spent weekly quality time in the "cool down" room. Justice Public was small, and Lainey swore the district created the room just for Zoey. She led with her fists rather than her head, and when it came to Mads, it seemed like she'd never stop swinging.

Madox was a little taller than Zoey. He had been diagnosed with Asperger's. He was incredibly intelligent, but life could put him into fits if certain conditions weren't just right, in his eyes. Their father left them because a child with special needs didn't fit into his plan. It was why Zoey had been in three fights this year, and why Lainey's future didn't go beyond the walls of Justice.

Madox had different triggers that would set him off. One of Madox's triggers was odd numbers. Their family had started calling him Mads when he was born, but it stuck because their dad named him Madox with one "D" instead of two like the rest of the Maddoxes in the world. Nothing set him off like his name or their father. When he got upset or would not be able to even something out, he would chant, "Madox five letters for Madox. Madox. Five letters should be six." "Madox. Five letters for Madox. Madox. Five letters should be six."

Lainey and her mother found out later that this chant happened to occur on the playground where all of the kids joined in. That was one of the many gifts their dad left them: the misspelling of his only son's name. If this ever happened, Lainey or Zoey would get as close to him as he would allow and remind him, "Mads has four, count one, two, three, and four. Mads has four." Then the rocking would start to get calm, the screams would begin to dissipate, and he would quietly work his Scrabble tiles Lainey had given him for stimulation. He made words as fast as he could with the small tiles, scramble up the letters, and then make another word. The special education teachers called it "stimming" and it was one of the only things that calmed Mads when he got like that.

The other trigger for Mads was any mention of his father. Lainey thought it might be because Mads blamed himself for their dad leaving. But Mads could see the way his father looked at him. He could hear the way his father talked about him like he wasn't there. The only one of the three of them who was blind to their father's faults was Zoey. She loved her daddy, and no amount of pain that he'd inflict would change that.

Justice, Nebraska was a blanket community just outside of Omaha. The town was forgotten by the big city, but the citizens of Justice had small town pride. Lainey's mom worked at First State Bank, and she could spout off the financial situations of all 1600 residents if she wanted to, but she would never cross that line. On weekdays, their routine consisted of Lainey's mom leaving for work at 7:30 and Lainey getting Zoey and Mads ready for school. On weekends, their mom worked at Church's — one of two bars in town. Lainey was in charge of putting the twins to bed. This routine wasn't as hard as it used to be when she was younger.

When Lainey approached her back steps, she pushed the stop button on her watch, and squinted at her time. 4:30 on the dot. She smiled and opened the back door to her house. "Mads? Zoey? I'm back!"

"We're playing Scrabble, Lainey! I've almost got him beat!" called Zoey. Mads remained quiet in what Lainey could only assume was full-strategy mode. Mads always beat Zoey, but Zoey's competitive spirit would not let her give up no matter how the game ended. It was that same spirit that kept her believing in her father, no matter how many times he disappointed her.

"Okay, I'm going out to the garden to see how it's doing. Let me know if you need anything until mom gets here."

Lainey grabbed her gardening tools sitting by the back door and went out to the garden. Although their house was small, the garden was something extraordinary. Lainey had planted ten rows of different vegetables and fruits. Tomatoes, lettuce, broccoli and more had begun to pop through the fertile ground. She took off her running shoes and entered the garden barefoot. The cold soil was a nice contrast to the hot August air. Lainey loved gardening. It helped her to pause, think, and reflect.

She thought about her upcoming week. She'd be a senior. Finally. It was the year she had been anticipating since kindergarten. She smiled while she pulled the weeds around the cucumbers, careful not to get poked by their tiny spikes. Looking at her watch, she noted it had been 20 minutes and the twins had been silent inside the house. This was suspicious, and she had to get ready for her mom's break between jobs anyway. She reached across the plants to gather her gardening tools and started to pack up when Zoey's voice interrupted her thoughts.

"He's gone again." Lainey, still crouching, looked just outside the garden and saw Zoey standing with her right hand on her hip. Lainey looked to the sky and sighed. Mads had started this new habit. He would sneak off when Zoey or Lainey or their mother would get busy. He usually walked down to the river behind the trees in a burrow constructed of felled tree limbs and leaves. Lainey had often found him stimming with his Scrabble letters, rocking, and repeating a number sequence. Even though she knew this town was small, she always felt the wind go out of her when he would just disappear. What if her dad had come by? Mads was the reason he left after all. Who knew what he'd do if he was drunk enough to find Mads alone. Lainey shook that thought from her head.

"Why didn't you stop him?" Lainey asked as she pulled the last of the weeds.

"I didn't notice he was gone until it was too late, and you told me to never go alone. After he beat me — *again* — I went to read in the living room and he must have snuck out. You know he's probably up by the trees again. It's his favorite place since those kids moved away," replied Zoey.

Lainey stood up and brushed the dirt off of her sun-kissed, summer legs. Her shoes were just outside of the garden. She put them on, and for a second time that day, took off toward the river.

She ran at a leisurely pace, and it was starting to feel good, again. Since this would be her last year in cross country, she had been training extra hard. Morning runs, middle of the day weight lifting, and evening runs with her team, when she could get away from her house, made for more work than fun. Jogging slowly toward the river was a nice change of pace.

As she got closer to the river, she could hear its current. The Missouri could be beautiful from afar, but if she got too close, Lainey could hear the anger in the fast-moving body of water. When she was able to finally see Mads's black hair, she noticed him sitting on a log. What made her heart stop was she could see he wasn't alone. Lainey ran faster. As she turned the corner, she could see the person with her little brother was an adult male who was holding something. As she approached, her heart raced, but her pace slowed. She was trying to act as though this wasn't greatly alarming. *Be normal. Most people are normal,* she told herself as she ran up to them.

The man was attached to a long rope and on the end of that rope was the furriest brown and black Australian shepherd Lainey had ever seen. Mads wasn't rocking or nervous. Mads wasn't screaming or listing his number sequence. Lainey noticed that Mads was smiling and petting a tail wagging, red-tongued panting dog. As she neared them, Mads acted as though he hadn't even seen Lainey. She got closer to the trio and saw that the man so close to her brother was probably in his mid-forties; he had a full head of dark hair and tired, hazel eyes. He had a five o'clock shadow that seemed purposeful. He was smiling with all of his teeth. People in this town rarely did that. Lainey found it strange she had never seen this man before, but she tried to shrug it off and get Mads back home with her and away from potential danger. She found her voice.

"Mads, it's time to come home. We've got to get you ready for your show," Lainey said trying to act like she wasn't incredibly bothered by a stranger talking to her brother. Mads looked up, seemed to consider Lainey's request to watch his favorite TV show, and then looked back down to the dog who fearlessly came up to Lainey with his tongue out, tail wagging. Mads was unusually content as he pet the dog in long, fine strokes.

The man looked up at Lainey and gave her a sweet smile. "Sorry, young lady. I didn't mean to startle you. I noticed, um, Mads, is that what your name is? Anyway, I noticed Mads out here by himself. He seemed upset. I've seen him out here a few times. I wanted to make sure everything was okay. I just moved in around the corner over there." Lainey looked where his finger pointed and noticed the For-Sale sign was gone from the Tuckers' old house.

"Oh, that's okay," Lainey said. "It's late and Mads needs to come home." Lainey paused. "Cute dog." As if summoned by her comment, the dog got closer and nudged her hand so that she would pet him. "What's his name?"

"His name is Royal. He's a therapy dog, so he loves people. Especially Mads over here, and apparently you as well."

Lainey couldn't help but smile and stay for a second longer. Royal looked like caramel and chocolate. He was as big as a wolf, but his eyes were as sweet as his owner's. She could see why he would make a good therapy dog. Lainey was sure she had never seen Mads so relaxed around strangers before. Especially those who were in his space.

"Lainey, can't we stay and play with Royal? He likes me." Royal walked back up to Mads and let Mads's hands fall on his back. Mads smiled, bent down, and hugged Royal with everything in him.

"No, buddy. We have to get back. Mom will be swinging home between shifts. You know her schedule is crazy. We've got to get to dinner. Thanks, Mr. um what did you say your name was?"

"My name is Mr. Newman. It was nice to meet you both."

"Nice to meet you too," Lainey said as she grabbed Mads's hand and walked away. There was something really nice about Mr. Newman. Why he would move to this town confused Lainey. There was nothing ever going on here, and the city is so close. Justice had a lot of character, but no outsider would ever know. Lainey had been exploring every nook and cranny of her little town since she was old enough to ride a bike. People like Lainey knew where to view the sunset, knew where to find peace, and knew where to hide when the world was too loud. But people rarely came this far south. Lainey thought it was because they preferred their worlds to be loud.

Mads held Lainey's hand until they got to the street. The terrain was a little lumpy by his spot in the trees. "Mads, I know you were just going off to find some peace and quiet, but you have to tell me before you do that next time. Also, don't talk to strangers. We don't know Mr. Newman. Who knows what could have happened?"

"No, Mr. Newman is nice. He likes me." Mads spoke as he skipped by Lainey. She couldn't help but giggle at his happiness.

Lainey sighed. It was times like this one that Lainey wished her mother wasn't always working.

....

Justice is a 60,000 word completed novel told from the parallel perspectives of a mother and daughter. Marissa believes she has turned into a small-town cliché, by birthing three children and marrying and divorcing her high school sweetheart by the time she is 43. Her daughter, Lainey, is about to spend her senior year at Justice High as a promising cross-country runner and creative journalist, and she uses her mother's life as a model of what to avoid in her impending adulthood. Both women's lives are about to be forever changed.

Jazz Beans

LUCY ADKINS

All day it's been beans.
I pick dishpans full, washtubs.
My back is permanently bent, I think,
my hands reaching, turning aside
the rough rounded leaves
searching for beans.

In the kitchen I wash away spider webs,
clots of blossom husks,
snip off the little pig tail ends
and snap — and I'm thinking these
are jazz beans, and snap my fingers
keeping time
to their music,
the sink now full of beans
water boiling a drum roll on the stove.
The Mason jars are white and hot,
the air filling with the steam of
dark, rank cooked flesh of bean
turning lime green,
row upon row,
making an entire bandstand of beans
jazzing it up on the counter.

At last, I sit at the table to stretch my back.
The jars stand at attention,
their round gold hats set flat on their heads,
glass faces shining,

the lids sealing one by one with
sharp, musical
pings.

They are happy.
They are jazzy.
They are full of beans.

Lookout
Photo by Barb Motes

last lullaby

TRACY AHRENS

wood veins on ivory sky,
back-lit by moon,
up-lit by snow.

two owls perched,
juxtaposed on limbs,
whispering to wake you from tormented sleep.

we sat on the floor,
embracing bare,
mesmerized by their duet.

you asked me to send one —
for peace.
a "genesis" swirled,
submerging you in strife.

i brought two.

spirits of your parents sang to you.
a last lullaby — soothing,
my mortal hands cradling,
tears cleansing your heart.

with a bow, they exited in flight,
aiming east as the rising sun climbed —
the resurrection direction.

together again,
they journeyed home.

two wise souls — free.

Word Images
Kristi Bolling

Second Chance

DUANE ANDERSON

Off in the distance, a short
distance from where I sat,
only two houses away,
the neighbor's tree
stands naked of any leaves,
but not because it is autumn

and all the leaves had left its
branches for winter.
No, the branches are bare
because the tree's life had ended,
part of nature where nothing lives
forever, not man, not tree.

It was not coming back to life,
so I said a prayer as they,
cut it down, then chopped it up
to be used as firewood,
something not all get a chance at
doing, given a second purpose in life.

Remember Where You Belong

STEVE BARBER

My brother and I stood in the yard by the back door to the farmhouse.

"Go ask him," my brother said.

"You go," I said. "He likes you more than me."

My brother climbed the stairs and went into the house. The screen door slammed behind him. I waited. Pretty soon he came back out.

"He says they are taking a nap and that we should go to the barn. He'll call us when he gets up."

"What if we can't hear him?"

"He says he'll honk the horn on the Ford. He says not to come back before he calls us."

"He never lets us do anything," I said.

We walked up the driveway toward the barn. I kicked at the dirt with my bare feet.

"It sure is hot," my brother said. Already the sun was high overhead and shivering like a globe of molten brass. Inside the barn the air was still, no breeze, and dust motes floated through the slivers of light that shone through the joints between the boards. The corrugated iron roof radiated heat, and the barn smelled like hay and dust and cow manure.

"It's too hot in here. Let's get out," I said. Sweat ran down my face. "Let's go get the mail."

"Yeah, maybe there's a letter from Mom."

We walked around the corner of the barn and up the long driveway to the county road, where we lay down on the asphalt in the shade of a giant black oak and waited for the mailman. After a while the mailman's green Plymouth sedan appeared at Schroeder's mail box, dropped off their mail, and then wheeled up and stopped, idling, in the shade of the oak. The mailman handed a *Farm Journal* and a packet of letters out through the driver's window.

"Here's the mail. Don't lose any of it," he said. Then he told us to watch out for cars and drove away.

"Why did he say to watch out for cars," my brother said. "We aren't dogs sleeping in the road."

We looked through the mail, but there were no letters from our mother. We walked back to the barn.

As we rounded the corner of the barn, we heard our grandfather calling, so we hurried to the house. When we got there, our grandfather stood by the back door in his usual denim bib overalls, long-sleeved blue chambray shirt, and a sweat-stained cap. He wore rubber irrigation boots with his pant legs tucked into them ready to go irrigate the alfalfa field. I handed him the mail.

"Can we go out to the river-bottom?" I asked.

"Where will you go?" He thumbed through the papers and letters.

"To Costanzo's," I answered. Costanzo's dairy was a little over a mile south toward town.

My grandfather frowned. "Don't bother the neighbors, and don't forget where you belong," he said. "You'll be home before supper, if you know what's good for you."

"Yes, sir," I said. My brother and I, shirtless, barefoot, and wearing patched blue jeans lit out across the orchard, down the crumbling riverbank, and onto the dry white sand of the riverbed heading south. The afternoon sun lashed the river sand, until it was almost too hot to walk barefoot there. Then, we ran to the shade of the nearest tree or to the clumps of mule fat that grew on the sandbars. When we came close to the ponds by Costanzo's, we ran to the water and jumped in.

Three ponds lay cushioned in the main channel of the Salinas below Costanzo's dairy. Two of them, twenty to thirty feet across, shimmered at the edge of a growth of sand bar willows and were no deeper than three or four feet. The intertwined roots of the trees kept the sand banks from collapsing and together with the watercress and milfoil provided cover for bluegills, sunfish and Sacramento Valley squawfish. We splashed around in these pools and on other days had caught fish with a net improvised out of chicken wire.

The third pond, underneath a tangle of low hanging willows and fringed at the shallow end with cattails, lay covered in a green blanket of duckweed. We poked a broken limb from a nearby cottonwood into the water in an attempt to gauge the depth, but all we could really tell was that the water was way over our heads at the deep end. We knew to stay out of deep water.

When the afternoon shadows of the willows crept across the sand, we climbed the riverbank, steep and brambled with cascarilla, creosote, and deadly nightshade, to the road where we pulled strings of wet algae off our jeans and started the long walk back to the farm. The sun had softened the asphalt, and we left shallow footprints as we dodged from shade to shade.

We ducked to the side of the road when an old brown Studebaker pickup rounded a curve and slowed. When it stopped, the driver, a large older man with a tangled fringe of black hair circling a bald head called out through the open passenger window.

"You boys want a lift?" The pickup shuddered, wheezed, and smoked in the middle of the road.

"Sure," I said. My brother and I stepped toward the passenger door.

"Hop in then," the man said.

The first thing that caught my eye when I opened the pickup door was a .22 rifle with the heel of the butt resting on the floor and the barrel leaning against the seat. I stopped. The driver caught my look.

"Don't pee your pants," he said. "It's for killing skunks and badgers." He pulled the rifle closer to him.

He wore a sweaty, unwashed, white, tee shirt that didn't quite cover a large pale belly that was crowded under the steering wheel. His blue jeans, faded and dirty, ended in ragged cuffs around worn brown cowboy boots.

"C'mon," he said. "Hop in. I ain't got all day."

I held the door while my brother climbed up on the seat. I got in after him. When I slammed the door, the man shifted the pickup into gear and started the truck rolling north. He clutched the steering wheel with large hands that had black hair on the back of his knuckles.

"You boys out smoking cigarettes?"

"Naw," I said. "We weren't smoking."

"C'mon now," he said. "I weren't born yesterday. Bet you was smoking cigarettes."

"We were swimming," my brother said.

The driver snorted. "Skinny-dipping?"

"What?" I asked.

"Skinny-dipping. No pants." He turned his head and stared at us. I looked at my brother.

"We don't take our pants off when we swim," I said. "It's so hot they dry out way before we get home."

"Yeah," said my brother. "They dry out fast."

The driver shifted the pickup into high gear and turned back facing the road.

"How old you boys?" he asked.

"I'm ten," I said. I pointed at my brother. "He's eight."

"Take two of you boys to make a man," he said. We rode in silence until he spoke again.

"You got any nekkid girly pictures down there in the trees?" he asked.

"Our uncle says there are trees in California that are so tall it takes a man and two boys to see all the way to the top," my brother said.

"Ha," the man said, but he wasn't laughing. "You got any dirty picture books?"

"Naw," I said. I moved closer to the door.

"There are lots of fish in the waterholes down there," my brother said.

"I don't give a damn about fish," he said. We were quiet then. I rested my arm on the open window. The warm air flowed over it.

"You boys like puppies?"

"I love puppies," my brother said.

"I wanted one for my birthday, but I didn't get one. How 'bout you?" He reached across my brother and squeezed my knee with his bristly hand. I jerked my knee away, and he pulled his hand back and rested it on his own leg. He frowned.

"I like puppies okay," I said.

"Well," he said, "we'll go out to my place. I got a bitch with a whole litter. You can pick one out."

"We have to go home," I said.

My brother nudged me with his elbow. "Let's go see the puppies," he said.

"Won't take long," the man said. "You can go home after that."

A yellow International pickup came the other way, driven by our neighbor, Armin Schroeder. Mister Schroeder raised a hand and waved as we passed. I waved back.

"Who's that?" asked the driver.

"We should have ducked down," my brother said.

"Mister Schroeder," I said. "He calls the house and tells everybody where we are."

"He's a blabber mouth," my brother said. "He gets us in trouble."

The driver took his foot off the gas. "Where's your place?"

"I want to see the puppies," my brother said.

I pointed to the large black oak a hundred yards farther on the right side of the road. "Driveway's across from that tree," I said.

The stranger slammed the pickup to a stop. "Hop out," he said.

"What about the puppies?" my brother asked.

"You can see them puppies some other time."

I opened the door, slid off the seat, and dropped onto the pavement. My brother jumped down. The pickup was already moving when I slammed the door. We walked down the long driveway toward the house.

"We could have got a puppy," my brother complained.

"He doesn't have any puppies," I said.

///

"The world is in desperate need of irresistible women: women who are willing to be enthusiastic, alive, and expressive—regardless of the circumstance; women who... speak up for what they believe in; women who feel at ease being intelligent, sensual, and compassionate all at once; women who... see everyone for who they really are—fellow human beings also in search of a great life, in search of love."

MARIE FORLEO

///

E Pluribus Unum

GARY BECK

Once we built a country
made it run,
worked on it all the time,
brought in lots of strangers
made them one,
now it's become a crime.
Separate this. Separate that.
The myth of unity
fraying beyond repair,
as different agendas
are more important
than the fate of the nation
and we finally resemble
the old world.

Memories of Vietnam

JOSEPH S. BENSON

(The names used in this story are fictitious. The people and the events are represented as accurately as I can recall them, fifty years later.)

As a Marine, Vietnam Veteran, many events are seared in my memory. Not all recollections of my tour in Nam are tragic or frightening. Many of the best relate to the exploits of our band of boys, who walked around in men's boots. It was essential that we carry on with bravado and find ways to entertain ourselves. Finding novel ways to have fun while in a war zone was a useful diversion.

Ronny Parsons was one of the biggest characters. Ronny was from Ontario, Canada, and played himself off as our resident mercenary. Even though he had enlisted in the Marine Corps, Ronny claimed he could go home at any time since he was not a U.S. citizen. It might have been true. With Ronny, I could not be sure.

Many of Ronny's shenanigans are almost legendary. He "requisitioned" a window unit air conditioner for our radio communications office. With a Corporal as accomplice, they went to supply with a story and came back with the air conditioner. The Corporal wore Captain's bars for this caper, and both of them could have been court-martialed.

Ronny was part of a convoy to Dong Ha and back. The group included two jeeps and a truck hauling Marines and supplies. The return trip included a third jeep. Ronny discovered an unattended vehicle that became his personal means of transportation.

A Marine from our Communications group was on mess duty for a month, working in the warehouse. That became an opportune time for Ronny to go "shopping." After making his selections, he came to get several of us to help haul cases of canned goods to our hooch (living quarters). This smuggling operation occurred in the middle of the afternoon on a typical work day. We happened to have a vacant living area in our hooch, which we made up to look occupied by another Marine. We hastily built a plywood storage locker and painted it a bright yellow. We stored cases of tuna, gallon cans of mixed nuts, canned fruit, huge jars of pickles, and sundry other dry goods in that canary-colored cabinet. We added a dorm-sized refrigerator to chill prepared foods. Occasionally, the Military Police (MPs) conducted nighttime contraband searches. These were "surprise" raids, but in our Communications group, nothing took place that wasn't recorded in the Comm Center. We were always alerted, sometimes, with minutes to spare, before the MPs arrived. When they "woke" us for their search and asked about the area with the yellow locker, we explained that Corporal Jones was on R & R (rest and relaxation for a week, out of country; the lucky guy was in Australia). We used that alibi twice that I remember.

One evening, at closing time for the enlisted men's club, we had a brief visit from Chief. I may have heard Chief's real name, but all I remember is Chief. It was all I ever heard him called. He was a Native American from Oklahoma. Chief was a big Marine with broad shoulders and a barrel chest. He was extremely good natured and loved his beer. It was common for Chief to stop by on the way home to his hooch from the club to see what we had to eat. Chief burst in through the east door of our hooch and barreled down the aisle to the refrigerator. He resembled a charging bull as he rushed toward the refrigerator. On this trip, he was happy to find a plastic container of tuna salad. With very little pause, he went on out the west door, into the night. Ronny called out to him, "Be sure you bring back that bowl, Chief." No one in our hooch thought any more about it.

A few minutes later, it was time for me to perform one of my nightly jobs. As a radio operator, I had a security clearance at the Secret level. Each day at 0000 (zero hundred hours; midnight), it was my duty to reset and test our crypto radio network (secure communication link using encryption technology).

It was a dark night. There were lights around the compound, but none were on along the course of my trip to the command bunker. None were deemed necessary. It was a familiar trip of less than thirty yards. I soon began to hear rustling and thumping sounds. The noise seemed to come from the vicinity of the well.

At some point before I arrived in Vietnam, someone thought it was a good idea to have a water well in our area. Two fifty-gallon steel drums had their tops and bottoms removed, and they were welded, end to end. A hole was dug in the sand to permit the long tube to stand upright. The outside of the structure was covered with two inches of concrete up to the top rim. The sand was backfilled around it with a few inches left above ground. Unfortunately, due to the sandy soil, it rarely held more than a couple of inches of water, even during the monsoon season.

I walked to the well to investigate the sounds. Even with limited light, I was able to determine what had happened. I ran back to our hooch, calling to Ronny, "Come quick! Chief's in the well!" We hurried back, and we could just make out the soles of the big Marine's boots. It had been clear that I couldn't haul Chief out by myself. Ronny and I each grabbed a foot and yanked a sputtering, vomiting Chief from the well, clutching the tuna salad bowl in one hand. He had probably been shoving tuna salad into his mouth by the handful, as he left our hooch. It didn't take long for his stomach to rebel at the new assault. Chief had gone to throw up and managed to drop the bowl into the well. Attempting to retrieve it, he wound up, head first, in a relatively narrow chamber he could not escape. In addition to beer and tuna, Chief managed to swallow a fair amount of brackish water from the bottom of the well.

After pulling Chief out and finding he only had a few scrapes and bruises, I went on to reset the crypto network. Spending evenings at the club was a daily routine for Chief. After his close encounter with the well, he didn't go to the club for several days. He resumed his daily schedule again before his scrapes were healed, but I don't recall him stopping by for any late-night snacks after that.

It was almost thirty years later when I reconnected with Ronny Parsons. After initial hugs and greetings, he took me to task for leaving him with a puking, slobbering Marine, who kept trying to hug him in gratitude.

I lost track of Chief, but wherever he is, I hope he is well and wonder how he remembers that night. Semper Fidelis, Chief.

Fall Grass
Photo by Barb Motes

Postcard

ALLISSANDRA BEQUETTE

In the evening, we walked through the neighborhood opposite ours. There was a distinctive line when you crossed this street, between where students like us lived and where the worries of others ceased to exist. Cleanly paved driveways, white brick and chandeliers over porches, neatly trimmed hedges and trees. To our right, a family was fussing as they got out of their luxury SUV, a mother carrying too many bags while children circled her, and a father making an outdated joke, as he got his papers from work out of the trunk.

"What's that like?" Kihyun asked me. He made a subtle motion to the strangers. The hint of a frown was tugging at his mouth.

"What's what like?"

"You know. Being a nuclear family. Living your life like it's an episode of a feel-good, all-American sitcom."

"I guess neither of us would know." He stumbled, the toe of his old sneakers catching on the brick below our feet. I held my arm out in front of him before he could fall. He cursed, shaking out his leg.

"Even their streets. Why have brick roads? This is the twenty-first century. It's inconvenient, and we moved past it for a reason."

"Some people can afford inconvenience," I said, pointedly. He snorted.

"Well, yeah. Some people." We crossed the street side by side, finally reaching our destination. Right outside of those housing districts was the Christmas Light Festival, woven among local shops and parks. It could very well become a postcard. I could see it in my mind. A watercolor, the dark blue bleeding into fresh snow. Splotches of yellow that fell onto passersby from street lamps that never went out. A sleeping landscape that made the passage of time seem like a dubious concept. He and I could have been in it, as well, if it was above the shoulders. His fraying jacket he'd bought with his first paycheck could be mistaken for a finer coat of wool. My hoodie with bleach stains on the sleeves and the scarf my mother made, when I was twelve, could be designed by an older gentleman in France. No one would be the wiser, when it was all so picturesque. Walking arm in arm with someone at Christmas time was familiar enough on its own to most, so perhaps, we could pass by without notice. We could be distorted figures in that four by six inch paper, edges never quite sharp enough to distinguish fortune from misfortune, and happy from not. We wound through the sidewalks, cleared of white powder long ago. He and I took turns pointing out amusing signs, shops that held promise in their wide windows, and disenchanted people. The cold air remained a distant burn, a steadily rising tide that only I seemed to feel. It should have been significant, but I couldn't bring myself to interrupt the dream in order to make it so.

That was, until my legs gave out, and I tumbled onto the pavement, barely avoiding crashing face first into the painted lines of the cross-walk. I immediately recovered myself, embarrassed although no one had stopped to stare. Kihyun hauled me upright. I staggered back into him, nearly knocking us both to the ground.

"I'm fine," I said, a premature reassurance that he didn't accept. He pulled me inside the nearest coffee shop, arms wound close around my shoulders to prevent another fall.

"Sit down," he said, tightly, when we'd plowed through the crowd. I sat, obediently, shaky legs demanding rest. His eyes flitted from my face to my body. "Are you hurt?" he questioned.

"No," I said after a moment. "Just bruises, maybe." He nodded and hurried away to the counter, ordering a hot chocolate with utmost urgency. The employee gave him an odd look. Now that I had gone still, it was obvious. The tiles underneath my feet seemed to be whirling, and the chatter of everyone in the shop was too distant to be real. My body seemed too heavy for the little strength that I possessed.

He returned with a mug, pushing it into my hands. Its warmth shot feeling back into my fingers, slowly crawling up into my chest.

"It scares me," he said, draping his coat over my shoulders. "You know?" I gave him an apologetic smile. "That's really all it takes to make you sick? I shouldn't have asked you to come with me. I should have known it was too cold."

"I just need a short break," I protested. "It's not your fault." He shook his head, jaw set.

"I just," he bit his lip, eyebrows furrowed, "think it's my responsibility to look after you."

"It's you who decided that," I reminded him, softly. "I never asked." He subsided, smiling faintly.

"I know." He slid a granola bar out of his pocket and put it on the table in front of me. I raised my eyebrows at it. "I won't change my mind."

"Not for anything?" It was only a running joke, harmless, but he straightened up like it was a challenge.

"Not for anything." He tapped the table. "Now eat."

I stared back at him. We were in a bigger painting now, fat, abstract strokes depicting panic in the soul. The harsh lighting of the shop left nothing to imagination. This was not a dream, anymore, but fact. This was an eight AM lecture on the Renaissance, too much coffee and an uncertain future. This was us.

This was all I wanted, in the end.

Mother, Culler, Teacher

J. ELEANOR BONET

Members of the Council, I am here because I must begin afresh, with purpose, and free of my self-wrought pain. I must expiate and mend the actions of my lifetime — and I have lived for millennia, as well you know. Perhaps, I seek absolution for judgments that I had no right to declare as truths, yet the power was mine, and I wielded it — you gave it to me. I was the one who believed only the pure could remain, only the pure could bear fruit and be allowed to survive. Purity was my measure of worth, but it was I who determined the definition of that purity. This is a burden I tire of carrying.

There were too many, you see. Too many for this small world to contain. This world, this gem, this blue and verdant Earth, like any good mother, feeds and tends her children, until there is almost nothing left of her. She is in each moment a caregiver, unable and unwilling to foresee her demise as the requisite result of that selfless nurturing. Of course, her progeny, blind to the cost exacted from the provider of such maternal bounty, consume her, exploit her, and yet claim to love her. She does not let them concern themselves with her condition because, as any loving mother does, she shelters them from awareness of her suffering. They believe life is short and should be lived in pursuit of self-satisfaction.

I am here before the Council of Watchers, who see all and do nothing, to tell you of the hell through which I am impelled to journey over and over again, while culling the children of this world in order to save their mother. I must act, so that she might revive and renew herself. She was created to be the life giver, while I was of necessity created to be the life taker. I am the single being, not of her issue, not of her body, and yet, it is I who love her most. I am the only being willing to sacrifice my personal peace, my very self, so that I might be her savior. And she hates me for it, even as she knows she needs me to be the bitter frost of autumn to her tree of life, felling the leaves to give way for the new fruit.

For eternity, we battle in this finite space, loving and hating each other; neither of us able to stop being and doing what we must, what we were created to do. She cannot stop giving life; therefore, I cannot stop taking it. We love her children in equal measure. We love each other but find ourselves forever embattled, although, there are moments when we see in each other our mutual salvation.

We are, as the moon and sun, cycling in and out of orbit with the constellations of dualities: joy and sorrow, love and hate, life and death. The endless, timeless contradiction of the sower and the reaper always act in the hope of someone among the children of Earth, awakening to her sacrifice, comprehending her needs, and striking a balance, so Mother and Culler might do our work in coherent harmony with humans, not despite them.

There is no greater being beyond us whom we would blame for our condition or from whom we would beg absolution. We are the essence of the two sides of existence, birth and death. Birth is the greatest joy and holds within it, the greatest sorrow, which is death, when it is believed to be a definitive ending of a life. We, she and I, share, extol, those moments as the most sacred of all else. But there must exist a point at which each can be revealed as reciprocally transformative, one flowing into the other. There must be given to humans a shared knowledge that neither is the beginning or end, and actions have consequences beyond the actor.

I propose to this Council a solution. Perhaps, there can be a third entity brought into being, a teacher, who will reveal to humans the value of both Culler and Mother and thus each would be respected but neither feared, a being who can open the hearts and minds of humans to the reality of life and death, as steps on the path of life's eternity within infinity. We two, she and I, pray there can be such a one who would save us both from torment. Is it so idiotic to hope for such a salvation?

It is for this reason, I am before you who have watched without judgment and action. I am petitioning for this gift. You have omniscient omnipotence, and we ask that you, by virtue of free will, alter existence, so there might be a kinder balance. Please, send us a teacher.

Theater: Observing the Influence

SARA K. BRADSHAW

To be an artist is to create, and to create is to understand, and to understand is to observe. In order to do art and to be a great artist, one must be an observer of mankind, life, and the way we interact with the world. By observing, one can hope to understand the world through art and help others understand it through art. It makes sense for an artist to be drawn to theater, because the word "theater" comes from ancient Greek: to see, to watch, to observe.

Theater is not just about entertainment. Through theater, actors help the audience understand the human condition. Theater is the most challenging art form, because the actor is observing people, while people observe the actor. With other visual art forms, one is creating and bringing to life ideas by using different materials and media. Through theater, the masterpiece one is creating and bringing to life uses oneself as the instrument. Theater has no boundaries; it is fearless and feared. Theater is vulnerable, personal, life changing, thought provoking, and transforming.

When I was 12, I saw an audition flyer for the Omaha Public Schools Summer Musical, *Les Misérables*. When I saw the flyer, I felt an instant connection, and I knew I had to try out. There was just something that resonated with me and awakened the observer in me. *Les Misérables* was my first official theater production. It lasted most of the summer with morning and afternoon rehearsals. I had the role of an orphan, along with another girl who is still one of my best friends. To put myself into a character and sing on stage with a cast, set, lights, with an audience watching was a surreal experience for me. The experience is what made me want to do theater as a career. The following year, I was part of the Omaha Public School's production of *The Secret Garden*.

My high school theater experience was an epic adventure. We did two plays and one musical per year. I was never as interested in acting in plays as I was performing in musicals, but I still wanted to be part of theater in some way. I auditioned for their technical team. My first show in high school was called *2222: The Zombie Apocalypse*. I was on the props crew, along with one other person, and it was amazing. I was able to use my knowledge of sculpture to create props for the cast and build sets. I went on to become prop head, along with my friend Katelynn, for the rest of my high school theater productions, including *The Good Fight, Princess Anonymous, The Giver, Cursing Mummies, The Girl in The Mirror, Wrinkle in Time,* and *A Midsummer Night's Dream*.

For the musicals at Burke High School, I could not be prop head, when I was doing crew, because I was always in the shows. My first musical in high school was *Once on This Island*. I was part of the ensemble as a peasant, but I was not as upset about my role as others were about theirs. In theater, there are no small parts, only small actors, and there were many parts to go around. We had a cast of 90! It was insane, but amazing. I became friends with many of the theater people during the show. What is amazing, yet sad, about big productions like musicals is that one will never work with the same cast and crew twice.

As the years went on, I started getting bigger roles. During my sophomore year, I played the Milkmaid in *Beauty and The Beast*. During my junior year, I was Queen Lilian and The Blue Bird in *Shrek*. For my senior year, I had my greatest role as Patricia Fodor in *Crazy for You*. Being part of those shows was amazing, and I made more and more friends as the production process went along. When I was not taking part in productions, I was a part of musical theater class, drama club, and other extracurricular theater activities.

As a child, I was bullied a lot. My peers picked on me, because I was not skinny enough. I had acne, I was quiet, and they observed me as an easy target. When theater came into my life, I found a place that did not pick on me for my flaws. It accepted my flaws and glorified them. To be different was to be great. Theater gave me a place to let me be me. It became my home. A cast is not just a cast, it is a family. We see each other's good and bad side, and love each other, either way. Theater gave me hope. Theater opened my soul and filled it with passion. Theater has been one of the biggest impacts on my life. I do not know what life would be like without it. In school, not only was I in theater, but I was in many honors classes and other extra-curricular clubs. At times, it was hard to balance them all, but no matter what, I prevailed. In the end, theater helped me. My social status in school went up. I met more people, and a lot of them helped me through school. Being creative in theater helped my grades. It gave me perspective.

Through theater, I was given many opportunities that would propel me into an amazing future. Every year, Nebraska thespians hold a State Thespian Festival, where over 300 thespians all over Nebraska get together for a three-day event filled with workshops, college fairs, auditions, competitions, and fun. The festival is usually held in Lincoln on the University of Nebraska campus, but this year it was held in Omaha. At the festival, participants compete in individual events for musical theater, acting, and tech. In the individual events, one performs for judges, then competes for a superior rating or a call back. If people make it to call backs, they get to make it to a final showcase, where they perform for everyone, and all superiors qualify for the International Thespian Festival. I went to the State Festival three years in a row, and I did a musical theater individual event twice. During my first year, I did well, but I did not get a superior rating, due to my nerves getting the best of me. My second year, I performed and got a superior qualifying for the International Thespian Festival, which is also held at the University of Nebraska at Lincoln. Thespians from all over the USA and other countries stay on campus. Over thousands of thespians see traveling high school shows, which perform in the Lied Center, go to workshops, and interact with fellow students. Just like the State Festival, individual event contestants perform for three judges, hoping to get a call back, and have the chance to perform for all of festival on the Lied Center stage. Without these festivals, I would not know as much as I do now about theater, performing arts schools, and career opportunities.

In college, things are a lot more challenging. When I first started, I was a music major, and I had a really hard time being happy. It was not what I truly wanted to do, but I loved music, and it was what everyone else told me I should do. Just being in the music building stressed me. The atmosphere was negative, and it was not helping me succeed. Halfway through the semester, I started to look into switching to theater, and I did. When I started my theater major, I was happier. The people were nicer and more accepting. If someone messed up, it was celebrated, and they were encouraged to try again, not scolded or criticized. I made more friends the first week in theater than I had the entire semester in music. The environment in theater is loving, caring, and supportive.

Theater is universal. It is love, passion, and family. Theater changes people's lives and has changed mine. It has given me a home and a career. With theater, one can do and be anything. Theater teaches people discipline, courage, trust, confidence, and selflessness. Theater helps bring stories to life. It makes the impossible possible. Anything can be achieved in theater. There is no status quo in theater, and anyone who wants to make a difference can impact the world.

Theater is a worldwide phenomenon. It is a platform for expression. Every day, it shares stories that are otherwise silenced. Actors take stands and share their experiences, promote their political views, and incite change. People are made aware of social issues and problems in the world. Theater is healing. It brings people together by telling stories, expressing ideas, and sharing resolutions. Theater takes us to new worlds and wakes us up from injustices of reality. Theater is personal, life changing, thought provoking, and transforming. On the stage, we are not "merely players" but observers and creators of change.

Croatian Spring

SUSAN GRADY BRISTOL

I sat in the Soviet jail, recalling events that led to my predicament. The dark dank cell in the pre-trial detention center in Zagreb smelled like a bad porta-potty after four days at a beer festival. The other five women in the eight-by-ten-foot cell stripped down to their underwear. I couldn't bring myself to do that, no matter the temperature. My stubborn streak didn't allow the heat to strip me of what dignity I had left.

How long had I been there? They allowed us to shower once a week, so that would make it five weeks. But I suspected that we'd missed a week or so. Am I ever getting out? The "pre-trial facility" seemed so permanent.

"I be here one year," a female inmate showed me the hash marks on the wall hidden behind a bunk. She pointed to another inmate who sat cramped on the top bunk with two other women. "She be here a-most two years."

The woman had been accused of black marketeering after trying to sell some of her possessions, and I was there for being at the wrong place at the wrong time with a camera.

Housed in a former fortress built hundreds of years ago, the center had no heating or air conditioning. With little ventilation, the cell felt stifling. It was hot in the daytime but cold when the sun went down.

When I first arrived at the center, the guards shoved me into a dark room the size of a phone booth, forcing my head against the cold wall. They said the accommodations were temporary; they had no other place to put me. "We rarely use this room." The cigarette-laced floor told me that was a lie.

I stood alone in the space for what seemed an eternity. My legs felt rubbery. I tried to sit, but that proved impossible. The best I could do was squat. By the time they came to get me, I could hardly stand.

It started two years ago in my Poli. Sci. class at the University of
Nebraska, 1973.

"A lot is happening in the world." Professor Rumsfeld stood before
the class. "I want you to select a country, describe the conflicts,
political structure and possible solutions to the problems."

I sighed at the thought of all the research.

"You might consider applying to study abroad for a semester to
really delve into the project. It's due at the end of spring semester, next
year."

My eyes lit up. The thought of researching a country, while
embedded in it, sounded appealing. I stopped at the library and
picked up some literature on world events.

"You should do it on Northern Ireland and the IRA." My boyfriend,
Marc, flipped through a *Time* magazine showing the British in Belfast.
"It would be so much easier."

"Belfast is too dangerous."

"But you're Irish. And they speak English there ... sort of," he
laughed. "Don't you want to visit your ancestral home?"

"I would rather see your ancestral home, Mr. Marc Novak. Besides,
I don't want to be like everyone else, picking Vietnam or Northern
Ireland. I prefer someplace more obscure, less well-known."

I discovered that Yugoslavia allowed more freedom than the other
Soviet countries. I wanted to find out how, and what it might mean
in the world arena. Might it lead to other USSR nations gaining their
freedom?

I turned in my initial assignment, explaining the background of my
project.

Professor Rumsfeld sat back in his swivel chair behind the desk.
"Gutsy move. Are you sure?" I nodded. "I think so. My parents have to
give me permission, but I'm sure they will."

The professor signed the paperwork, then added, "I suggest you
do thorough research before deciding to go. It's not like heading to
California."

"I dunno. California can seem foreign," I laughed.

"Right." The professor narrowed his eyes. "Eastern Europe can be a dangerous place. Be cautious as you proceed." He rose and opened the office door, escorting me out. "And seek information." I promised I would.

A month later, it came. The envelope. I didn't want to open it, yet. I was afraid it might be a rejection. I needed my friends to help bolster me. "Are you heading to the Schnitzel and Stein?" I ran down the dorm hallway after them. They turned and waited at the elevator.

"We're meeting the guys there. I think Marc is coming. You two seem to be an item these days, Sue." My roommate smiled.

"Yeah, maybe. I kinda hope he's there tonight. I need to talk to him."

"Ooo. Tell us."

I just smiled.

We arrived at the college hangout and found our usual table. I chose to sit at the end. Soon the guys arrived. Marc smiled when he saw me. I pulled out a chair for him. He scooted close and put his arm around the back of my wooden seat.

"It came today." I slipped the corner of the envelope from my purse, so only he could see.

"Have you opened it, yet?" He studied my face, as he spoke.

"No. I wanted to wait until I saw you. I'm a little scared."

I looked around at the others at the table. Engrossed in their own conversations and flirtations, no one paid attention to us. Wanting to wait for the right time and not ready to announce anything to the world, I needed a private moment with Marc. "Let's order a beer first."

The Schnitzel and Stein was crowded. Eight of us "regulars" enjoyed tipping a few on Friday and Saturday nights. The establishment, once an upscale German bistro, became a hangout for the students, as the college campus expanded and took over more land. No longer surrounded by businesses and office buildings, the restaurant-turned-pub found itself in between two student parking lots. The owners hired a sing-a-long band in an attempt to maintain the previous ambiance, as well as, provide a friendlier atmosphere to discourage brawls. Every weekend, four guys arrived carrying a banjo, guitar, and trombone. They wore panama hats with red, white, and blue bands. Bright red garters held their baggie white shirt sleeves in place. They looked like they stepped out of a time machine, in garb from the 1890s.

The musicians pulled the old upright piano out from the wall and tuned their instruments. The piano player passed out mimeographed copies of the lyrics to "East Side, West Side," "Toot, Toot Tootsie," "Let Me Call You Sweetheart," and other songs from bygone years.

Our beers arrived, the others still uninterested in Marc and me. Gingerly, I opened the envelope, afraid of what the contents might hold. Marc peered over my shoulder, as I unfolded the letter. "Your request for a grant to study abroad in Yugoslavia has been approved."

I touched the embossed seal of the University of Zagreb at the bottom of the letter. The largest and oldest Croatian University, established in 1671 by Emperor Leopold I, the institution would be my temporary home.

Marc grabbed me, attempting to hug me in the chair. I smiled a tentative smile. Now what?

"Guess what, guys." Marc turned to our friends, who were predicting which song the band would begin playing. "Sue's going to Croatia."

"Really? How did that happen?" The "Five W" questions bounced back and forth. I felt overwhelmed. I didn't know the answers myself. I knew I'd have to talk to Mom and Dad. I was relieved, when the music started and the questions ended.

Ragtime seemed to fit in with a rowdy beer-drinking crowd. After singing along with the band for about an hour, my friends ordered another pitcher and passed it around. As "In Heaven There is No Beer" rang out, we rose from our chairs, waving our steins to the rhythm of the music. We knew the "Flying Dutchman" would be next. At the final lyric, "and when we're gone from here, our friends will be drinking all the beer," the guys grabbed the girls and pulled us onto the dance floor.

With two girls and a guy in the middle or two guys with a girl in the middle, the group stepped together in a circle of threesomes. I found myself locking arms with Marc and his roommate, Steve. Step, step, hop. Step, step, hop. We followed the other dancers in a circle, the music slow and simple. Suddenly, it changed, and we jumped into a fast do-si-do. At their mercy, I hoped my partners didn't lose their grip. Smaller girls flew off the floor like the swing carousel in a carnival. Somehow, I managed to stay aground with only a few stumbles.

At the end of the dance, we dragged ourselves back to our seats, flushed and panting. I took a drink of my beer to cool off. I felt tipsy and giddy. We sang a few more songs, then "Goodnight Irene," which signaled that it was closing time. Marc and I swayed, "Goodnight, Irene, goodnight, Irene. I'll see you in my dreams."

"I'll be fine," I told my parents. Marc still had relatives in Slovenia and Croatia, and wasn't Tito considered a benevolent dictator?

A WWII veteran, Dad worried. In the news, examples of the KGB bringing citizens in for questioning appeared almost weekly. Stories of being sent to Siberia to do hard labor horrified people in the free world. I pointed out that most of the cases were in countries other than Yugoslavia.

The university assured Mom and Dad that the agreement between nations protected me. I was given a list of rules to follow while abroad. I'd need to check in at the US Embassy in Zagreb.

I made copies of my passport, airline tickets, student ID and health insurance information. I hoped I didn't get sick while I was there, because I barely knew how to navigate the health care system in the United States, let alone a foreign country.

I scanned the list of precautions. *Be aware of your surroundings. Don't wander through unfamiliar areas alone. Remain alert. Don't wear expensive jewelry. Keep cameras out of sight. Staying on campus was strongly encouraged. Avoid drinking alcohol. Observe local student behavior, and try to mimic it.*

Would I have any fun at all? Was this a mistake? But I was determined. I wanted to know about Yugoslavia, first hand, partly because of Marc's heritage, but also because it was unique in the USSR.

Stay away from demonstrations or any kind of civil disturbances. Protect your passport.

Could I remember all the rules?

Saying "goodbye" to Marc at the airport was hard, but he smiled and said I would love his ancestral land. He still had family there. "My cousins know you're coming. Here's their number."

He'd been to Zagreb, when he was in junior high. "Be sure and see Mount Medvednica. It means Bear Mountain." I joked about the Russian bear.

Arriving in Zagreb held much excitement and mystery. I could hardly wait to take pictures. I remembered the caution about cameras. I'd wait until I settled in. There would be plenty of time for this shutterbug to shoot.

Over time, I acclimated to the new surroundings with the help of other students. I felt secure enough to venture out and do some sightseeing. I decided to go see Mount Medvednica and the castle ruins at its base. I grabbed my camera case and headed out to explore. I wondered about finding someone to go with me, but it was a mild winter-to-spring day, and no one was around to ask. I decided I'd be fine on my own. After studying three months in Zagreb, I'd picked up enough of the language to ask basic questions. I hid my camera under my nylon jacket and headed out.

As I neared the main square in downtown Zagreb, I heard shouting and pandemonium. Turning the corner, I was startled. Hundreds of police in long, dark, trench coats held clubs. They pushed against a crowd carrying signs in Croatian that read: "Better the Grave than a

Slave." Their dark gray military-style caps with black visors sat low on their heads, partially covering their eyes.

I felt myself being pushed from behind. More protesters arrived. I wanted to take a picture, but did I dare? With as much stealth as I could muster, I eased my camera out of its case. Holding it under my jacket just enough to avoid notice, I snapped a series of pictures. I wasn't getting the shots I wanted. Only lower body. I moved it a bit higher. The zoom exposed, I snapped three more photos. I was caught in a new wave of protesters. Losing ground, the police backed up to the periphery. I found myself in the middle of the crowd. I turned and saw a policeman glaring at me. He moved toward me. I tried to ignore him, moving away, intending to get lost in the crowd.

It didn't work. He grabbed the camera from my hand, breaking the strap as he pulled it.

Another policeman arrived at his side. They spoke, rapidly, and I couldn't understand.

They yelled at me. I stood still. One grabbed my arm and pulled me, forcing me down the street to a parked van. The other opened the back of the van and shoved me onto a bench seat, snagging my jacket on a sharp edge of the door handle. Both sides of the van were equipped with cold flat metal seats. The slats dug into my legs. Eight disheveled people with glum, expressionless faces sat next to me. Frightened, I tried to become invisible. I sat very still, not saying a word. I hugged myself for warmth, as well as security.

The van approached a looming, stone fortress that stood on the hill. The gray skies added to the sinister nature. None of my friends knew where I was. Would they know to come look for me?

I thought of my parents back home. I was glad they didn't know. It would kill them. Tears formed, as I thought about my family.

Mama lived by the heart, not logic. Irish and the eldest daughter of a Pennsylvania coalminer, superstitions and old sayings colored her conversation almost daily. Some of her folklore rang true. "It's going to rain. The leaves are upside down." And it did.

"The caterpillars are fuzzy. We're in for a bad winter." A few months later, we'd have a blizzard. Or a ring around the moon signaled a change in the weather.

I thought of her adages about itching. "If your eyes itch, you saw something you shouldn't have." It was true.

The sleepless nights in the putrid, cold, jail cell did nothing for my state of mind. The other prisoners stared at me, as if I were a zoo animal. Our crowded cell housed six women. Even with the bunks stacked three high, there wasn't much room to move around.

The guards yelled at us and demanded obedience. They chastised the Croatian women more than the rest of us. I kept quiet and was pretty much left alone. A guard sneered at me, saying, "Goli Otek," jabbing me in the chest with his finger. I asked one of my cellmates what that meant.

Her eyes grew wide. "Bad place." She described it as a desolate island prison for political dissidents. I thought of the movie, *Papillon*, starring Steve McQueen.

I tried to put Goli Otek out of my mind. Evening arrived, and the temperature dropped. Moisture dripped from the rock wall, adding to the chill. One bunk had a blanket. The others laid bare. The mattress, two-inches thick, atop metal slats, cut into my body. Two people slept sideways on the narrow bunks, legs hanging over the side. The toilet, situated in an inconvenient area, wasted space. Sometimes, one of the women would be forced to sleep on the floor, if her bunkmates were angry with her. I tried to be invisible and not make any waves, but being American, I had two strikes against me. Everyone smoked but me, and the air was thick. I developed a cough. The others, convinced I was ill, made me sleep on the floor. A guard took pity and gave us two more blankets. I got the holey, smelliest one.

"We live in a toilet," one of the inmates muttered. The scurry of mice could be heard at night. Undefinable insects and vermin swarmed the cell.

The weekly shower came due. It didn't matter. "Only one shower working," a guard laughed, as we trudged down the hall. We all had to share the same shower. I suspected that the guards watched, as three or four of us struggled to wash our naked bodies under one showerhead.

The same food arrived each day. Breakfast — stale brown bread and tea. Lunch — cabbage soup, mashed potatoes, and more stale bread. Supper — fish soup and bread. At least, the soup helped warm us a bit. Once in a while, a carrot would show up in the soup. Probably so the prison officials could claim they gave us vegetables.

Tears formed, as I thought about my mama back home. Her sayings covered many situations. What would she say about my situation? "Good things come to those who wait?" Probably not. "Life is 10% of what happens to you and 90% how you react to it." Maybe. "After every storm, there is a rainbow." Was there a rainbow, or was I stuck in the storm?

Mama believed that itches predicted certain things. If your nose itched, you would kiss a fool. If your right hand itched, you would make a new friend. If your left hand itched, money was sure to come your way. If your ears itched, someone was talking about you. If your feet itched, you would travel. If your eyes itched, you were about to see something you shouldn't.

Well, the itchy eyes sure panned out. Seeing the demonstration and taking pictures landed me in prison. My feet itched, but they were dirty, red, and scabbed with athlete's foot fungus. Maybe, I was about to travel. Where? I'd hoped it would be home, but Goli Otek loomed in my head. Every day, I wondered if anyone would rescue me.

I began humming to break the tedium and to maintain my sanity. After a while, I realized I was humming "In Heaven There Is No Beer." A Croatian inmate studied me. She jumped from the top bunk and squeezed by me to the door. She looked through the peep hole, as we often did, trying to see what might be going on out there. She coughed.

She must be getting a cold, I thought. Great. Now, two of us have to find space to sleep on the floor.

I continued to hum, lost in my thoughts of home and longing to see my friends and family.

A guard called her name. She trudged from the cell and followed. She was gone a little over an hour. Upon her return, she flashed a toothless grin. The guard pointed to me and yelled for me to come. I hesitated but rose and followed. First her and now me. Something is up. I tried to think positive. Maybe, they're allowing some exercise time. Better yet, maybe someone has come to rescue me.

He took me to a dim interrogation room. My heart skipped a beat.

The warden sat behind a metal table covered with papers and a big stamper. What's that about? A single white light flickered over an empty chair. "Sit," he pointed. I complied. It's nice to be able to sit on a chair for a change, even a hard metal one.

He yelled something at me.

"I don't understand. I'm an American."

"Who you signaling?" His English hard to discern.

Confusion engulfs me. "What?"

"Who. A Slovene?"

"I don't know any Slovenians."

His voice rose, and he slammed his fist on the desk. "You signaling. The woman told us."

"What woman? I wasn't signaling anyone. I don't know anyone."

It was then that I realized the toothless woman must've said something, but what? And why did she think I was signaling someone?

"You hummed secret song. One famous by a Slovene singer in the U.S."

"What? Who?"

"Frankie Yankovic. You have conspirator in cell. Tell us who it is."

"Frankie who? What are you talking about? I was just humming to pass the time."

"We know you contact someone. The song is code. What did you sing?"

"In heaven there is no beer?"

"You very funny lady. You go to the box. You go to solitary confinement."

Just then, a man in a business suit arrived. He looked at me. "Thank God! I found you." Facing the desk, he pulled out an identification card and flashed it at the warden. "I'm from the US Embassy." He handed some papers to the warden. "This woman is an American citizen. I demand that you release her now."

The captain pored over the papers for what seemed like an eternity. He grabbed the stamper and pounded the paper several times. Were they really releasing me?

The warden rose and scowled. "You may go."

I left with the embassy official, grateful to be out of that stink hole. "I must smell to high heaven."

The emissary smiled. "We'll have you clean up before boarding the plane home."

"How'd you find me?"

The man opened the car door. "It wasn't easy. Your roommate said you'd gone off by yourself and weren't back, yet, so I called around. I heard about the demonstration and wondered if you might've gotten caught up in that. I talked to a lot of people and finally found you. The warden was in the process of moving you to Goli Otok. Fortunately, Soviet bureaucracy moves slowly, so I was able to track you down."

I thought of the toothless woman and my close call. She had talked about me. I thought my ears itched because of bug bites, but Mama's adage was right. Someone was talking about me. Mama sent me the message, and now my feet itched. I was heading home. Hallelujah.

Feminism Is Knowing We Are All Equal
Image by Amanda Caillau

Gardening Sestina

LIN BRUMMELS

*(A sestina is a poem with six stanzas of six lines and a final triplet, all
stanzas having the same six words at the line-ends in six different sequences
that follow a fixed pattern, and with all six words appearing in the closing
three-line envoi.)*

Cucumber vines wilt in hot summer sun,
peach ice cream melts in the damp kitchen,
pressed linen dresses droop when dew points
jump, smiles dissolve in rising air pressure,
no one wants to press clothes these days,
bunnies hop happily around the peach grove

eating over-ripe fruit as it falls in the grove,
July darkness cools, heat returns with the sun,
emerging red globe forewarns a hot summer day's
melting, we eat peaches and cream in the kitchen,
chase rabbits from the garden under pressure
to protect vines from invasion at all points,

sweating as soon as we step into rising dew points.
Rabbits and a few deer live in the nearby grove,
nightly feast on lettuce and fruit without pressure,
fade into brush and tall grass as soon as the sun
peeks over the horizon and floods the kitchen
with morning light signaling the new day's

beginning, time to plan an agenda for today's
gardening with special efforts at weedy points,
first listening to doves' coo from the kitchen
window that overlooks a fine view of the grove,

sit with coffee in hand waiting for the sun,
enjoy the early morning quiet without pressure.

Dawn breaks after passage of a low pressure
system that didn't bring rain to ease the day's
watering plans to rescue plants from the sun's
heat, again forecast for the nineties and points
higher, we hang our rumpled linen in the grove,
scare the deer and rabbits we see from the kitchen,

step outside into warm damp and close the kitchen
door to keep cooled night air inside, resist pressure
to eat over-ripe peaches from the bounteous grove,
remember, it's not an emergency, nor end-of-days,
avoid people that turn up their noses and point
fingers; just smile and pick cucumbers in the sun.

All too soon fruit's gone from the grove and days
shorten, the kitchen garden slows down and even points
of view change as pressure-system clouds cover the sun.

Fine Lines
Writer's Critique Group
meets the 3rd Thursday of each month at
Concierge Marketing
4822 S 133rd St., Ste. 200
6:30–8:30pm
Bring 6–8 copies of your writing for peer editing.
We start and end on time.

Lumière

JAYME BUSSING

Who should know the flames
Of love better than the candelabra?
Wax fixed where hands once touched,
Casanova and Maître' d I remain.

You came unannounced,
Setting the hearts of the castle
Aglow, engulfing this château
In the deadliest of wildfires.
Even my flames could not compare.

Bright, beautiful, and kind, you were
The solution to our woes and prayers.
A pairing unmatched. Unfit. Necessary.
The day you ran was the day my
Flames diminished.

When did my candle start burning for you?
My heart untamable, suddenly kindled.
Yet, I watch from aside, face wan and waxed,
So you might become a bride, and I a man.

Whose Key Is This?

WILLIAM CAMERON
Buffet Magnet Middle School

Whose Key is that? I think I know.
Its owner is quite sad though.
It really is a tale of woe.
I watch him frown. I cry hello.

He gives his Key a shake
And sobs until the tears make.
The only other sound's the break
Of distant waves and birds awake.

The Key is long, ridged and deep,
But he has promises to keep,
Until then he shall not sleep.
He lies in bed with ducts that weep.
He rises from his bitter bed,
With thoughts of sadness in his head,
His idols being dead.
Facing the day with never ending dread.

A Mother's Watershed

MARY CAMPBELL

Motherhood is the wide, green river curving
through the heart, beginning to beginning,
watering the tilted plain and surging through my
veins, emerging now and then, mysteriously salinized.
It burns the skin; the eyes turn into lakes, emitting rivulets
that carry off the residue of transitory misery or happiness,
neglected joy, and bittersweet remembrance.

At too great a distance from her watershed I am bereft, without
a home or compass. Safe beside her, I am known and cherished,
strong and capable, refreshed, refreshing, blessed, eternal. Just
tonight she has reminded me that it is time to fill the bottles from
her wells. That must be why I am so thirsty. I'd forgotten: There's
no virtue in the kind of sacrifice that weakens me. I, too, am
mother of a hundred streams. Depleted, how can I be generous?

Everything I plant in gardens on her slopes and in her valleys
flourishes, oblivious to drought and flood, in sun or shade. Her
spirit thrives in maple trees and terraces of pungent herbs, in
groves of lilac, vines of wild rose. Hers is a subtle presence,
growing lush just as the summer wanes, in towers of
chrysanthemums, in harvesting of apples, pears, and plums.
Because of her protection, by her foresight, in her love and grace —
thus am I snug all winter long. She has put up enough for
sustenance and liberality, for fellowship and charity. *Don't worry,*
I can hear her murmur. *God is good, there are provisions in the
cellar, and abundant game runs in the wood.*

There is neither benefit nor leisure for indulging in the shame of
having taken her for granted, nor should I blame myself for

offering a song or fragrance not the same as hers, for of necessity our courses separated long before (I thought) they ought to have. Unable to go back, impelled by currents I had no control of, I have faced implacably great cliffs of stone. Had I not known she waited on the other side, I might have stayed and gathered to myself the streams that chance and gravity had given me. I could have settled like a placid lake in such a Canaan, if it were indeed the Promised Land and it had been my destiny to populate that fertile valley. But the bottom would not hold; I must go on or be absorbed, and I was born to sing and on the strength of just one chorus, honed to honesty, could slice through bedrock, if need be, to force my way beyond the granite gates and flow again beside my source.

And I had generations to propel to greatness of their own in time, not mine to choose, thank God for that; thank Heaven that I finally knew how many rocks I need not move. The hurdles would make way for me or not, regardless of how hard I pushed, without respect to karma or the stories I'd created, saying, *Stumbling blocks, remove yourselves and go impede somebody else.* As it turned out, they were as porous as the sand. I simply drifted through, emerging purer than before. I left behind (for compost) death and other sediment. What better could I do but flow in ease and lightness toward the source, to motherhood herself? Why should I race to reach a destination foreordained in any case, when there are peace and apricots along the way?

Oceans

BUD CASSIDAY

In an ocean of stars
dandelion puffs float

like soldiers dropped
from airplanes

over France
those many

ages ago,
like metaphor

burning through
the sky a hole,

like tears
that never touched

the ground,
or a heart —

yet make oceans.

Snowing Against Season

YUAN CHANGMING

In the wild open west, flakes keep falling
Like myriad baby angels knocked down from Paradise

Blurring the landscape behind the vision
Hunting each consonant trying to rise above

The ground. The day is brighter, lighter and
Softer than the feel. Soon there will be

Dirty prints leading to everywhere (or nowhere)
And no one will care how the whole world will collapse

In blasphemy. The missing cat won't come to
Trespass the lawn, nor will the daffodil bloom

To catch a flake drifting astray. Nobody bothers even to think
About where the season is held up on its way back, how

The fishes are agitating under the pressure of wintry
Water, why people wish to see more and more snow

A Child Can Feel Pain in an Adult World

GENEVIEVE CHEREK-GARCIA

This is my true story. When I was a very young child, I liked to look at the beautiful postcards my father sent from France to my mother. They were embroidered silk flowers, all colors. One day, I asked about them, and my mother told me my father was in the Great War, World War I, that seemed to be the mother of all world wars. I was born 19 years after the war, and adding years to that, I was now old enough to ask questions. Yet, despite the horrific things he went through, when he got a break, he stopped at a little shop in France, remembered my mother, and sent her the most beautiful postcards I have ever seen or have seen since. He stayed in the war to the finish, but during breaks, he stopped at little shops to always send more postcards home, as Mom had a box of them. To this day, they sit in a metal box, tied neatly with a piece of yarn. Both parents are deceased.

Another war and another episode, World War II, and I was 3. By this time, my beloved brother packed his things neatly in a suitcase, and I never saw him again. Where did he go? He was gone! My mother and father's grief at his departure, knowing what he might have to go through, was probably too much to explain to a young person. After all, my father went through it 26 years before. One day, my brother did come back, and I learned a new word, "furlow." He was so happy to see me and in his joy threw me up into the air and caught me. Then, he was gone, again. We had letters to remind us he was somewhere in strange places. I couldn't figure out why he would be there in the first place.

He came back to stay in 1945, and by then, I was 8-years-old and an avid reader. I knew all about war, all the letters mom sent to him overseas, and his letters sent back, things like he is "going to the front," Nazi's, and German invasions. Years later, I learned my brother was in the Battle of the Bulge, and an old picture showed him driving a tank. I never blamed God for war, I knew at a young age there were disagreements among men, that men run countries, and not knowing any other way to solve their problems, war is the solution. Peace came, eventually, but there were horrible consequences left on both sides.

When he returned from the war, he got a job in a meatpacking plant and left for work late in the afternoon. I sat by the window everyday watching him leave, and he was gone. I can still see the curtain blowing in the breeze, as I waved goodbye. Thoughts returned to me. Is he coming back? Each day, I greeted him when he returned. I went through this every day, until time healed those thoughts, and I grew up.

One day, he took his wallet out and showed me a picture of a little girl. He said to me, "I carried your picture all over Europe."

That is how much he loved me. He taught me "never give up" and "always keep your job. It is a safety net and will protect you when things fail." I had those seeds planted in my brain for many years, and my attitude in life has always been to never give up.

Story Tellers

JACOB CLARYS

I believe in the importance of being literate and learning how to appreciate an education. Storytelling and learning from each tale are important to me. Reading for pleasure is a must-do activity for a wholesome life, and reading well has shown me how to pay attention when telling stories of my own.

I go to church almost every Sunday, like most Catholics, but while most people are dying to get out, I am intently listening to the parables that are told. Not only do I want to learn their religious content, but it intrigues me how these same stories have been passed down for hundreds of years, inspiring people in different ways.

The best teachers are story tellers. People learn almost all of what they know by listening, and what better way to learn something, than through stories. As a child, some of the most memorable times that I had, were lying next to my mother, fascinated, while she read *Little House on the Prairie* to me and my younger brothers. Learning lessons through the eyes of Laura Ingalls Wilder was truly amazing, and I hope children now get that same experience.

Not only am I fascinated with stories in church, but in school literature as well. I wrote a book report my freshman year of high school on *Animal Farm*, which was written by George Orwell, and to this day I still remember every detail about the book and what it meant. The story of the animals on the farm was written by an author who was anti-communist and hoped to show all its dangers to the public. By using suspicious animals representing their unnamed people counterparts, he crafted a story that was not only entertaining but informative as well. I truly appreciate good story tellers and writers, because they are some of the most influential people on the planet.

I Was Justified in Being Upset

ALEX COLE

Having the freedom of creative writing helps grow minds and is almost "a religious-like devotion." It makes one's thoughts visible and more comprehensible. Therefore, creative writing makes life easier to process.

Whenever I go to therapy, I tend to talk about my rumination issues and the anxious jumbled up mess in my head. My anxiety can get to the point where all I want to do is lie in bed and not worry about anything, but that's almost always impossible, because I end up thinking about it anyway.

As cheesy as it sounds, my therapist always recommends journaling. It doesn't have to be in a neat and organized leather-bound volume. Most of the time, my "journaling" is just scribbling on the side of my agenda notebook. The writing tends to be in incomprehensible paragraphs, but just being able to get the noise out of my head is therapeutic. Once in a while, the sides of my pages are not enough to contain what is going on in my head, and I need to bring out the big guns. In these situations, my thoughts are formally crafted, as if I was preparing for a debate, and end up being a novel all their own.

One of my biggest mistakes in high school was letting my counselor talk me out of creative writing. I am a creative type, so naturally, I was excited to take a creative writing course. In my school, students have to talk with their counselors when making their schedules for the following year. When I went into the meeting, the counselor's eyes went straight for creative writing. I was already taking two other art classes, because my focus was to be an art major, and I thought creative writing would help contribute to my future major.

Something that is popular in my school system is to pressure students to take as many AP courses as possible, so they can say we have the most students taking AP classes. Instead of following my passion, I let my counselor pressure me into taking AP Biology. In doing so, I ended up barely passing the class, only got four hours of sleep a night, and lost my All American status because I couldn't keep up with the class work. I had already taken AP World, AP US History, AP Language, and AP Literature. I didn't need AP Biology for any credits, and I wasn't interested in the Sciences.

When my art teacher found out about my situation, he went down to the principal's office and yelled at him for pressuring kids into AP classes. (Turns out I wasn't the only one.) He, of course, apologized later for blowing up, but it was nice to know that I was justified in being upset.

*"Do not grow old, no matter how long you live.
Never cease to stand like curious children before the
Great Mystery into which we were born."*

ALBERT EINSTEIN

Smarty, Smarty, Smarty

ED CONNOLLY

I meet with three of my sisters about once per month for brunch. We catch up on stories and reminisce. This last time, the sister, one year younger, asked if I remembered "Smarty, Smarty, Smarty." It brought back some memories. You can determine if they were good or not.

A long, long time ago, my sister and I sang a duet in a talent contest at the local school. I'm not sure how I got forced into this, but I'm pretty certain it had a lot to do with my sister getting revenge for something she imagined I did to her. She was 6, and I was 7. I don't sing very well. As a matter of fact, when I go to church, the minister asks me not to sing.

The name of the song was simply "Smarty." This fit my sister pretty well. Smarty Mouth would have been better but that's just me. The song is from 1908 and was originally sung by Ada Jones and Billy Murphy in 1914 and recorded on a gramophone. No, I'm really not that old, though sometimes I feel that way.

Ada recorded a lot of songs, like "Don't Get Married Any More, Ma," and "All She Gets from The Iceman Is Ice." The "Smarty" song is about a boy and a girl, and she apparently caught him kissing another girl. My sister sang the first verse, and as much as I hate to admit it, she did a pretty good job. We then sang the chorus together ("you're nothing but a smarty cat so there, there, there"). Then, I sang the second verse, after which we sang the chorus again together.

That ended the song, and we're supposed to exit stage left. My sister began to go off the wrong way. Being the more mature person, I had to grab her and guide her the correct way. Okay, okay I was pretty pushy as I knew she had just ruined any microscopic chance that we had of winning anything.

We did end up winning third place. She falsely claims that the reason we got third was because the judges liked the pushing and shoving at the end of our song. She says that is why we got $15.00. I say that her confusion on which way to exit the stage cost us first place, which was worth $50. That's $35 more. In today's dollars, that is $365 more. No small number to a seven-year-old boy.

That wasn't the end of this adventure. We than went to Lincoln and auditioned for a TV talent program. We didn't get a call back. My sister had serious delusions. She thinks the reason we didn't get a call back was because we didn't have the pushing and shoving at the end. I think I'm being a realist in saying we really weren't that good, and "you're nothing but a smarty cat, so there, there, there."

The Lost Child

BEV CRANSIER

Why am I so afraid to create on paper what has been my constant underlying passion since I was a young teen of 16? What is it that I am so afraid of? Failure? Rejection? Could be. Or is there more to it than just those insecure feelings?

A story I heard recently struck a chord in my heart and memory when I listened to a fellow writer describe an incident, which involved her young grandchild. She described her grandson's reaction to a prism of light reflecting its beams on a wall, as that of awesome wonder and pleasure. It carried me back in time, when I remembered a young child who approached the wonders of life around her in that same inquisitive way. Various thoughts stirred within me, as I questioned what occurred during her lifetime, which caused her to lose that ability to look at life in such a wondrous way. I felt a strong suspicion that her passion was still very much alive somewhere deep within the recesses of her soul. Over the years, I have caught quick glimpses of her passion. Now and then, I have experienced her ebb and flow and a vast range of emotions. Often, I find myself pondering about possible past circumstances that may have stifled her passionate true feelings, especially now as she fades into the life of a middle-aged woman.

I remember many years ago how she used to sit for hours at her bedroom window and fantasize about the leaves on the pink dogwood tree just outside her room. She would envision the leaves dancing and nodding in conversations to each other, keeping rhythm with the gentle breeze. In her mind, various conversations took place between the "family" of nodding leaves, and she could entertain herself for endless hours. The birds flying to and fro in the trees and bushes would also catch her eye, and her imagination would run wild again creating stories about each of the various bird "families." The little girl would visualize in her mind what activities occurred in their nest "homes" and how excited the young birds became anticipating their parents' return with food in their beaks as a prize for them.

Occasionally, she would catch a glimpse of her neighbors' shadows as they would travel from room to room in the house next door. She envisioned a large gigantic storybook entitled *Life* existed in the heavens and represented each family in the world. "Each home had a story to tell," she would say to herself. On each separate page of the giant book, a home was represented in the story of life. At the end of every day, when family members in all homes represented shut their eyes for sleep each night, angels in the heavens closed the gigantic book of life for yet another day. As a young child, she was awestruck by that concept and pondered on it quite frequently, playing out the various characters in her mind's eye.

Her childhood home was situated on a dead-end street with the backyard bordering a grassy marsh which boasted cattails in their season. Her family home was next to the last house on the block on the marsh side. The reed marsh ran on the outside perimeters of her backyard and curved around the adjacent neighbor's yard to establish the boundary for the dead-end street. The distance between her parent's lot and the houses on the opposite side of the marshlands was approximately 1½ miles apart from each other. Quite often in the early mornings while getting ready for school, she would take time to daydream and gaze at the houses across the marshy grasslands. Sitting at her bedroom window, she would watch the shadows cast by moving figures in lighted rooms within those homes. As she watched those shadows, her creativity would take over as she imagined the various activities taking place within the families living in that neighborhood. It was an impressionistic and innocent time in her young life.

At that point in her life, she didn't realize her passionate imagination was a gift to be encouraged. Without her realizing it, experiencing a private world of imagination all her own set her apart from significant others in her immediate world. She felt so different from her siblings and the other kids at school and thought that maybe something was wrong with her. Should she talk to someone about it, she thought to herself? She didn't know who to go to for Mom and Dad were always so busy, and she just wanted so badly to fit in and be "normal." She often craved the attention of others, and in a family of five children, it was difficult for her parents to evenly distribute attention to all of them. This was no fault of their own — they were just unaware of the deep craving for recognition she particularly needed and desperately wanted in a private world all her own.

She remembered a particular way she would strive for attention would be to dramatically induce antics so she would be the center of attention. When she would proceed with one of these antics, she would more often than not receive a disapproving look from one of her parents, signifying it was unacceptable behavior, or worse yet, feel the jealous look from one of her siblings. Even if her reward of attention was captured for only a few moments, or the attention she received was negative in nature, a feeling of success would encroach her spirit.

Her parents cared for her and her siblings well — as much as any children could be cared for in a middle class family of the 1950s. Her family was not well off financially by any means. However, her parents worked very hard to provide a comfortable living environment for their five children. They loved their children very much, but in that day and time, love was not always spoken aloud, but shown in various non-physical ways. Not shown — but known. Despite the knowledge that she was loved, she still felt lacking — a feeling that has haunted her to this very day. At times, she still feels disconnected and yearns to be in touch with the world around her, only to be fooled at times by a phantom connectiveness. It puzzles her.

She grew up in a family atmosphere of Virginian-type manners of "Yes, Ma'am," "No Sir," "Please," and "Thank You." Manners had been engrained into her life from early years on and added dimension to her personality. But, also engrained in her continually was, "What would the neighbors say?" mode of thinking. That would definitely curb any mischievous or negative behavior patterns right down to the quick! Even to this day, that particular mode of thinking, which was engrained in her so long ago, reflects her restrained and aloof performance in both outward appearance and behavior patterns. It had squelched her spirit.

Her older sister would describe her as passionate about everything! The young woman could identify with that, for when she felt something about anything it was with all her soul. Whether it was a happy emotion or despair, inquisitiveness or withdrawal, her emotions would range so dramatically from high ups to low downs.

Years later, it was discovered she suffered, and still suffers, from Attention Deficit Disorder which caused various learning and social disorders in her life. After all these years, that recurring feeling of being different invades not only her creative world, but also rears its ugly head in her social skills and how she perceives the world around her. The young woman had to learn on her own, through painful trial and error, what worked successfully for her and what caused negative reactions from those around her. She has learned to adjust to her world by learning new behavioral patterns that compensate for her feelings and actions. These compensation patterns help to guide her through life's various issues and everyday occurrences with others and life in general. Every single day of her life, she continues to struggle with this issue of living in a much different world than others. A different beat of life's "drum" is what she hears, and she is forever searching for creative ways within her daily grind of life to appease her restlessness.

She was born to think outside the lines, but social expectations of her young days clipped her creative wings, and dutifully she succumbed to what was expected of her. Trying so hard to please her parents and everyone around her, the effort instilled a behavior pattern of passivity for approval to include those in authority positions. Her early social environment created an inner child who strived to be a people pleaser, and at times it spills over into present day.

I look back today at that child's life and realize I killed my creative self. I sold myself out without even realizing I did so. How can I revive my creative child? The passion to write has been inside me since I was 16 years old — I am now 50. So many years of creativity have been lost. Is it too late for revival?

A characteristic I have developed over the years from my many different struggles in life is that of being a survivor. I have decided to rise above my fears and losses by beginning a journey of discovering this lost, creative, and fragile child within me. She's still here with me — just hiding behind a memory. I catch a glimpse of her occasionally playing creative "peek-a-boo" with me, and I am confident and optimistic that she will be unveiled.

Recently, I had the wonderful experience, and one of which I consciously chose to happen in my life, of participating in a journaling group. The messages I heard from my fellow writers were echoes of "Give up control," "Take a risk," "You do have a voice," "Look at your soul through writing," and "A lot of it may be junk — but that's okay." These words were a healing balm for my soul's passionate fire to write without fear. The gift of my opinion being valued was given freely by this group, and I was confirmed positively, even though I was a stranger among them. Their unconditional acceptance of me being just where I am in my writing activity provided the catalyst I needed to begin my "lost child" journey. I intend to accomplish this journey through the practice of a new habit of journaling.

If I come face to face with fears that jump out at me from the lined pages of my journal — so what! I have the power to just close my journal until I am stronger, or more inquisitive to open the "door" of my journal once more, peek in, and start my walk again. My new journaling friends enlightened me to the fact that it was the worst that can happen to me! During my journaling process, I will sometimes just crawl at a snail's pace, and other times, I will sprint like a champion marathon runner breaking the ribbon at the finish line to claim first prize! Shakespeare wrote many centuries ago, "To thine own self be true." How that phrase rings clearly to me now as a reminder of what I must do to find my "lost child."

I am anxious, through the encouragement of my fellow journal writers, to begin this journey with all the passion that my heart holds. When I write, I am my happiest — my soul sings and soars! I have so much to share with others, and I feel obligated through this vessel of my life to use that talent. So be it! I will not be afraid of the shadows of a lost child's passion from this day forth!

The Boy Scouts of America: Misconstrued in Society

BENJAMIN DALTON

The Boy Scouts of America announced on October 11, 2017, that they would become "The Scouts of America." This was done because of a controversial change that would allow girls to become Cub Scouts starting in 2018, allowing females into the "Scouts BSA program," which is just the old Boy Scout program/curriculum. There was an outcry from a lot of people. The negative attention came from those who probably did not know or understand the program. Those same protestors are probably just as knowledgeable as those who think most of the male adult leaders in Boy Scouts are pedophiles, abusing an innocent system to get closer to young children. All of this has led to a culmination of gross misunderstanding from the public view on what the Boy Scouts program really is. The common stereotypes among new issues have caused an outcry of hatred that could be easily solved, if our society would experience it like those who are in the program have.

The Boy Scouts of America (BSA) has been around for over 100 years, starting in 1910; however, it did not originate in the United States. The Boy Scouts Association was created in 1908 by Baden-Powell. W.D. Boyce was an American entrepreneur, who was assisted by a scout, when he was lost in the London fog. When the boy refused a tip because he was a Boy Scout, he became enthralled in the concept of it all and started it in America. It became the fastest growing youth organization in the United States. The program underwent a lot of reconstruction in its early years due to questions that arose after its popularity. How old do children have to be to join scouting? Should eight-year-olds and seventeen-year-olds really be doing the same program? These questions created the two different programs of Cub Scouts and Boy Scouts.

The Cub Scouts would become a program open to boys in elementary school grades, kindergarten through sixth. Then Boy Scouts would take them through until they were eighteen-years-old. Cub Scouts would focus on activities such as basic fundamentals of camping and learning a variety of basic skills that helped them in life along with playing different sports, doing crafts including pinewood derby cars, and learning communication skills. Boy Scouts emphasize adventure and the enabling of skills they practice. They found the split in age made it more appropriate, and it still gives the chance for new Boy Scouts, who are age eleven when joining, to see sixteen to seventeen-year-old scouts in their same troop setting examples of what they should strive to be like.

I started Cub Scouts in third grade in Pack 490. The meetings were held at my school. I started doing it because my brother, who is four years older, just started doing Boy Scouts, and I really had no say. My time in Cub Scouts was over before I knew it, and I was on to the real deal, Boy Scouts. The troop I joined was based out of my church, which was right across the street from where my Cubs Scout pack met. Troop 476 was where my brother was, along with a lot of other people I knew from my Cub Scout pack. This made the transition easy. My brother and his age group of friends were very impressionable on all of us and helped us to learn what Boy Scouts was all about.

Boy Scouts is the greatest program available for youth to learn respect, reliability, and the value of being thrifty. The Scoutmaster of our troop, Jerry Kline, did those three things to the extreme. Most people would be confused by why he was even there. Our Scoutmaster was 30 years old, unmarried, with no children of his own, and had no connection or relation to anyone in the troop. However, not once have I, or anyone else, been made uncomfortable by him in any regard, because he had a mission. Mr. Kline wanted to give kids the chance to grow into adults they never could have imagined. Every time we saw him, he surpassed people's expectations they had of him.

He turned boys into men. He created a boy-led environment that allowed us to grow and communicate like adults.

The "boy-led troop" is not a common thing in scouting. It was very unique to our experience. Every troop has positions like Senior Patrol Leader (equivalent to a president), a treasurer, and a quartermaster (takes care of troop gear such as tents). While entering our troop, instead of a boring adult telling the Boy Scouts what to do for a couple of hours once a week and one weekend of every month for campouts, there are fellow scouts showing us the ropes of what to do and how to do it. This enables older boys to become leaders of younger boys and create a strong brother-like bond between the boys in the troop.

Being a Boy Scout can get anybody made fun of by classmates, as I did, relentlessly. However, it provides a much deeper understanding of the world. Between the Scout Oath and the Scout Law, the two main principles of scouting, boys learn to respect those who might not always show the same respect back. They learn to take care of themselves. The highest rank of scouting is the Eagle Scout. This is an emblem of character and represents Scouts for the rest of their lives. When scouting first starts for a boy, the adult leaders talk about how the boy should want to reach the Eagle Scout, because of how it looks good on college and job applications. I would argue that is the least important part of the ordeal.

Scouting is an adventure. Scouts will learn to do marvelous things they never thought they could accomplish: fight through adversity and earn the respect of their peers, while growing into well-rounded individuals. The memories and life lessons they learn are what get them jobs and into college. I, myself, am an Eagle Scout and am incredibly proud of that fact. However, I would rather go the rest of my life holding those memories and lessons, than ever flaunt my Eagle badge, as a reason why I should be picked over someone else. Once a boy becomes an Eagle Scout, he always is one. The skills he learns and the activities he experiences become like invisible tattoos that only other Scouts can understand. I've spent most of my life explaining the honor it was to become a Scout.

Equality for All
Image by Amanda Caillau

Sweet Dreams

JASMINE DALRYMPLE

It's just a dream. It's just a dream — I keep telling myself. My eyes jolt open, and my heart begins to race. I'm in near sweat from that nightmare. The rhythm of my heart is racing as adrenaline pumps into it. It feels as if I am about to have a heart attack. I sit up in my bed, taking deep breaths trying to calm myself. The warmth of my bed has a comforting effect on me and helps settle my nerves. That is the fourth nightmare I have had this month — flashbacks of an incident I experienced as a child. That childhood event is haunting my dreams. I have no reason to be frightened. It was long ago, but what disturbs me the most is the fact that I keep dreaming about it.

I sit in my bed thinking about why all this is happening to me. I come to the conclusion that it's because of all the stress I've been going through these past few weeks. I'm a staff writer for a newspaper here in New York, and things have been pressing down on me hard. I've been assigned to write an *interesting* column that's due by the end of the month on a horrifying event people have experienced. The reason my boss is making me write such a ridiculous column is that Halloween is right around the corner, and he wants something to spook-up the paper.

I don't dare say that I haven't even started, but it's true. I haven't been able to write a single sentence on the subject. Maybe, it's because I don't know anything horrifying, or perhaps, it's just writer's block. But sitting in bed wasn't going to make that assignment disappear. I swing the covers off and slide into my house slippers. I walk over to the window and draw the curtains letting in the morning sunshine. It's a beautiful area where I live. I purchased this apartment after I graduated from NYU. The city noises can be a bother, sometimes, but I'm up on the tenth floor, so I can't hear those obnoxious horns honking.

I walk into the kitchen and begin to fix myself a cup of coffee. I pour some French vanilla creamer and stir it. I take my mug and walk over to my desk facing the window. I like to be able to look out the window when I'm writing.

I log onto my computer and begin checking my emails to see if I have any queries from my boss on my upcoming column. I like checking my emails in the morning, so I know what I have to do for the day.

I scroll through and see nothing unusual, just typical Monday emails of advertisements and store discounts. I gaze down and see an email sent at midnight.

The sender's name read Nance. *Nance?* I thought to myself, I don't know anybody named Nance, at least not someone I can recall. I clicked on the email and saw it was addressed to me, Elyce Murray, and Allie Smith.

My eyes widen when I see the names of two friends whom I haven't seen in years. They were some of my closest friends growing up in Illinois. I haven't kept in touch with any of my friends except for Elyce, who occasionally texts me to wish me a happy birthday or Merry Christmas. I haven't spoken to Allie since high school. We had a couple of falling-outs in our teenage years and never reconciled.

I scrolled down to read the email.

> *To: Christine Prescott, Elyce Murray, Allie Smith*
> *From: Nance*
>
> *Hi, Girls!*
>
> *Long time no see. It's me, Nancy Cypress! Sorry for such a late email, but you're all hard to find. I've been up making funeral arrangements for my parents. Both of my parents passed away. I'm inviting you all to the funeral, which will take place this weekend. We have lots of catching up to do. Please email me back to confirm.*
>
> *Love,*
> *Nance xoxox*

Nancy Cypress. I can't believe I have come back in contact with Nancy. I haven't seen or spoken to her in years, much longer than Elyce or Allie. I can honestly say I forgot about Nancy. I'm not sure what Nancy is up to these days, but I think she is still living in Cypress. Nancy's family owned Cypress Woods and a house in the woods. The woods have been in her family for over a hundred years. Allie, Elyce, and I use to go out to Cypress during the summer to stay with Nancy and her parents. I can't believe her parents are dead. I remember them so vaguely; all I recall was them being really nice and great parents to Nancy.

I wonder what happened.

I begin to contemplate the email and whether or not I should reply or keep my distance and not attend and focus on my work.

I decide to give Elyce a text and see if she knows about the email. I log off my computer and grab my cell phone and text Elyce asking:

> *Hey Elyce, I was wondering if you'd by any chance got an email from Nancy Cypress about a funeral for her parents?*

I hit send and waited for her to reply. I wasn't sure if she still had the same number, but I used the one she texted me on a few months ago to wish me a happy birthday.

I wander around my apartment anxiously waiting for her reply. I gaze at the clock and see that it is nearly twelve o'clock. Instead of pacing around waiting, I need to occupy my mind and decide to take a shower. I take my mug back to the kitchen and run the faucet to rinse out the coffee left inside. I set the mug upside down on a clean hand rag and head to the bathroom.

The shower is a refreshing start for me. I feel much better about myself and ready to get to work. I slip into some jeans and a flannel and towel-dry my hair. It is a little damp but not completely wet. I've been avoiding using any hot tools on my hair for a while now. I'm trying to grow out my hair, and I've been doing a great job so far.

I head back to my desk and take out my notebook and folders that hold the story I am working on. I pick up the pencil and begin to write, then hear a *ding* from my phone — a text has come through.

I grab my phone and see Elyce's name. I unlock my cell phone and click on the text from my notifications.

Hey, Can I call you???

With those three question marks, I assume Elyce didn't know. But of course, I'm not going to stop her. I reply with a *Yes*.

I set my phone back down and walk back to my desk. I figure Elyce might take a while to call. Before I can sit down, the phone rings and buzzes on the table. *That was quick*, I think to myself. I scurry to the phone and see Elyce's name. I answer it. "Hello," I say.

"*Chris?*" I hear Elyce say slightly confused on the other end. She must've thought my voice sounded different. The name *Chris* sinks into my mind. I haven't been called that in years. That name brings back memories. In fact, Nancy Cypress was the one who nicknamed me that years ago. Allie and Elyce eventually caught on to it and started calling me Chris, too. I never liked *Chris*, because every Chris I knew was a boy and far too masculine for me. I preferred my real name, Christine. After hearing Elyce say *Chris* after all these years makes me realize that it's stuck with me.

"Elyce, hey it's *Chris*," I say trying to spit that name out of my mouth.

"Hey, Chris! It's been so long, how are you?" Elyce's voice changes to excitement. "I'm doing fine, just trying to figure things out."

"Oh, believe me, I know what you mean. I can't believe Nancy's parents died. It's unbelievable."

"I know, it's crazy to believe it. But death gets you unexpectedly."

"Exactly what I thought when I read the email. Are you going?"

"I'm not sure. That's why I called you. I wanted to know what you were doing?"

"I'll go if you go. It'll be nice to see everyone again. Plus, we haven't been back there," Elyce paused. "Well, you know, since that thing happened to you."

I feel my throat tighten up, hearing those words. I can't even remember what Elyce is talking about. I know something did happen to me in Cypress Woods, but I don't remember what. I paused for too long, leaving Elyce's voice echoing my name. *"Chris! Chris.* You still there?"

"Yeah, sorry. I got to get back to work. Talk later?" I said.

"Of course."

"Bye."

I hang up the phone before she can say goodbye. I am frazzled by what she said. I can't seem to recall what she was referring to. I'm not sure if my mind intentionally cut that out of my memory or if I can't simply remember. Whatever it was will be coming back to me soon.

"The road to hell is paved with works-in-progress."

PHILIP ROTH

The Element of Inspiration: The Experience of Hope, a Journey, and Success

MITCHELL FEAGINS

Without any effort there is no progress, and with no progress there is no satisfaction. It's hard for people, including myself, to find the effort for certain things. There are many things that get people to make that effort. One of the factors of effort is inspiration, which is the will to act along with a previously produced feeling of confidence. Inspiration is the thing that breaks hesitation; it gets you off the couch, metaphorical or not. Inspiration is a mute voice in one's heart and mind. To me, every bit of effort requires some form of inspiration. There are many things that most people would not do if it was not for something that was in their head telling them to act and that everything would be okay. Someone's own personal path in life has been steered back and forth, and a lot of the time it is due to something in their head, telling them to go the way they want to. Inspiration puts people on the desired path. Through this metaphorical road of life there are many victories along the way. To me, inspirations are a beacon of all sorts of possibilities for the whole world. They happen more than once because something in their mind that told them to act and to go the way they wanted to came through for them. Without any inspiration many of the most world-changing idols would not have acted. And with none of these idols, there would be no change and progress. Inspiration is change and progress. Inspiration gives hope, a journey, and success.

Without hope there is no life-changing journey or success. It is the first step of the lifetime experience. Hope creates strife, an act without it is passionless and has not as much worth as one with hope has. Inspiration is a big element of hope; it tells the darers of life that what they want to do is possible and that it has been done before. Hope is courage; it is the dare to act. Without hope, there is no act which leads to no wanted journey and no wanted success. I believe that inspiration and hope go hand-in-hand. Inspiration creates hope, and with that hope there is a passionate act. When others look upon passionate acts, they become inspired. It's a cycle of internal satisfaction and real-world progress. These people want to act, but maybe they just need a boost of confidence. Inspiration tells them that their dreams are possible and that they matter. I believe that an act of hope is the hardest step for many, myself included. Hope gets me and a lot of people out of the comfort zone and it puts us in an alien place. Most people are not just going to try to start a journey without any signal of hope because they fear that it could all go wrong. Inspiration creates hope, a window of possibilities and opportunities.

For a lot of people, including me sometimes, the journey is the best part. All of the experiences along the way are the most memorable. After the first step of the experience has been completed, where to go? The answer is to keep going, go somewhere. Continue attempting daring acts, go where your heart belongs. There will be mistakes but also many victories. Depending on the way one looks at it, mistakes themselves are victories. Mistakes are gifts of new knowledge and experience. Hope is not a chore, because it is consistent and throughout the journey until the very end. Inspiration is that strife to keep going. It is the journey itself. Throughout the journey, one will look back to the things that inspired the trip`. Along with victories, there will be so-called 'mistakes.' Mistakes are a different kind of victory, the reward they bring is not apparent until further along the road. Unlike mistakes, victories have sudden positive results. With mistakes, there must be the will to endure the sudden hardship that comes with it. To endure the knowledge it brings is an alternative victory. When these mistakes hit, remember what inspired this journey that led to this mistake. Did the thing that inspired the journey also have mistakes? Remember that hope will stay until the end; it keeps the journey in motion. Inspiration and hope will stay throughout the journey.

At the end of the dream that started the experience, the final goal is what the dreamers set out for in the first place. Success is relatively the last stage of this experience. Success is the dream finally becoming true, a humongous gap finally filled after so long. To me, success is either the main goal or the side goal depending on the journey. Either way, it is a reward for starting the first daring act of hope. When the big wish becomes reality, it gives people more reason to try to keep succeeding and carry onto more journeys. When success occurs, the experience comes full circle. In some ways, success can be inspiration too. Success inspires others; it tells them that it's not impossible, just like what happened to the original inspirer. An act of success or just an act in general, can inspire others. What is there to do after success? The best option is to start yet another experience. Get more hope, start another journey, and maybe even succeed. Take the knowledge gained from this experience and use it for more purposes, inspire others.

Inspiration gives people hope, a journey, and success. Inspiration is that thing in one's head that tells them to go for the metaphorical stunts. Taking that first leap of faith starts the experience, because it is hope incarnate. Carrying on after that leap and taking many others is the journey. And fulfilling the desires wanted in the beginning is success. Inspiration can start an experience of a lifetime, and it can alter the future. It is a cycle that tells the people that their dreams are possible and they have to chase them. Inspiration gives a boost of confidence, without which many well-known inspirational idols would not be where they are. With no hope, many people would not dare try the first stunt of courage. Without a journey, there would be no steering of the path to a desired destination. With no success, there would be less confidence and will for the lifetime experience. Without inspiration, there is no effort.

Inspiration steers people to the needed window of opportunity. Inspiration matters, and it is what helps people survive. In my own humble opinion, inspiration is a needed factor of living life. Inspiration helps people, me included, get through the day. It pushes people out of bed every morning. There's a well-known poem I think perfectly describes inspiration, *Do Not Go Gentle into That Good Night* by Dylan Thomas. In this poem, there is a line that says *"Rage, rage against the dying of the light."* This line is repeated throughout the poem. I believe it is about fighting against death in someone's final moments. Something in this being's life inspired him to keep living, fighting for more life until the very end. Inspiration keeps people living and the world turning. It helps people find a much more satisfying way of life.

"We need poets to change the world."

JUSTIN TRUDEAU

Take This Dog

KRISTI FITZGERALD

"Take this dog" she said
"please"

Judy
from the rescue place
handed you to me
and the smell rising off
of you
made my eyes water

"take this dog" she said
"please"

Your hair was
shaved to the skin
and you were
covered in scabs

"take this dog" she said
"please"

Your eyes were full
of sadness,
your tail tucked
between your legs

"take this dog" she said
"please"

You rubbed against me
and rolled
on your back.

You licked my hand
and stared into my
eyes with your soul

"take this dog" she said
"please"

You lifted your
leg on my couch
and ran from
the cat

"take this dog" she said
"please"

You put your paw
on my arm
and lifted
your eyes up
waiting
for me
to love you
and I did

"take this dog" she said
"please"

You tucked your
head beneath my arm
and wriggled
against my side
your floppy foot dangling
in space

"take this dog" she said
"please"

You snorted a lot,
and your tongue
was always
hanging out,
and you
wagged your
entire body
when you were happy

"take this dog" she said
"please"

You went on
adventures with us
and slept next to me
on the bed
you would stare at me
as if to say
'mama, I love you'

"take this dog" she said
"please"

the vet said to me,
"kidney failure,"
when you were
too young
and my heart
broke in two

"don't take this dog from me" I said
"please"

I held you in my arms,
your tongue was
a heart
sliding out of your mouth

and your eyes said,
'don't worry, mama'
and my heart
broke in two
again

"don't take this dog from me" I said
"please"

I rescued you
but that's not true
because we both
know
you rescued me

Fountain of Fire
Photo by Derek Burdeny
derekburdenyphotography.com

Mr. Creevey's Library

LAYLA FLEMING

Buffett Middle School, Grade 5

It was Halloween night. My friend Jackson and I had plans to go trick or treating for some delicious chocolate candy. Olivia, our friend from the neighborhood who was homeschooled, saw us walking and asked to join us. We stopped at four houses and one of them gave us full-size candy bars. We then see a light through the forest across the street.

"There must be more extra-large candy bars if the house is that hard to find!" said Olivia.

We ran into the forest, but before long we didn't know where we were. Finally, we reached the light, but it was not a house it was an abandoned library. The library stood still in the moon light, its silence making the warm breezy night air chilly and raw. Nothing but darkness could be seen through the weather-beaten windows and chips of grey paint lying on the ground below. Olivia went first into the library. We told her, "This is crazy," but she didn't listen!

The forest was creepy. We were scared outside in the dark. Jackson followed Olivia inside, and I wasn't going to stay outside by myself. We tiptoed inside. Olivia saw a book floating towards her. She grabbed the book out of the air and began reading aloud. It was an old nursery rhyme book. We told her to stop reading, then suddenly a ghost appeared! The ghost seemed nice at first. He said his name was Tom and that the owner, Mr. Creevey, would be very angry if he found kids in his library. Olivia was still holding the book Tom told her to finish. Reading the nursery rhyme, he had a weird looking smile on his face.

Olivia looked hypnotized and kept reading, until she suddenly fell to the ground. Tom disappeared. We didn't know if she was dead or alive. Jackson checked her pulse and felt nothing.

"She's dead!" he yelled. Jackson then picked her up, and we ran as fast as we could back to town. When we got to Olivia's house, her mother began crying, as Jackson laid her on the porch. Just then, Olivia awakened, singing the nursery rhyme. Her mother quickly grabbed the king-size candy bar and told Olivia to eat it. Jackson and I were confused, but seconds later, Olivia returned to her normal self. Olivia remembered nothing of the night but the delicious taste of chocolate peanut butter crunch.

Everything seemed to go back to normal after that night except Olivia wouldn't talk to Jackson or our other friends. She would only hang out with me alone and was often sad. I long forgot about the evening, until ten years later, when I was walking down the same street. Out of the forest, two ghosts appeared, singing the nursery rhyme. I ran straight home and locked my doors. The next morning, I went to Olivia's house to tell her about what I saw. Her mom answered the door and began crying when I asked for Olivia.

"She has been dead since that horrible night ten years ago!"

Turning Darkness into Light

TRANSLATED BY ROBIN FLOWER

I and Pangur Ban my cat
'Tis a like task we are at;
Hunting mice is his delight,
Hunting words I sit all night.

Better far than praise of men
'Tis to sit with book and pen;
Pangur bears me no ill will.
He too plies his simple skill.

Often times a mouse will stray
In the hero Pangur's way;
Often times my keen thought set
Takes a meaning in its net.

'Gainst the wall he sets his eye,
Full and fierce and sharp and sly;
"Gainst the wall of knowledge I
All my little wisdom try.

Practice every day has made
Pangur perfect in his trade;
I get wisdom day and night
Turning darkness into light.

....

The author's name is unknown, although we are sure it was written by an
eighth-century Irish monk, who was living in St. Gallen, Switzerland. This
is the earliest written Gaelic poetry that has survived.

Leo

MARCIA CALHOUN FORECKI

What was the name of that soldier Leo brought home after the war?
Ellie had thought about him all morning. Not Leo, the other one, the
unknown soldier.

He had dark curly hair and a tight stomach. Jack? Jimmy? Jake? Ellie
went through all the J-names she could think of, even Jedidiah, until
she stopped and wondered what made her so sure his name started
with a "J" at all.

*His ears stuck out from his head. I'm certain of that much. All that hair
on top of his head balanced out the ears, though.*

This was Ellie's third Thanksgiving without Leo. He had awakened
one morning with his right leg swollen to twice its size. It was a blood
clot, a deep vein thrombosis from sitting behind the wheel of a truck
for too many hours for too many years. Not like today with all the
rules and restrictions, rest times, and what not. Back when Leo started
driving, it was strictly pay by the mile, and the more the merrier.
Before Leo could get an appointment with the only doctor he had
seen for 30 years, the clot broke free in the leg and didn't stop until it
reached Leo's heart.

Ellie cut butter into flour with two knives for pie crust dough, as
she always had. Her mother had shown her how to crisscross the
knives, so the butter and flour formed little balls the size of early peas.
Marianne, her oldest daughter, bought Ellie a special tool for cutting
butter into flour. It was good for nothing else. *What a waste,* Ellie
thought, when she saw it. She tried using the cutter once or twice,
but it felt awkward in her hand. Besides, she had to think about it,
when she used the gizmo. When she used two knives, her hands took
over, and Ellie was free to think about other things. By the time she

replayed her wedding in her mind, or Marianne's first day of school, or getting a flat tire in the rain on the way to the hospital to deliver her son, Gregory, the pie crust would be rolled out and in the pan with perfectly fluted edges.

For Ellie, cooking was like driving had been for Leo. He always said he had done it for so long that he didn't have to think about the clutch or the gears or the steering anymore. He could think his thoughts. Ellie invited the daughters and daughter-in-law together to make Christmas cookies the year before Leo passed. Alice was Gregory's wife. When Alice rolled out the dough, she concentrated so hard that her tongue stuck out a little. Ellie had to stifle a laugh and started singing "Joy to the World," all four verses.

Apple and pumpkin. Two pies were plenty. Ellie had already made a coconut cake earlier in the afternoon. It came together almost by itself. The first coconut cake Ellie ever made took her half a day and leaned a little on the platter. She had made it for Leo's Army friend, the first time he came to share dinner. Coconut was Leo's favorite, of course. The friend insisted on helping with the dishes. Leo took the radio out on the front porch and smoked, while he listened to the Kansas City Athletics play the Yankees.

"Come on out here," Leo called. "Score's tied and beer's cold."

At the time, Leo's friend's lips were planted softly on Ellie's lips. He just turned her around at the sink and kissed her. Not a "thank you for dinner kiss." It was a "there's more where this came from" kiss. *Whatever was his name?*

Ellie never had problems with names or dates or places before. She remembered every trip the family had taken, where they stayed, and what the motels had been like. She could name every neighbor who ever lived on the block where she and Leo made their home. She cooked from memory, never from recipes, and her meals always came out right. Was this the beginning of some change, some milestone to indicate that she was getting older? How could she forget the name of the one man she had ever touched except for Leo? Was it time to start giving up things like hosting the family Thanksgiving? Were the girls ready to take over? Was Ellie ready to pass it on?

Alice always brought a relish tray and two cans of cranberry sauce. "When are you going to let me make the pies?" she always asked. *When you learn how,* Ellie always thought but never said. Apparently, it helped Alice to believe that Ellie wanted to do the pies herself, rather than the truth, which was that Alice couldn't make a pie crust to save her soul. Leo told Ellie that she should let Alice make the pies. "How's she ever going to learn, if she don't make a few clunkers?"

Ellie set a beautiful table on Thanksgiving. She took pleasure in hand-washing the fragile dinnerware that Leo sent her from Taiwan during the war. He was with the occupation troops so he could get great deals on china, silk kimonos, and tea sets. Ellie had three. Two sets were boxed up to give to Marianne and Alice for Christmas. *Whether she wanted them or not,* Ellie thought.

Ellie went to bed early. She drank a short glass of bourbon to help get her to dreamland. But, this night, even the hooch didn't help. Her thoughts kept flip flopping between making the stuffing for the turkey and washing dishes with Leo's friend. He ate with them, often, and sometimes, the dishwashing took an hour.

Leo never helped wash dishes. He barely set foot in the kitchen after breakfast, and he only ate his breakfast there, because Ellie refused to serve eggs and bacon in the dining room. Leo considered the kitchen a female sanctorum he was forced to enter once each day. When Leo wanted a glass of water or a beer, it was "Ellie bring me a beer," or "Can I get some fresh coffee in here?" Sometimes, even now, all these years later, when Ellie put her hands in hot sudsy water, she thought about those stolen kisses from Leo's friend. *What was his name?*

After Leo passed, Ellie's son, Gregory, bought her an electric dishwasher and tore out a perfectly good cabinet to install it. After Gregory demonstrated how to use it, Ellie never touched it, except when the whole family came to eat. On her own, she rinsed out the few dishes she used by hand.

Ellie always roasted her turkey breast down. It was juicier that way. She flipped it over twenty minutes before serving and basted it with real butter to get that magazine-picture golden crust everyone admired so. She had made a whole flock of turkeys over the years, just that way. She had never had any trouble whatsoever, and she had no reason to think she would have any problem this year, either.

By 12:30 on Thanksgiving Day, everyone had arrived at Ellie's house. The grandkids were playing a game on the living room floor. Marianne was draining the potatoes, and Alice was opening one of her cans of cranberry sauce.

"Gangway," Ellie called, as she lifted the roasting pan out of the oven and set it on the wooden cutting board. "It's time to flip the bird," she said.

The girls laughed, as they always did.

Marianne called to her husband, Dwight, "Mom's flipping you the bird."

Dwight and Gregory laughed, as they always did. This year, the grandkids giggled, too. That was new.

As Ellie worked on the turkey, steam rose and fogged her bifocals. No matter. She didn't need to see what she was doing. Cooking was instinctive to her by now.

When Ellie lifted the turkey to turn it, her wrist suddenly went weak on her. The turkey started to fall. Alice yelped. Ellie caught the hot bird in her apron. She kept it off the floor, but the dripping juices were burning her legs. Marianne grabbed a dish towel and wrapped it around the turkey, as she lifted it back into the pan.

"That's why you girls should wear aprons," Ellie said, as she rinsed her hands in the sink. Alice ran to the bathroom and returned with a damp wash cloth. She wiped Ellie's legs. "You go change, and let us finish in here," Alice said.

Ellie hesitated a moment. She had never turned her kitchen over to anyone before. Not even when she was sick. Not even when she had a newborn on her hip. The kitchen was her domain, her haven, the place where she felt confident. It was the place that kept her biggest secret.

"I guess you can handle it," Ellie said. "I brought the meal this far."

Marianne turned to her mother. She held a stick of butter wrapped in a paper towel. She was buttering the turkey breast just the way Ellie always did. "In fact, Mama, I was going to tell you later, but next year Thanksgiving is at my house."

"All of it?" Ellie asked.

"All. You'll be the guest of honor."

Alice picked up the hand mixer and put it into the potatoes. Ellie couldn't believe her eyes. Didn't Alice know that she was about to take a shower in potatoes and milk and butter? Before letting the mixer rip, Alice turned to her mother. "You can still make pies, if you want to."

"Pies? They're a piece of cake," Ellie laughed.

In her bedroom, Ellie pulled a clean dress out of her closet. She felt something she couldn't identify right away. Was it relief? Yes, it was. Relief and a little sorrow at passing Thanksgiving on to the next generation. What kind of menu would the girls come up with? It was a cinch there would be some kind of rice dish. Marianne loved rice. Ellie fluffed up her hair, after pulling the dress down over her head. Leo hated rice. After being in Japan all those months and eating it every meal, he refused to let Ellie bring rice into the house. Leo's nameless friend laughed and said he wouldn't mind rice, but only if Ellie cooked it and if he could eat it with a fork instead of chopsticks.

Leo had introduced his friend to his cousin Eileen. He invited them both for Thanksgiving one year. Eileen insisted on helping with the dishes. Leo's friend rocked little Marianne in the living room. "I'm so glad to see he likes babies," Eileen had whispered into Ellie's ear. Ellie said nothing. She just scrubbed the roaster with steel wool, as hard as she could.

After changing her dress, Ellie returned to the dining room, where she sat down to her last home-cooked turkey dinner. She enjoyed it more than any meal she had cooked in years. After the meal, the girls helped Ellie put the food away, but Ellie refused to let them wash the dishes. After everyone had gone home, Ellie sat alone at the kitchen table and dozed to the hum of the electric dishwasher.

Wide awake in bed that night, Ellie thought about passing Thanksgiving to the next generation. They wanted to make their own traditions for their own families. The young ones had passion. They stuck out their tongues, when they did difficult things. Ellie needed to find something new to do, something she would have to concentrate on, something that would make her tongue stick out a little. *What would it be? Genealogy? Growing orchids? Ceramics? Just what I need: ugly pots of orchids all around the place.*

Ellie wanted to do something hard, something she could never master. She needed a carrot on a string on a pole so long she could never bite it. If she did conquer some new challenge, she would find another to take its place. Ellie saw herself swimming the English Channel. When she reached France, she would turn around quickly and swim back. She would write a cookbook describing every dish that could be made with onions as an ingredient. Train for a marathon. Learn to play the piano. Number the stars.

Ellie decided to start off more modestly. She would make a list. Before she forgot any more names, she would make a list of everyone she had ever met in her life. Next to their names, she would list where she met each person, how they were related, and to the extent possible, what happened to them. If she didn't know, Alice could help her look people up on the thing, on the Internet, the Google. It would take months to make such a list. Years. As Ellie kept meeting new people, in doctor's waiting rooms and estate sales, the list would never be complete.

Ellie rose from her bed and walked to the dining room. From the bottom drawer of the hutch, she drew out some writing paper. She sat at the table and wrote her name across the first line of a blank page: "Eleanor Constance Brennen. A List of the People She Met and Why They Are Important to Her."

Where to begin? Her parents were the first people she had met, of course. Ellie started with them. She wrote all she could remember, which took hours. Next, she started remembering Leo. They had met at a carnival. There was only one place left on the Ferris wheel, and Ellie's friend, Rosemary, was too chicken to ride, so rather than wait until the next turn to go with Rosemary, Ellie asked the tall kid behind her if he wanted to share a seat. Leo had shrugged, and when they stopped at the top of the wheel, Leo leaned over the bar and shouted to his friend below, "Hey, Monty. Look at me!" *That was Leo's friend with the protruding ears and mop of hair. Monty.*

He married Eileen, and they moved to Oregon or Alaska. They lived in a town with the word Bay in the name. Ellie thought she should send them a note, let Monty know Leo had passed. What was the name of that town? Something Bay or Bay something. It had something to do with babies, she was certain. Oh, yes, Coo's Bay. She wondered when she first heard of the town who Mr. Coo was and how he came to have his own bay.

It was nearly 3:30 in the morning when Ellie rose from the dining room table and carried her coffee cup into the kitchen. She rinsed the cup with hot water and dried it. *Next year, all I have to do for Thanksgiving is show up with two pies.* There was that mixture of relief and sorrow, again.

Leo loved Thanksgiving. He would make Pilgrim hats for the children and then the grandchildren. He helped to tear stale bread for the stuffing. He even roasted chestnuts in the fireplace for Ellie in the evening, when the dishes were washed and the children slept. Suddenly, Ellie felt glad she was giving Thanksgiving to the girls. It wasn't the same without Leo. He's the one who first came up with the line about flipping the bird. How Leo could make her laugh. Besides, making a turkey dinner for ten people was a big chore. Once a person loses her passion for a thing, it's just so much work.

Ellie never encouraged Monty's kitchen necking. Never discouraged it, either. It was flattering to be wanted. It made her feel she was still in the female business a little bit. What did the Commandment say? Don't covet your neighbor's wife, or your husband's Navy buddy. Same thing. She never coveted Monty, even though he kissed like he was born for it. Monty would lean in and give Ellie a couple of baby smacks. Then, he pulled her close and landed his lips on her like a leaf meeting the grass, soft and easy. Monty didn't grind his mouth onto Ellie's, like boys in high school did. He pushed easy like a breeze on a pond. *Funny,* Ellie thought, *I can relive those kisses like they happened this morning, but I couldn't come up with his name all day.*

The idea hit Ellie, just as she was falling asleep. It was the perfect project. Here was her passion, her masterpiece. Ellie rose from her bed and opened Leo's closet. She dug deep into a box on the floor. The box contained remnants of her children's school days. Ellie brought some boxes up from the basement in that flush of cleaning she experienced just after Leo's death. She wanted to de-clutter in anticipation of moving on with her life. But, move on to what? As she couldn't answer that question, the boxes went into Leo's empty closet.

Now, Ellie knew what she wanted to do, must do. Somewhere, in the box of old school art projects and report cards, were several partially used Big Chief tablets. Ellie saved them from the end of the year, thinking the kids could use up the empty pages, when they started school the next year.

"I can't use a third-grade tablet in fourth grade," Alice said. Maybe it was Marianne.

"The pages are all blank, ready for fourth grade work," Ellie reasoned, but to no avail. Apparently, the tablet carried the indelible mark of third grade, and Alice could not use it in any other grade without danger of losing what she had achieved the year before.

Ellie was finally glad to have the pulpy paper in the tablets. To her, the blank sheets were like a paved road stretching far into the distance. The promise of a future. Ellie opened the cover. Her new passion, the endeavor that would carry her through the seemingly empty years ahead was to write a book, a romance, a tribute to a wonderful, desirable man.

It would be difficult, but that was precisely the sort of undertaking Ellie wanted. Something she had to work at, lose sleep over, and pour her soul into. This would be an emotional journey, a self-examination. Ellie even had a title: *Forbidden Kisses.* The book would tell the story of the love affair of a wife and her husband's best friend. It all began with stolen kisses in the kitchen. Ellie needed all of her imagination to take the story from the innocence of a few kisses to a smoldering work of fiction. Ellie was wide awake, now. She drew on her flannel robe and tied the belt with a yank of determination.

Ellie awoke the next morning at the old desk in Gregory's bedroom. Her neck was stiff from lying on her folded arms half the night. Her cheek stuck to the top sheet of a Big Chief tablet when she raised her head. The page was empty but for a small circle of saliva.

All that day, Ellie thought of Monty. She brewed coffee, made her bed, and washed the tablecloth from Thanksgiving dinner, all without effort or thought. Her hands moved through the tasks on their own. Ellie imagined encounters with Monty, stolen moments in the kitchen, secret meetings in the corner booths of dark restaurants. While she picked through the turkey carcass to find meaty scraps for making soup, Ellie's mind focused on a tearful parting scene at a pier, as Monty prepared to sail off to battle. In her book, Monty was the ship's captain, and the war had just begun.

The after-Thanksgiving sales started that morning, and Ellie wanted to pick up some new tinsel. She planned a small tree this year. Dragging a big tree into the house and decorating it alone had been difficult the year before. This year, Ellie intended to simplify. The grandkids might be disappointed, but they would adjust when they saw packages

with their names on the tags stacked on the coffee table. Let their
parents sweep up pine needles until Groundhog's day. Ellie was finally
finished with that.

Ellie wandered around the new K-Mart store. *What did I come in
here for?* she thought. She had come for something very specific, but
she couldn't remember what it was. Laundry detergent? Depends?
A weed whacker? Ellie smiled; she always thought "weed whacker"
was the funniest term she ever heard. It didn't matter. Ellie was
content to wander the aisles. Her mind was occupied with imagined
romance anyway.

Monty lay in a Navy hospital, his hands bandaged from the burns
he suffered pulling a young sailor from the burning engine room, after
his ship was struck by a kamikaze plane. The young sailor stumbled up
the stairs, pulled by his courageous captain. The young sailor, named
Leo, vowed to name his first born after the man who saved his life.

In her story, Ellie had rushed to California to be at Monty's
bedside. She took the train and peered out the window through
trails of rain, as if the whole world were crying. Poor Monty. It was
agony for him to speak, because his throat had been burned when he
breathed in super-heated air in the engine room. Still, Monty had so
much to tell Ellie.

You see, Monty had not been completely honest with Ellie. When
they met at the little tavern where Ellie worked as a waitress for her
father, Monty failed to say he was married. Now, he felt he must tell
her. The kisses they had shared were forbidden, and Monty needed to
make a clean breast of it to Ellie, and very soon now, to his Maker.

As Ellie walked away from Monty's bed, her eyes flooded with
tears. She could not see the young sailor in the bed by the door.

"Please, Miss, can you reach my water cup?"

Ellie looked over and saw a handsome young sailor with bandages
over his eyes. In feeling the bedside table for his tin cup, he had
knocked it onto the floor. Ellie retrieved the cup and took the sailor's
hand, placing the cup in his palm. Her fingers brushed his. She stood
as if paralyzed by the sailor's bed.

"Step up, lady. This line hasn't moved in five minutes," a voice behind Ellie growled.

"Sorry," Ellie stammered. She rushed ahead and placed her items on the check-out counter: fifteen spiral notebooks and a box of number 2 Ticonderoga pencils.

"Don't they make Big Chief tablets anymore?" she asked the cashier.

"If it's not in the ad, it's not on sale," the cashier mumbled.

Driving home from K-Mart, Ellie's mind wandered back to her story. She focused on the young sailor. He had a sweet voice and a tantalizing half-smile.

"My name's Leo," he said.

Ellie turned the car into the driveway and parked beside the azaleas Leo had planted as a surprise for her first anniversary, years ago. Ellie realized her book was not about the dashing captain but about the young sailor. Every good writer knows to follow the characters and let them tell their own story. Ellie wrote about Leo, remembering so much of the life they lived together. It was a humdinger of a steamy romance, and Ellie hardly made up any of it. She changed the title, too. She called her book *Love for a Lifetime*.

"Use what talents
you possess: the woods
would be very silent if no
bird sang there except
those that sang best."

Henry Van Dyke

I Am From

CECILIA FUNES PETIT

I am from Comayagua, Honduras,
where the blue and white bleeds out through the calls of citizens.
I am from a place where a phone may be your last breath, and
the cries of mothers burying their sons repeat through the streets.
I am from a place where danger becomes beauty,
the sites of mountains trailing off into the horizon,
sites of oceans that become bright blue.

I am from a place where the smell of baleadas hit your nose,
tasting the warm homemade flour tortillas, and
creamy beans captivate your taste buds.
I am from a place where gangs are powerful, and
7,000 migrants march for a better life.

I am from a place where childhood memories
remind me of the simple life, I used to live.
Scars evoke how I miss my country.
I am from French and Norfolk ancestors.
Petit and Funes shape my DNA background.
I am from Comayagua, Honduras,
a place that shows my culture is Catracha.

Walls of Stone

JOANN GARDEN

Walls are built instead of bridges
Walls of stone that span the ages

Walls upon which children stand
And shed their blood to stain the sand

The drops of blood become the stones
Picked up by a child and thrown

Or used in walls we hide behind
Or used by demagogues to blind.

Throughout our time the human race
Has hurled stones and found no peace.

Let us tear down the walls of stone
Defang the demagogues that roam

Use the stones for building bridges
Between the nations, across the ages.

Mumble

NANCY GENEVIEVE

"Mumble," he called it. He wanted "mumble." And I gave him potholders.

"No. Mumble," and I gave him pans.

He shook his head NO with a pure patience that as a neophyte mother I felt unworthy of receiving, I offered him books and brushes, even oranges and an eggplant.

I rhymed words, "Mumble. Stumble. Tumble. Fumble." But not one noun appeared in my mind or leaked from my mouth.

In his eighteen-month certainty, he did not elaborate. He held his arms skyward; however, and I picked him up, kissed his nose, and tickled his cheeks with my eyelashes until the laughter rolled up from his belly and saturated the air with its joy.

When he stopped his mirthful celebration, he placed one of each of his hands on each of my cheeks and made sure I was looking, really looking, into his eyes before he spoke, "Mumble," he said. "Mumble."

"I know my precious son, 'Mumble.'"

His eyes danced. He believed that I did understand.

But I didn't. Not really. I knew he wanted *mumble*. But what was *mumble*?

Then from a gift beyond my mind that I would grow to trust like his good heart, I set him on his own feet and held out my hand and said, "Mumble."

He took my hand, and this time, for the very first time, he led me to HIS destination. Hand-in-hand, we walked out of the kitchen, through the living room, down the hallway, and into my bedroom. He pulled back the curtain, which hid the overly stuffed area in this university apartment and acted as a door to our family's only closet, and pulled his hand free from mine and pointed to the upper shelves, "Mumble."

I shoved the desk chair to the closet. He gave me his best, new-tooth smile.

Finally, whatever it is, it is on these shelves.

Shoe box after shoe box full of treasures were retrieved from the shelves: pictures which needed scrapbooks, a fossil collection from my childhood, and unanswered letters from high school friends. As I opened each lid, he shook his head NO and waited.

I began a conversation I knew we could have, would have, someday. But for now, I spoke both parts: "I know you know what you want, and I would give it to you.

"I want mumble. It is on that shelf. In that box.

"Here, look; do you want ribbons to play with? Red ones? Green ones?"

He folded his arms more or less over his chest, and I laughed. He was talking to me in non-verbals, as clearly as I had ever heard them.

I ran my hand over each box and waited for his response. Well, his lack of a response. Until my hand rested on the box which served as my sewing basket. Then, over and over, he repeated, "Mumble. Mumble. Mumble."

"What the...?" but I brought it off the shelf and placed it on the chair's seat and lifted its lid.

He peered over its edge. I brought items out for his inspection — thread, buttons, even scissors. Finally, in the bottom was my silver thimble.

When I held it in the palm of my hand, dawn broke.

His whole face glowed with light. He heaved a contented sigh and took the thimble and put it on his forefinger, exactly where I always wore it for those quick repairs.

He walked out of the room, saying softly over and over, "Mumble. Mumble. Mumble."

I held my tongue and did not remind him, again for the first time, *Don't put that thimble in your mouth.*

Arctic Blast

JOAN GIVENS

I tune into KGUN 9, Arizona's ABC station, hearing words like wind chill index and *Arctic blast*. I shiver, even though I'm 1,300 miles away. It is not that long ago that I watched school cancellations scroll across the bottom of my TV screen in Nebraska.

I remember an early October storm, when freezing rain clung to tree branches. Bent down with weight they couldn't support, branches snapped, bringing down power lines. People read by candle light and huddled under comforters for warmth. The power stayed off for a week, and families lost all the food in their freezers.

I recall walking across a parking lot on my way to an early child-hood education meeting. I slipped on black ice, scraping my knee, tearing my nylons, and making me forever uncomfortable on icy walkways. That incident contributes to my living in Green Valley each winter.

I remember even earlier times when driving in snow was a chal-lenge, one I gladly undertook. I wasn't afraid to venture out and congratulated myself when I made it up the icy hill.

As a teenager, ice skating at Miller Park pond was a season-long activity. Trudging up the steep hill to the ice house to warm myself by the heater in the middle of the room was fun. Then, bravely skating down that same hill to the pond below was challenging and invigo-rating. I practiced skating backwards, gliding on one skate, and quick stops on the toe of my skate.

I sit here now immersed in memories. As a young person, I wel-comed winter, with its snow forts, snowball fights, sledding, and ice skating. Even as a young family, we relished days off from school to play in the snow.

How much has changed, from delight at seeing those snowflakes fall to dread at what they might mean. When did fear slip in? When did caution overtake joy?

Hispanic in the USA: I Am

ROXANA GOMEZ

Society thinks Hispanics are meant for picking fruit and fixing gardens, but we are so much more. Hispanics receive criticism from politicians, because we are not natural born citizens. Hispanics have been discriminated against ever since the Mexican-American War was won by the United States. Every race experiences discrimination. Hispanics experience it every day.

The first Spaniard to set foot in what later became the United States was a conquistador named Juan Ponce de León in 1513. He first arrived at *La Florida*. Within the three decades of arriving in the Americas, the Spaniards were the first Europeans to reach the Appalachian Mountains, the Mississippi River, the Grand Canyon, and the Great Plains. They even began to sail along the East Coast, up the Atlantic Ocean, as far as Maine. Hernando de Soto also came to the Americas. He traveled through Georgia, North Carolina, South Carolina, Tennessee, Alabama, Mississippi, Arkansas, Oklahoma, Texas, and Louisiana in 1540. That same year, Francisco Vásquez de Coronado led over 2,000 Spaniards and Mexican Indians across what is now known as the Arizona-Mexico border. The conquistadors did not just come to America to explore. They came to settle, make homes for people, and create an empire.

Once the Mexican-American War was over, the United States got 55 percent of Mexico's land, which included California, Arizona, New Mexico, Texas, Utah, Nevada, and small sections of Colorado, Kansas, Oklahoma, and Wyoming. The people who were already settled in automatically got citizenship. In 1850, California was divided into two sections. The northern part was meant for Whites, and the southern part was for Hispanics. The whites named it "Californios."

In 1931, the racism and violence began. Mexican-Americans were told to move to the urban barrios in the poor areas. Police officers and immigration agents would go around town and grab Mexican-Americans. Regardless of their citizenship or immigration status, they were loaded into vans, and taken to Mexico.

In 1848, Hispanics received discrimination. They were arrested, illegally deported, and lynched. Many white men would accuse them of doing things to white people. So many accusations were made, but court trials seldomed happened.

In 1851, Josefa Segovia was accused of murdering a white man. The townspeople marched her through the streets, made a fake trail, and lynched her. Over 2,000 men came together and watched her die, while shouting racial slurs. Even children got accused of rape and murder. In 1911, a fourteen-year-old boy named Antonio Gómez was arrested for murdering a white person. A group of 100 townspeople gathered to try him, and instead of giving him jail time, they lynched him and dragged his body through the streets of Thorndale, Texas, for everyone to see.

When the Great Depression began, nobody was working. Anglo-Americans accused Mexicans and other foreigners of stealing jobs from Americans, who feared that the Mexicans and other foreigners would end up stealing all the jobs, and the economy would not get better. Immigrant agencies ended up deporting over 2 million Mexicans to Mexico, even if they were American citizens. They even went to hospitals and got Mexicans who had an active illness or disability and dropped them off at the border.

In the South, Latinos were not allowed in restaurants, movie theaters, and schools. In the beginning of the 1870s, Latinos were expected to attend separate schools. Many whites thought Latinos did not know how to talk, read, or write, but that was not true. In the 1940s, a young Latino girl named Sylvia Mendez was rejected from attending an all-white school in Orange County, CA. Her parents fought back and filed a lawsuit against the Orange County School District. Their goal was to win the case, so all children may attend the same schools, no matter what race they are.

When the case was occurring, there was a statement saying that Latino students were dirty and carried diseases that can put white students at risk. Judge Paul J. McCormick took seven months to make up his mind. On February 18, 1946, he said that school districts discriminated against Mexican-American students, and that violates their rights of the Constitution. Thanks to Sylvia Mendez and her lawsuit, she won and ended segregation in the Orange County School District. Once she attended school with other races, she got harassed by her classmates. Other parents in Texas and Arizona began to hear about the case, so they filed for lawsuits against school districts and successfully won. Brown vs the Board of Education banned segregated schools throughout the country.

Latinos are still discriminated against. It got worse, lately, because President Trump made a comment that Mexicans were rapists and drug dealers, and they are only here to steal jobs. I have seen videos, the news, and social media about people yelling at Hispanics, because they are not talking in English, and in America, we speak English. I saw a video of an older Hispanic man, who was walking, and out of nowhere, an older black lady threw a brick at him, telling him to go back to his country. That is not okay; they should not harass people by the way they look or the color of their skin. This is not all right.

Last year, when I was working and ringing people up at my cash register, I heard a white lady yelling at a young Hispanic girl for speaking Spanish to her mom. The lady's voice began to get louder, and she said, "We're in America. Speak English." The Hispanic girl was not having it and began to get up in her face to defend herself and her mom. My manager ran to the two arguing women and asked the lady to leave the store and apologized to the Hispanic girl about the older lady. My manager said that no one should act like that to someone who was not doing anything wrong.

There was also a video of an older white lady yelling at a Hispanic mom and her children, because they were talking in Spanish. A bystander defended them, which I thought was nice of her. She ended up telling the lady to leave the store, because they deserved to be there just as much as she did. Just a couple of weeks ago, my older sister was working, and she was helping an older white man. He wanted to deposit something, but he did not want to show her his license, because she might steal his information. The man began to yell racial slurs at her and at the other employees. He wanted to be helped by someone who was white, and there was only one there who was working. They ended up asking the man to leave the bank, because of his harassment to the employees, and he was no longer able do business at the bank.

People may not be paying attention to the news about Hispanics getting deported or being harassed in public, but it is happening every day. Some stories may not make it on the news or social media. It is heartbreaking, because these are innocent people, who want to have a better life for themselves, especially for their children. My parents came so my siblings and I could have the opportunities they never had.

Where I Want to Be

ELIZABETH GRAHAM

(*An original villanelle*)

The thought of the ocean puts me at ease
Waves flowing over the glittering sand
Nothing is better than feeling the breeze

In winter, the top of the sea will freeze
The entirety of the sea is grand
The thought of the ocean puts me at ease

To think of those who've traveled through the seas
Travelers had the sea at their command
Nothing is better than feeling the breeze

I watch the swaying of the big palm trees
The bright moon shines its light onto the land
The thought of the ocean puts me at ease

Those who look at the ocean say it frees
I would say the ocean is a dreamland
Nothing is better than feeling the breeze

Someday soon, take me to the ocean please
I don't need to do anything but stand
The thought of the ocean puts me at ease
Nothing is better than feeling the breeze

My Historical Travel: Boston

ELIZABETH GREUNKE

Throughout my life, I have taken history class upon history class. It was not until my eighth grade year that something sparked and made me fall in love with this subject. Ironically, the movie that made me deeply interested in history was *The Patriot*, which is notorious for being one of the most historically inaccurate movies. Nevertheless, it is still an interesting movie. I am most drawn to the Revolutionary War era, because I love learning about the past events and how they shaped the United States into the country it is today. Because of my deep love of history, I want to travel and see the places first hand.

There are a lot of components that make history interesting and worthy of seeing. I am fascinated by the historic roles of women. Some of the iconic women who had a role in the U.S. Revolutionary War were Abigail Adams, Molly Pitcher, and Anna Strong.

Abigail Adams was one of the first known feminists of her time. She actively pushed for women to be educated and to be known as more than "their husbands' wives." She is also very well known for a letter she sent to John Adams during the Continental Congress, declaring that he should not forget about the ladies. Molly Pitcher is a name given to women who ran water to troops on the fields in the midst of fighting. Throughout the span of the Revolutionary War, many women did just that, giving them the name Molly Pitcher. One woman who took on this name was identified as Mary Hays. Mary ran pitchers of water to soldiers fighting in the legendary Battle of Monmouth. My favorite historical woman is Anna Strong, who was a spy in the Culper Spy Ring. She made a huge impact on the war, as the ring is one of the biggest factors as to why we won. Seeing how these intelligent and courageous women contributed to the war effort encouraged me to better myself. They influenced me to be the best person I can be.

The atmosphere and everyday life during the U.S. Revolutionary War was also very intriguing. That may sound like an oxymoron, but it is impressive how they carried on about their lives without the technology we have today. They only had the bare necessities to help them live. No toilets, lights, or cooking appliances. Instead, they had chamber pots as toilets, candles as lights, and a fireplace as an oven. When I think of a town in that era, I think of little wood shops that sell textiles and pubs that housed drinking soldiers. Reading about places like that is one thing, but being there is another. I could only imagine visiting those places.

In the summer of 2016, I made my way to the East Coast with my grandma. We went to Boston, which is said to be the most walkable big city in the United States. Since I was young, my grandma and I had gone on trips together. We have been to Branson, some cities in Iowa, and Nebraska. She had some reward points to travel to a destination, and she asked me to go with her on a trip. We chose to go to Boston, because of my love of history. We stayed in Boston four days, July 10–14. When we arrived, we stayed in a hotel in the heart of Charlestown. The first day, we visited the USS Constitution, which was a warship used in the War of 1812. Although it was not used in the Revolutionary War, it was still extremely fascinating to tour. Next, we walked around the city. I thought it was beautiful how the old buildings and the skyscrapers were mixed together. We then discovered Faneuil Hall, and we ate there each night we were in the city.

The second day in Boston, we went on a trolley ride around the city, to help us understand where the historical places were. We visited the Granary Burying Ground, which was founded in 1660. We saw the graves of Samuel Adams, John Hancock, victims of the Boston Massacre, and Paul Revere. Then, we did a "bells and bones" tour, which included touring a crypt underneath the church next to the burial ground and a bell tower where one of the original bells made by Paul

Revere is hung. We stopped by the historical house that he lived in later. After that, we went to the Old North Church, which was where they lit the famous lanterns to signify when the British were coming. The church was absolutely stunning, with white and gold accents. It was fascinating to see the reserved church pews, for the ladies and gentleman, dating all the way back to 1724.

The third day in Boston, we went to a Boston Tea Party museum, which was different than most, because it was on an actual boat. We threw a "crate of tea" into the harbor like the actual Boston Tea Party in 1773. However, the crate was made out of a foam material and a string was attached so it could be pulled out of the water. We then went to the Bunker Hill Monument, which was just steps outside our hotel. I climbed all 294 steps to the top and was awed by the beautiful skyline. We ended our night at Faneuil Hall, which is a huge food court. It had food from clam chowder to Greek food. The food court was a long, big building, and outside there were buildings that had clothing stores. It was my favorite place to eat new food and to shop.

On the fourth day, we strayed from downtown and went southwest. We took the subway to the Boston Commons Garden and other historic churches. The Garden was in full bloom and was really beautiful. There were swans, statues, and old, gorgeous trees. We saw the First Baptist Church, which was founded in 1665. Inside, I found a sign that used Fs instead of Ss. The practice of using "F"s instead of the "S"s dates back to the Old English language, and I thought the sign showed how truly old the church was. We then went to the Trinity Church, which was such a beautiful church, and it looked similar to a castle with vines growing up the bell tower. Next, we went to the Green Dragon Tavern, which was a hub for all of the patriots during the war, including The Sons of Liberty. While we were there, we saw a man dressed up as a Redcoat soldier drinking at the bar.

On the last day, we visited the Old State House in the heart of the city. The inside was a museum of old paintings, clothes worn by John Hancock, and other artifacts from the war. The interesting, yet sad thing about the old building, is the basement of it is now part of the subway system. Outside of the front door was the spot of the Boston Massacre, which was symbolized by a brass circular stone in the ground. This Old State House was so beautiful, and I am so glad we stopped in. Next, we took a ferry tour of the harbor. It was a slightly chilly summer day, so it was a very pleasant ride.

History was the main reason I went on this trip. I was so excited to travel to a historical place and see the history firsthand. I saw all of the historical buildings I wanted to see, and it absolutely made my love for history grow. Boston showed me a part of the world I have never experienced before, and because of that, I really hope I can visit other cities like it. I mixed enjoyment with passion on this trip, and I am so grateful for the opportunity to go to this beautiful, historical city.

The Sun and the Stars: The Infinite Importance of Exploration

BOMAN R. GROFF

In his memoir, *Wind, Sand and Stars,* Antoine de Saint-Exupéry states, "Now the clay of which you were shaped has dried and hardened, and naught in you will ever awaken the sleeping musician, the poet, the astronomer that possibly inhabited you in the beginning" (11). Saint-Exupéry was a French pilot in the early twentieth century, whose passion for aviation brought him to explore the world from a unique perspective and reflect on the personal importance he found in life. The core of the author's statement is a warning: do not waste the opportunities that life presents, seize them as a chance to explore. Nearly a century later, Bertrand Piccard and André Borschberg have taken Saint-Exupéry's philosophy to heart. The two Swiss pilots will be the first to circle the globe flying the *Solar Impulse 2* — a plane powered completely by solar energy. The *Solar Impulse 2* is not only a source of environmental breakthrough, but also a symbol of exploration and challenge. Demonstrating a passion for flight, adventure, and innovation, Piccard and Borschberg reflect Saint-Exupéry's philosophies and experiences shaped by his time as an airmail pilot. Indeed, the worldwide flight of the *Solar Impulse 2* further validates the importance of exploration and personal reflection that Antoine de Saint-Exupéry modeled in the twentieth century.

Broadly, exploration can be defined as the investigation of the unknown. Typically, exploration is thought of in concrete terms, such as mapping undiscovered lands and seas, or space exploration. Within any field, there are a vast amount of unanswered questions, leaving exploration with a much greater significance than it is given. Too often, initial exploration is tinged with ignorance, and the reflection truly needed to investigate the unknown is missing. Christopher Columbus is a modern archetype for exploration, but he mistakenly labeled the New World as India. Ironically, Columbus, the explorer, mislabeled a continent by failing to search for a deeper meaning. Antoine de Saint-Exupéry shares a confrontational statement to those unwilling to explore: "You are not the dweller upon an errant planet and do not ask yourself questions to which there are no answers" (11). Observation from a new perspective, fresh attempts at unsolved problems, and the discovery of the human condition are forms of exploration and reflection that are infinitely important. Whether abstract or concrete, true exploration is to create meaning in life.

Antoine de Saint-Exupéry was born on June 29, 1900, in Lyons, France, and discovered a spirit for aviation early in life that would follow him throughout his career. In 1921, Saint-Exupéry joined the military and became a pilot a year later. After completing his time with the military learning flight techniques, he enrolled as a student airline pilot with the Latécoère Company in Toulouse, France (Healey). During his time with the company, Saint-Exupéry delivered mail and "helped establish airmail routes over northwest Africa, the South Atlantic, and South America" (Editors of the *Encyclopedia Britannica*). Like pioneers of any task, Saint-Exupéry's career was a dangerous one. The canvas planes utilized in the twentieth century left pilots in constant danger of crashing, where they could be stranded for days on end.

One constant danger for the French pilot was the plane itself. The technology supporting flight was not as sophisticated as what is now found in twenty-first century airplanes, and the engine would often breakdown or separate entirely from the bottom of the plane. For example, Fig. 1 shows a realistic sketch of The Breguet 14, a plane utilized by Saint-Exupéry and other French pilots in the 1900s. Although widely utilized for flight in France, "The Breguet 14 ... frequently broke down. The instruments and gas tank would often become clogged with sand" (Healey). Following a plane malfunction and crash, pilots who survived would be stranded in the mountains or desert until another plane was able to reach them. In short, the planes utilized in the early twentieth century were one source of adversity faced by Saint-Exupéry during his travels.

Sketch of the Breguet 14 in flight (Trussel)

In addition to plane malfunctions, Saint-Exupéry's success in flight was at nature's whim. Storms and a lack of visibility were two difficulties that led to some of Saint-Exupéry's most physically and mentally demanding experiences as a pilot. Early in his career, the pilot describes a cyclone he encountered along the coast of Argentina as, "physically, much the most brutal and overwhelming experience I ever underwent..." (Saint-Exupéry 49). The explorer was battered by 150 mile per hour winds and nearly driven into the Atlantic Ocean. On this account and many others, rather than brushing off the ordeal, Saint-Exupéry found meaning, concluding that, "The physical drama itself cannot touch us until someone points out its spiritual sense" (62). The harsh weather that Saint-Exupéry experienced brought him to realize the importance of reflection on experience. Without reflection, exploration of any kind holds no significance. Indeed, the storms that Saint-Exupéry faced during flight helped him realize the importance of reflection.

Secondly, clouds and a lack of visibility were subtle events in nature that influenced Saint-Exupéry's philosophies on exploration, inspired his novels, and led to one of his most well-known crashes. In a flight from Paris to Saigon, Saint-Exupéry crash landed in the Sahara Desert. In *Wind, Sand and Stars*, the cause of the crash is clearly due to a misjudgment in altitude because of the lack of visibility. Following the crash, he and his mechanic wandered in the desert for over three days until they "are rescued at the last moment by a passing Bedouin tribesman" (Boyne 69). Nearly dying of thirst and heat exhaustion is a harrowing experience for any individual, but for Saint-Exupéry his suffering was an opportunity for exploration. Saint-Exupéry takes his hardships and forms art. The author draws on time in the desert as inspiration for *The Little Prince* — a worldwide best seller. In addition, regarding *Wind, Sand and Stars*, Christina Healey observes, "these crashes and forced landings take place in the Sahara desert, and the author uses the arid desert landscape and desert-dwelling peoples to give his story an air of exoticism and adventure." In short, Saint-Exupéry explores his perspective on misfortunes found in the clouds to find inspiration for his art.

What made Saint-Exupéry an explorer and philosopher? What molded him into a beloved author? The answer is Saint-Exupéry's ability to explore and reflect upon the significance of his experiences. He drew on his times of isolation, plane crashes, and hardships as a pilot to reflect on the meaning of life and delve into the world from a unique perspective. Antoine de Saint-Exupéry explored adversity to discover the beauty found among the stars, sand, and wind.

In modern times, a similar situation has arisen in the world of aviation that further validates the importance of exploration and reflection. Swiss pilots André Borschberg and Bertrand Piccard began a journey on March 9, 2015, to pilot a completely solar powered plane around the globe. The *Solar Impulse 2* will not use fuel and will circle

the globe in a span of five months. Borshberg and Piccard will alter-
nate flying the plane between each of the stops, with only one pilot
in the plane at any given time. The pilots hope to revolutionize travel
with environmentally safe solar technology. They call their plan
"Exploration to Change the World" (*Solar Impulse*).

The goal of the *Solar Impulse 2* and its crew is no small task.
Borschberg and Piccard will take turns piloting the plane that "will
operate like a glorified glider. During the day it will climb to 27,000
feet, drawing energy from the sun and storing some of it in ultra-
efficient, purpose-built, lithium-ion batteries. At night, it will glide
slowly downward to as low as 3,000 feet, drawing as little power as
possible from the battery reserves" (Fields). Glorified glider sums up
the plane's characteristics quite well. The plane weighs as much as an
SUV, four thousand pounds, while a commercial plane of the same
size weighs twelve thousand pounds. The light weight makes the plane
more energy efficient, but also more vulnerable to powerful winds.
The *Solar Impulse 2* travels at a pace that made the 215 mile trip from
Abu Dhabi to Muscat, Oman, take thirteen hours, and some flights
will take as long as five days to complete (Chappell). This will be the
shortest of the twelve flights required to circle the globe, which means
the pilots will have to function for long periods within the experi-
mental plane.

To reach their goal, the pilots must overcome a vast number of
obstacles. The most pressing hardship that Borschberg and Piccard
face is the need for sleep on long distance flights. The pilots have
explored this issue and created a unique solution. Autopilot and
resting techniques will allow the men to rest for twenty minute
periods. In an interview, Piccard explains his solution to sleep: "I
developed a self-hypnosis technique, where the body is asleep but the
mind is alert to changes. This allows me to take 20-minute naps, 10
times a day, with the plane on autopilot. If it leaves a predetermined
envelope of flight, an alarm and vibrations in my flight suit will wake
me" (qtd. in Schiffman). Borschberg will use meditation for the same

purpose. By exploring the fields of technology and alternative rest, the pilots have discovered a unique perspective to problem solving, similar to the intellectual explorations of Antoine de Saint-Exupéry in the twentieth century. Indeed, Borschberg and Piccard model the importance of exploration by finding a solution that allows them to simultaneously monitor their flight and rest.

In addition to abstract exploration, Bertrand Piccard reflects on the importance of the flight, which closely models the reflections and philosophies of Saint-Exupéry. On the *Solar Impulse 2* website, Bertrand Piccard states:

> *Adventure is not necessarily a spectacular deed, but rather an "extra-ordinary" one, meaning something that pushes us outside our normal way of thinking and behaving. Something that forces us to leave the protective shell of our certainties, within which we act and react automatically. Adventure is a state of mind in the face of the unknown, a way of conceiving our existence as an experimental field, in which we have to develop our inner resources, climb our personal path of evolution and assimilate the ethical and moral values that we need to accompany our voyage.*

Piccard reveals his true nature in this quote and the heart of exploration. He is proclaiming to the public that he is prepared to explore the capabilities of solar powered flight and the limits of his mind. Piccard's reflection displays his willingness to ask questions to which there are no answers, just as Saint-Exupéry did within his books a century earlier. Undoubtedly, by referring to adventure as a state of mind, Bertrand Piccard further validates the importance of exploration that Saint-Exupéry modeled in *Wind, Sand and Stars*.

All things considered, the worldwide flight of the *Solar Impulse 2*, and the reflections of Andre Borschberg and Betrand Piccard, confirm the importance of exploration that Antoine de Saint-Exupéry modeled in the twentieth century. Through the hardships of his career as a French airmail pilot, Antoine de Saint-Exupéry developed powerful philosophies on the meaning of life. Saint-Exupéry saw the adversity of his lifestyle as a source of exploration. In his hardships, the pilot discovered inspiration from his unique perspective. The pilot drew from these experiences to become a world-renowned author, with his most notable works being *The Little Prince* and *Wind, Sand and Stars*. The revolutionary flight of the *Solar Impulse 2* is further validating the importance of exploration established by Saint-Exupéry. Through the power of exploration, the Swiss pilots Andre Borschberg and Betrand Piccard are overcoming the myriad of adversities associated with a worldwide solar flight. By utilizing their unique perspectives to search for answers, the pilots are making history and revolutionizing environmentally friendly transportation. Piccard's abstract views on adventure are closely intertwined with the reflections of Antoine de Saint-Exupéry, which captures a timeless relevance to each of their efforts. The intertwined stories of Saint-Exupéry and the *Solar Impulse 2* express the need to awaken the astronomer, poet, and musician that all individuals may become through exploration.

WORKS CITED

Boyne, Walter J. "Wind, Sand and Stars." Aviation History 19.1 (2008): 67–69. Academic

Search Complete. Web. 3 April 2015.

Chappell, Bill. "Solar-Powered Airplane Embarks on Attempt to Fly Around The World." *NPR*.

NPR News, 9 March 2015. Web. 3 April 2015.

Editors of Encyclopedia Britannica. "Antoine de Saint-Exupéry." *Encyclopedia Britannica*.

Encyclopedia Britannica, Inc. 22 September 2015. Web. 3 April, 2015.

Fields, Helen. "Light MAKES Flight. (Cover Story)." *Discover* 35.5 (2014): n.pg. *Academic*

Search Complete. Web. 4 April 2015.

Healey, Christina. "Antoine De Saint-Exupery." *Antoine De Saint-Exupery* (2005): 1. *Primary*

Search. Web. 3 April 2015.

Mathiesen, Karl. "Swiss pilots attempt first around-the-world solar flight." *The Guardian*. The Guardian News and Media, 9 March 2015. Web. 3 April 2015.

Saint-Exupéry, A. *Wind, Sand and Stars*. Antoine de Saint-Exupéry, 1939. Print.

Schiffman, Richard. "Sun-Powered Adventurer." *New Scientist* 255.3009 (2015): 1. *Academic*

Search Complete. Web. 4 April 2015.

Solar Impulse. Solar Impulse SA, 2015. Web. 3 April 2015.

Trussel. "Saint-Exupéry on Stamps." N.p. N.d. Web. 3 April 2015.

///

*"This is going to hurt; revising a story down
to the bare essentials is always a little like
murdering children, but it must be done."*

STEPHEN KING

///

Good Girl

SARAH GUYER

I am a good girl.
I have expectations.
I am expected to get grades to fear,
To uphold the mantle I raised in third year
I am expected to take hard classes — no tears
That's weak.
AP is requested, granted, stress with
A sticker on top, letting me know that I've bested
A tuition stamp.
95th percentile.
Class rank 5, close but so far
Not valedictorian, close but no cigar
And so I languish just beneath the bar
I've set for myself.
Whose expectations?
At first, my parents — "you can do better than a "B"
Elementary school math, "2" plus "1" is "3"
Middle school, "A" squared plus "B" squared is "C"
Squared.
Downgraded.
Further and further in this black-hole spiral
trapped in a tidal wave of stress and denial
While friends live for laughter from a video gone viral
That I've never seen.
Social life.
Securely set, on the back-left burner
For friends sometimes, my heart will yearn, "her
Priority is her grades, she'll never flirt —
She's smart."
Isolated.

One word — intelligence — split from the masses
Up a few steps, brownie-point passes
Resentment because I take all hard classes
And pass them.
Work ethic.
Getting good grades doesn't mean it comes easy
All nine periods, a teacher to please, he
Wants more and more as the work overwhelms me
But I do it.
I finish it.
Just because I finish tests the fastest
Or my comments on class are 'bragging words' blasted
To inferior feelings grown cumbersome and fastened on the status
      ladder
I'm pushed to the top
Not off of the ladder, perched on the top rung
Or even beneath that, where sweeter songs have been sung
I'm nearing the top, choking on strings that have hung
For years now.
Strings that are people
Who "can't" move on their own
Friends in whom depression has made its home
Smiles with homework questions, my answers in stone
In their belief
That I am superior
Better
I am exalted by a chorus of bitter voices
that are exonerated from all of their choices
by cares of the material sort, loud noises
of the world surrounding them, distracting them,
they are poised at attention, a military salute,
to not caring enough or not being a snoot, and I
stand alone, my morals taking root
To fulfill my expectations.
I fulfill my expectations.
Because I am a good girl.

understand in depth
the power of persistence
from canyon rivers

New Snow Rims Canyon
Haiku and photo by Kim McNealy-Sosin

Night Terror

LEILONNI HAGLER

In the eerie sky, there were angry storms with booming thunder and
 lightning,
Trees falling with fury, windows cracking, absolutely frightening.

Families crying at the rumble of earthquakes and gaping holes,
I cried out for help but even they were lost souls.

I felt agonizing fear; no shelter was safe.
There were ravenous beasts and monsters alike, just waiting for the chase.

Houses were being consumed by the sweltering fires despite the
 pouring rain.
The storm raged on and battered the ground, the earth twisting in
 tormenting pain.

And we. We were helpless. No roof protected us from danger,
The clouds opened and cast down their anger.

Hungry flames surrounded me, sparking up in dry piles of clothes,
My sanctuary was suddenly a burning grove.

And as I tried to outrun the raging cyclone, my hands began to
 tremble,
For lurking and breathing down my neck was something dreadful.

My eyes jolted awake, my body convulsing now,
Tears running from my swollen eyes, sweat dripping from my brow.

I glance around, trying to find familiarity in my room,
The dark prowls in silence only granting a sliver of light in from the
 moon.

My heart tries to settle down, but still it beats hard against my ribs.
It's just a night terror, yet I fear for everything that lives.

I Prayed for You

MOLLY HALLIGAN

I always prayed I would have a child. I wasn't sure if my prayers would
come through.
I simply prayed for a baby in my arms. I didn't know I was praying for
you.

When I found out you were coming, it was July 31.
You were nothing but a speck then. But I still loved you more than life.

I couldn't wait to find out more about you. To see you on the ultra-
sound screen.
I was 16 weeks and 4 days pregnant. It was October 31, Halloween.

I saw your profile, your legs and your arms. I heard the sound of your
heartbeat.
I fell even more in love with you then. But what came next knocked
me off my feet.

"Your daughter's kidneys are not doing well", the doctor told me with
concern in his eyes.
"If she survives, it will be rough." He left me alone in the room to cry.

That's how I found out I was having a girl. Hidden in a sentence I
never expected to hear.
I should have been excited, celebrating and happy. Instead, I was
consumed with fear.

The next several weeks were the darkest of my life. The news wasn't
getting any better.
I went to appointments week after week, and I just kept getting sadder.

I couldn't plan for your arrival. I found myself crying all the time.
I tried to go on with life untroubled. But "if she survives ..." was stuck
in my mind.

I turned to God through my anger and sadness. Prayer being the only
place I found comfort.
I asked Him to heal you, to hold me, to help us. But I still couldn't see
through the hurt.

I thought I was going to lose you. This sweet child I wanted all my life.
So many prayers had been said for you. And finally we got a good sign.

Your little body had started to heal. One small improvement at a time.
I was given more hope than I'd had in weeks. We no longer feared for
your life.

As time went on you got stronger. We knew you were going to be okay.
I thanked God every day for you. But still I continued to pray.

I prayed that you would be happy. That you would always feel loved
and cared for.
I prayed for God to help me navigate life as a new mother.

Now you are here and you are more than I ever dreamed. You're beautiful, special, and sweet.
You are so much like your daddy. I have never felt more complete.

It's almost Halloween again. The date will always mean something to
me.
But this year is so different from the last. You are here and things are
just as they should be.

Your life has been surrounded in prayer. God has been by your side
this whole time.
My sweet little miracle; you are His child, as well as mine.

My First Ex-Friend

AMANDA HANSEN WEIGNER

Kristen. She had once been a bright young girl who, even with a horrible mother, had her future in front of her and her best friend beside her.

I was *once* her best friend.

I still, to this day, don't honestly recall exactly how the two of us met, other than it was at G. Stanley Hall Elementary School located in the heart of a small town known as La Vista. We pretty much became fast friends at the age of six, even though she had Mrs. Rothe and I had Mrs. Moenssen. Our friendship began the first night I stayed at her house. Ironically, she lived right down the street from my house. I remember we had stayed up almost all night spilling secrets to each other that we swore never to speak of to anyone but ourselves. One of the first things I remember about her room was the countless Barbie dolls she owned. The majority were still in their original pristine boxes, such as her Special Edition Barbies who always appeared in extraordinary ball gowns that shimmered through the fiber-plastic covers.

My Barbie dolls were always played with, and sometimes, I'd purposely let the family dog, Rascal, chew the heads off a few. Kristen never did understand the humor I always saw in that. While Kristen was always dressed up in sparkly dance outfits and trying to wear her mother's heels, I was a true tomboy at heart, though when we became friends, she talked me into playing Barbies with her. Just as well, it was also Kristen who convinced me years later to quit playing Barbies at the age of 10. I was upset that in all the years we had been friends, for all the times I was happy to let her play with my Barbies that my parents had just bought me, never once did she ever let me even lay a finger on any of her Barbies that hadn't been worn and played with. As one could see, this had been just the start of the deterioration of our blossoming friendship.

I chose to keep my friendship with Kristen, based on the absurd idea I had that I could help her.

Since being in the same Girl Scout troop where her mother, Adrienne, was our leader, I couldn't help but notice that Kristen never seemed to be able to hold her own in an argument with Adrienne. All Kristen could do was cry while Adrienne continuously yelled instead of comforting her own daughter. I hated how her mother went about raising her. I hate it more, learning that her father, for all the good he resembled, still couldn't keep his wife from deteriorating the backbone I wanted my best friend to own. Kristen began to grow more within her mother's shadow. I still believed I could help her, even when nobody believed I could. Our bond, strange as it may have seemed, was unlike any I've ever had. I remember how we could spend countless hours discussing more satisfying current events like why the Backstreet Boys let N'SYNC steal away their iconic boy band turf, or how Lindsay Lohan could platonically say that she was never romantically involved with Aaron Carter even though it directly led to his break up with Hilary Duff. We would talk about what was happening at school to convincing our parents to kidnap each other for the coming weekends. I just always assumed that we would be the best of friends for years to come.

I'll be the first to admit that I was completely wrong.

While we were in fourth grade, I had surprisingly struck up a friendship with Cassie, a girl who was in our troop, and was a new addition to the popular crowd. We became fast friends after both attending the birthday party sleepover of our mutual Girl Scout member, Megan. Megan's family had just moved into a house from living in an apartment for most of our elementary school years. Like Megan and Kristen, Cassie was also a member of their dance team, a team made up of every member of my Girl Scout troop, with the exception of myself.

Befriending Cassie was a godsend during most of fourth grade. She and I would plan sleepovers (mostly at her house) including coloring hour, watching Sailor Moon, playing pranks on her little brother, to gossiping over who we secretly hated within our troop, to who we crushed on at school. Cassie quickly became one of my best childhood friends. Before the end of that school year, Cassie came to me at recess with a startling ultimatum. I had to choose between being Kristen's best friend or Cassie's. I couldn't be both, and to me, that was wrong.

I went to my mom for these kinds of questions all the time and this time was no different. She would always tell me that you can be anybody's friend, just as they can be anybody's friend, and that two friends don't have to get along to remain mutual friends of another. I came back to Cassie the next day, telling her I choose to be both her friend as well as Kristen's. Cassie walked away and has refused to talk to me since.

Today, I understand that Cassie was right, in the sense that I should've walked away from my friendship with Kristen, but she was wrong to think that I would choose between two friends. That experience served as many lessons down the line about who to trust as my friend over when to trust them. and what to share with them. In the years since, I am beginning to wonder why I ever felt I needed friends. For all the good they bring into my life, the majority seem to leave just after breaking away more pieces of why I'm afraid I'll never be able to mend, entirely.

The thing about the deteriorating friendship I shared with Kristen is that, as the years drifted by, I began to remember less and less of the good times, easily remembering the more not-so-good times. I continuously allowed her and her mother to walk all over me like I was their personal doormat, doing everything from scraping their six-inch heels to dumping on me whenever they felt like it.

When we were roughly eight years old, I learned that the church the Grainger's once belonged to had been torn down. I opened my big

fat mouth to invite them to join the church my family belonged to:
Trinity Lutheran. Not a day goes by that I don't regret that decision.
Adrienne became a far greater mess than she had been running our
Girl Scout troop into a hole not even my mother could dig us out
of. Although I've gotten older and far wiser than I was over a decade
ago, I've come to notice that it really never was Kristen with whom I
had deep concerning issues with. It had been her mother, Adrienne,
all along.

See, Adrienne has always and *will always* have her daughter's back,
literally. One example happened the day after Christmas in 2002.
Our mutual friend, Emily, came over to hang out. The two of us were
sprawled out on my bedroom floor with my seventh grade yearbook
primed for doodling. When we got to the page that had all three of our
hideous school pictures on it, we each took a sparkling gel pen to draw
devil horns, a mustache, and a devil tail to go on Kristen. We laughed
hysterically at ourselves for what we had just done. Later, we contem-
plated giving our dear friend's (Kristen) house a ring, pretending to
be KFC, telling them that their chicken order was out on the loose. I
knew I was never any good at prank-calling, and while Emily was no
better, we still both figured we'd get a nice laugh out of it from her end.

Wrong, again.

Not only did Adrienne become suddenly very upset with me, she
also strangely requested (more like ordered) me to physically walk my
way down the street to their house just so I could apologize to Kristen
in person. That was out of line and not at all right of her to make that
call. Kristen and I had been friends long enough, at thirteen years old,
we were more than old enough to handle a minor dispute between
ourselves without parental interference. It was obvious Adrienne
knew it was me before she even picked up the receiver off the base.
I had been well aware of their newly-equipped caller-ID at the time.
Still, I marched my way down the street, up their driveway, all the way
to the inside of their doorway at the foot of their staircase. All I can
remember is feeling so stupid for even agreeing to be there in the first

place; while all Kristen could do was stand there, allowing her mother the floor to do all the talking she damn well pleased.

"What kind of friend are you to treat my daughter that way?"

"Did you even apologize to her?!"

"If you don't straighten out your act, kid, you'll no doubt end up like your brother!"

All that, just for a joke that was meant to be *funny.* It was that day, that particular moment when I realized that neither mother nor daughter could handle sarcasm well.

The line about my brother really hit hard, as well.

See, my brother never did graduate high school. He also never got his license. He did, however, turn his life around by the time he was 25 years old.

He grew up. He got married. They had my adorable little nephew.

All was well and especially happy.

Then he got sick. *real* sick.

Cancer.

Six months.

He died the *day* after *Christmas.*

Adrienne *hated* Jerome.

One time, our parents were off to a Christmas party for Dad's work. They were going to stay at the Double Tree hotel. Jerome was in charge of baby-sitting Rochelle and me.

He loathed having to watch his sisters. Kristen had been invited over with Mom and Dad's approval.

Regretfully, we spent the evening yelling and screaming at Rochelle (she was only a toddler) just because it was what Jerome would do had he been there.

He actually skipped out of the house and walked across the street to the neighbors to smoke or drink. I was proud he left me in charge. So, there we were, ALL ALONE in the house. I don't recall that we ate, since we weren't old enough to use the stove.

When it came time for Adrienne to pick Kristen up from the house, she made sure to express her opinion of my brother to our mother by telling her that "your son will never amount to anything!"

My mom let that sink in deeper than she should have.

Needless to say, my brother may not have gotten his GED, but he did find the love of his life, had a beautiful baby boy, as well as her older son. He died a family man, a loving man.

Kristen and I remained friends until the middle of eighth grade. Since then, we have gone our separate ways. To this day, our parents still live in the same house they did back when. Over the years, I took notice that when she would walk her dog, Princess, around the block, she would cross the street to the side my parents' house is on and continue walking, until she got to our neighbor's yard, then cross back (directly across from my parents' house), walk a few feet, then proceed to cross back over to our side, then continue walking the block as normal. For some reason or another that I cannot put my finger on, I still can't fathom why she would do that.

Once, while I was taking some ASL (American Sign Language) courses over at the local Metro Community College, I ran into her younger brother, Derek. He always was nice and also loyal to his sister. I saw that he had been walking to and from school. I politely asked him if he wanted a ride. He said yes, but with respect to his sister and the history he knows we both had, he politely declined, then waved me on.

Over the years, I have wondered from time to time, what our lives would have been like had we remained good friends instead of sworn enemies. I only considered us enemies for about the first three months after we stopped being friends. I was hurt at what actions took place for the two of us back in middle school.

I remember I was sitting in Mr. List's math class, taking our Algebra exam to see what class we would need to sign up for the following year up at the high school. I was positive I would end up in Algebra 1 just like my brother. I would have been wrong. In the middle of taking the exam, the eighth grade counselor, knocked on the door and kindly asked that I be removed from my exam to deal with a social problem that had been brought to her attention. I was not at all happy when she walked me back to her office to find Kristen sitting in the corner. I was told to take the seat next to her; I did.

She then proceeded to ask both of us why the three of us are wasting these minutes of our time. I wasn't about to talk. I had no intention of furthering our issues within school. We were done. Over. Why couldn't she have just left it all alone?

That was so not like her back then.

In short, it has been so long now, that I can't even remember what the conversation was even about aside from the deterioration of our friendship.

What I do remember is that after Kristen excused herself back to class, the guidance counselor pulled me back aside and kindly told me that I handled that very well, and that she was sorry I had lost a friend to her anger and toxicity. I then told her that while I was sad that the two of us were no longer friends, I was glad to not be near her anymore.

Once high school set in, we both soon found our places. I was in the marching band as well as Forensics and Bowling. Based on yearbook photos over the four years, she had been in multiple choirs, student body clubs such as Leos Club, etc.

The only thing about her that bothered me during those four years was when we would pass each other in the hallways. She had the tendency to whisper ugly words.

I mentioned a few to my mother who was a Paraprofessional at the school back then. She, then, brought it to the attention of the school principal, but since it was not deemed as truly threatening in any way, he asked my mom to drop it.

And, it really wasn't. Just words thrown out in mid-air that I could choose whether or not I would catch it or let it fall. Once I began letting her words and whispers bounce off me, she slowly began to stop. By my senior year, I had forgotten all about her.

Now, I really don't have a single clue about her life after high school. Other than that she has moved in and out of her parents' house more than I ever could. She *still* finds it hard to walk across my parents' driveway. According to my folks, her dad, at one point, suffered cancer.

Now, had we still been good friends, I would have been there for her. I lost my brother to cancer a decade ago.

That is still the difference between us two.

She was never the friend to take the time to think about others above herself. Everything had to eventually come back to reflect on her in a positive way. She would take credit where credit wasn't due. Still, I can't exactly blame her as she had only to learn from her mother. I do wish their family well.

(*I do honestly appreciate that our circles hardly ever cross, if at all.*)

Cattail on a Pond
Photo by Nia Karmann

The Connection

PATRICIA HARRIS

Before a song became a song, it was Writing.
Before it was Writing, it was a bunch of words.
Before it was a bunch of words, it was a word.
Before it was a word, it was letters with sounds.

Before it was a song, it was a poem.
Before it was a poem, it was a jumble of words.
After it was a jumble of words, it took order.
With the order came rhythm and rhyme.
With the rhythm and rhyme came a melody,
And then the poem and the rap became a song!

*"We are made whole by Books, as by
Great Spaces and the Stars."*

MARY CAROLYN DAVIES

White Wolf on the Wall

KATHIE HASKINS

Her eyes follow me as I walk
　　from the living room to the dining room.
She peers at me through a stand
　　of bare winter trees.
Her thick white fur blends perfectly
　　into her surroundings.
Ears perked in alertness,
　　eyes steady,
I can almost feel the cold wetness of her
　　black nose against my cheek.
She calms my restless nerves.

I call her
　　Serenity.

I Strive to Live

ANNA M. HENG

Freshman at the University of Nebraska-Omaha

"Affirmation" means to tell the truth about ourselves and how we support other people. Emotionally supporting one another is so important. Supporting one another is an important thing to do in our lives every day!

I include every person who gets left out. When I was little, I was often picked on for my clothes or shoes, because they weren't name brand like the other kids wore. They were from Walmart. I was in the first grade, and the girls in my class would not let me watch them play dolls, because my parents couldn't afford to get me a doll. In the third grade, I waited patiently every day for the swings, and I never got on them, and when I did I never had anyone to play with me. When I was ten years old and the fastest kid in my class, the boys asked me to play football with them, so I did. Now, every time I see someone left out of a conversation, I go talk to them.

When I see kids with no one next to them at the lunch table, I go sit with them. I don't want people to feel the way I felt, when I was little, because those guys were there for me when no one else was so I will do the same for them. My belief in God helps guide me in the right way in my decisions. At a young age, I was taught right and wrong. Every day, I strive to do the right thing and avoid the wrong one, and my faith helps me keep on this path. Helping others and being with lonely people is a perfect example of me trying to do what God wants me to do. I strive to live the best life I can possibly live.

Take Out a Piece of Paper

ANALISA JACOB
Graduate of Omaha Central High School

Of the four years in high school, I think my junior year was the worst of all. Deadlines, due dates, and curfews were all thrown at me in one big package. "This is the one year colleges look at, so make it count!" screamed the counselors, but every time a counselor, or a peer, or teacher said that to me, I asked myself, "Make it count for whom?"

I wanted this year to count for me. This is why I took creative writing. Without creative writing, I would have missed out on some of the most impressionable experiences of my life. The people, the stories, the poems, and all the glory that came in and out of that class every day were impressive. We became a family, a family of writers. Not a day goes by that I don't thank my lucky stars for taking that class.

I can't say that it was fun and games; the junior year isn't supposed to be. At one point, I never wanted to come to school. I had no desire for it, but as time passed, so did that phase.

Without creative writing, I would never have taken the time to understand people. Creative writing taught me about myself, and I studied the people around me, more than I studied the eight parts of speech. I learned to accept, respect, and observe my fellow peers. I can't imagine my junior year without a creative writing class. I think I would've gone insane.

I am grateful for the opportunity to be in that class. I am grateful for the friendships I made. I am grateful for having a dedicated teacher who refused to see me as anything less than special. So much encouragement, so much love, and so much devotion came from that teacher. What did I learn? I learned respect for others and dedication to the writing craft, which I am still working on. This wonderful experience will always remain with me. "Write on."

Creation

LAUREN JAMAIL

I want to write.
I want to fill wonderful words into your eyes and ears.
I want to worry you with inspiration.
I want you to feel the words in your chest.

I want to create.
Something that wasn't there before.
Something original.
Something new and exciting.

I want to be innovative.
I want to excite your mind.
I want to send a tingle down your body from my words.
I want to fill your brain with new ideas.

I want to construct.
Something that is inexperienced.
Something that is a virgin to the paper I'll write it on.
Something even strange.

I want to formulate words like a professor.
I want to write in the now.
I want to write for the future readers.
I want to make it new.

I want to generate.
Something that will change the future generation.
Something that will spark young minds.
Something that is unused.

I want to be an author.
I want to change the world with my words.
I want to write.
I want to create.

Culture
Photo by Tracy Ahrens

Back to Vegas

TONY JOHNSON

When I was young, I was so lost. Not a whole lot different now that I'm older. Still lost, just a different kind of lost.

When I left Nebraska to go back to Vegas, I was broken. I was heart-broken, I was financially broken, I was self-esteem broken … pretty much every kind of broken you could be.

Rochelle dropped me off at the bus station. She gave me twenty dollars for my travels. Back then the first thing I thought about was where I could buy a bottle of vodka to drown my sorrows. Turns out it was in Kansas City, but that's a whole different story.

Anyway, I got to Vegas with $16.92 in my pocket and a small back-pack with all my worldly belongings. No plan at all, nowhere to stay, just me.

My brother George picked me up from the bus station. He asked me what my plan was. I said I didn't know, I guessed I'd start selling weed.

He told me then that it wasn't a good plan, and even today, I'm not so sure. He might have been right. He usually is.

There were a few hitches in my plan. (1) I had no money. (2) I was a horrible alcoholic. (3) I had no money.

I got to the neighborhood on Tropicana and Jones and it amazed me that the same dudes were still on the same corners doing the same thing. It's a pretty rough competition to be the Man.

I hung out with my sister Audrey the first couple of days. She was with some crackhead white dude, but they had a half-gallon of cheap whiskey. The more I drank the worse my decisions usually got. Long story short, he called me a n — r. I told him I'd show him a n — r. I reached straight into his pocket and snatched his money. At the time, I was pretty big, and I loved to fight, so I dared him, basically. Don't you know, the second I turned away from him there was a policeman standing about six feet from me? He had to have seen the whole thing. I just stepped around him and started walking. Maybe, he saw it in my eyes that day. Maybe, he just didn't want that kind of problem. That instant might have held the worst or the best decision of my life.

I come from a family of pimps, prostitutes, gangbangers, drug dealers — society's "problems." What I was taught is if you're gonna do the wrong thing, do it the right way. If I had caught a robbery charge and become a felon that day, it might have changed everything. Either I would have done a hell of a lot more time in prison by now, or I would have been saved a lot earlier and have been successful right now. Who really knows? You don't know your destiny until after you get there. We think we control so much. Fate? We have no right to tempt it.

I walked across the street, bought a case of forty-ounce beers, and started handing them out to everyone in the neighborhood. I remember the look in their eyes when I was telling them I'm quitting drinking and this is it. No one believed me.

I got back to where I was staying. These old heroin addicts let me crash on their couch for a few days. Rick's brother Basco was in bad shape. I remember talking to him before I went to sleep that night. I told him I was gonna take over the neighborhood. You know what I saw in Basco's eyes? When he told me he believed me and he wanted to see me shine, Basco was telling the truth.

I can see it in everyone's eyes in the first ninety seconds after I meet them. It's completely my decision whether I deal with you or not. So if I deal with you there is no blame-shifting if something goes wrong. Good or bad, I made that decision.

The next morning I was hung over. Normally, my first decision would be to grab a beer. I was tired, though. I knew what I had to do. Ryan was on the way, my oldest son. I had no place to live, no clothes, nothing! Rock bottom. I felt a stirring in my soul.

I didn't drink for about a year from that day. I started walking to Labor Ready. I'd work eight hours for $32, usually work that only illegal immigrants would do. I just had to. I grinded and grinded, and finally, I had a little over $200 in my pocket, a cell phone, five white T-shirts, and a couple pairs of jeans.

I bought a half-ounce of weed for $150 dollars at scale.

My dynasty began. I look back, today, and yeah, there's a lot I'd like to change. There's a lot I wouldn't, though. I helped a lot of people but took a lot of losses. I became cold because of the parasites who latched onto me because they saw my shine. Would I not go in that direction and try to be a square instead, though, if I could go back? Sad to say, I just don't think so. I'm just not cut that way.

We are who we are. There's a time that the streets will choose you, when you're young and gullible. You believe them when they say they'll always be there. Then, there's a time you have to decide what you're willing to risk to get what you want.

Me, I'll take the gamble every time, if the consequences are less than the rewards. You might be different, but I think I know me a little, today.

I know one thing.

I know the streets don't love me.

I know I really, honestly, wholeheartedly love the streets.

I've been stabbed, robbed, and had my head literally run over by a truck. I don't blame the streets. I blame myself for being so stupid, as to get caught slipping.

Yeah, what's the word I'm looking for? Self-destructive? Yeah, that's me.

Stories on Wealth Inequality

JOHN KESSLER

In Alain de Botton's *Status Anxiety* (2005), he writes about differing perspectives on poverty and wealth. The stories offer a terrific window into some of the common beliefs of people from different classes. The divide between the rich and the poor is as great as ever, and as the middle-class wanes, we worry about the stability of society. One way we can manipulate this divide is through governmental control. Communism hopes to equalize the peaks and valleys of wealth through government ownership and communal employment. A meritocracy hopes to allow the people of great skill to rise to the top of the economic food chain and hopefully enhance society with their ability. Knowing different belief systems toward wealth and poverty is important, because they form the eventual government systems we adopt.

In Alain de Botton's three stories about failure, we learn about how society viewed the poor throughout history. In medieval or pre-modern society, there existed the nobility, clergy, and peasantry. John of Salisbury describes the peasantry as a pair of feet and the rich as a head. This notion encapsulates the feelings of the time towards wealth. The poor are perhaps dirty and stinky but still vital and necessary, nonetheless. Alain de Botton gives examples spanning the late middle ages that exaggerate this idea of necessity to the point of reverence.

The second story on failure explains that poverty is not connected to morality or the lack of righteousness. This is identified by the fact that in Christianity, Jesus was a poor carpenter and is directly connected to God. The poor of the time were more naturally beholden to religion. Need often precedes prayer, and the rich were more independent. Independence from prayer means they are independent of God, and the possibility that a life might be had without a dependence on God was evil.

The third story is where we see the notions that once lent dignity to the labor of the poor, fostered a culture of victims and blame. The poor now believe they are captured in systems, which ensure their low status and they are being robbed by deception and plunder from the powerful. This story, which starts in the late 1700s, shows the rise of Marxism. With the wealthy no longer being literally appointed by God in the view of the people, and great abuses of labor in the age of industrialism becoming common, there was a great strain on the peasantry at the time. Karl Marx would be the spark that started the fires of many revolutions. He explains in his manifesto that "the proletarians have nothing to lose but their chains."

It is easy to see how these connected beliefs through time culminate in the ideas of communism. People are born into wealth classes that may either guarantee their struggle and possibly shortened life or provide them with shortcuts and luxuries that help them succeed. Many children grow up with hunger being a regular part of their lives. Some are born into even worse circumstances and do not reach adulthood. For these things to still happen, especially in places where a happy existence is now relatively easy, should weigh on the conscience of us all. The problem is there is often no clear way to help. It is common to hear about charities where tiny fractions of donations ever actually result in aid. We also cannot go around scooping homeless people up off the streets and giving them a job at some business to cure them of their poverty. Communism really does appear to be the easy fix to our issues in this case.

In Alain de Botton's next three stories about success, we are offered a different view of wealth from the perspective of those who have great wealth. In 1723, Bernard Mandeville posits that the rich contribute the most to society. He perhaps plants the seeds to the ideas of trickle-down economics by explaining that the spending of the wealthy provides employment and great benefit to those beneath them economically. In this story, the rich are painted as fools who support their enormous egos with their dollars and whose greed acts as charity. The wealthy are only good for society.

Thomas Paine introduces the theme of the second story with his ruminations about the idiocy of hereditary positions of societal rank and employment. He explains how disastrous hereditary appointment would be in government or science. That great writers would not likely have sons capable of finishing their works. Napoleon shared Thomas Paine's views and saw to the abolishment of feudal privileges. He appointed people he found talent in to positions of his government and reformed the education system to allow for subsidies to the poor. Thomas Carlyle, who was disgusted by the "Idle Aristocracy," imagined a system in which people were no longer born into their position in the world, but instead came by their inequalities honestly. This system would be known later as a meritocracy.

The last tale of success blames poverty on the failures of the poor. Social Darwinists believed that the rich were naturally better than the poor. They do not accuse the poor of being morally wrong, but rather simply less than. They insisted that the suffering and deaths of the poor were good for society and natural. The alpha beasts of the human jungle naturally would rise to the top of the socio-economic ladder and dominate, thereby furthering us as people. It is easy to see how this mindset may become popular among people in such dominant positions already. Andrew Carnegie described charity as better thrown into the sea. He viewed the poor as lazy and drunken. Valuable men of the race do not require assistance in his opinion.

The ideas that lead to a meritocracy have a very logical timeline. With the European nobility's abuse of hereditary classes and failure to uphold those given positions respectably, it was almost an inevitable revelation. Most people would agree that the people who earn their wealth deserve it. Again, most would agree that criminals have earned whatever situation they find themselves in. What about, however, the children of these people? Do children deserve to be born into poverty? It can be questioned whether someone really deserves to be born into wealth. The person who earned that wealth would take it as a benefit of his hard work that his children be well supported. Most people do not believe we should have enormous wealth or power if we did not work for it. So, we arrive at the natural solution to these issues being a meritocracy.

It is not an easy task to end world hunger or mitigate corruption of the wealthy, but by knowing the view of the people from different classes, we can find compromises that work and help each other. The most extreme examples of poverty and power have diverse effects and implications on us all. Through our organization and governments, we can try to mitigate the most negative effects. In these two timelines of success and failure, we have not arrived at a single solution. No one has invented a system which can solve the persistent issues of human society. Our capitalist government still allows for people to starve on the street and for people with mental and physical conditions to be uncared for. Corporations and the powerful still control narratives and outcomes of political issues. In foreign governments, human rights abuses are much more common and corruption more acceptable. We are closer to finding a system that benefits all classes than we ever have been. It is the best time to be alive in all of history. Fewer people starve, and there are fewer wars than before. This is largely due to the evolution of these systems of belief toward inequality and wealth.

Somewhere in Between

NEHA KHALID

The summer sun blazed overhead scorching its victims. Dust swirled, filling every hole, covering skin, and stinging eyes. Lungs filled with dirt then quickly expelled them in a vicious cough. The ferocious wind fought against anyone outside, sweeping hats away, and causing hair to slap against their tired, worn faces. The wind sneaked around, stealing when people weren't looking. It rolled luggage away, overturned the tiny children, and blew against starched clothing. The citizens tried to fight it by pulling their shirts down and trying to keep a grip on everything they had brought, for fear of it being gone, but they rarely succeeded. Normal chaos reigned over the Benazir Bhutto Airport. Everything was in rapid tangles with one another, except a small lone leaf drifting in between citizens, lost.

Freezing air blasted through the vents causing the visitors to shiver and tremble. They pulled their long, luxurious coats tighter around their bodies, clutching their carry-ons. The smell of pungent antiseptics mixed with a variety of brawny colognes and flowery perfumes, caused a haze of odors to choke those who passed through. The cacophony consisted of screaming babies, tense mothers, and bellowing fathers. People rushed past one another, bumping and pushing. Elbows hit arms, legs stepped on feet, but no one cared. They were all too busy racing the clock to get to their destinations. Organization controlled the O'Hare International Airport. Towering guards, with energy crackling through their tasers, guarded the doors, monitoring those who came through and stopping those who didn't conform to their expectations. Everything moved swiftly and smoothly, except a small lone leaf drifting in between people, lost.

I pulled on my jeans, cursing myself. They were riding up about an inch, exposing my lower ankle. Every few steps I would try to pull them back down to try to cover that patch of skin but to no avail. It became a pattern, watch the black tiles, count to 5 and then pull down one leg of the jeans. Watch the tiles again, count to 5, and pull down the other leg. Once in a while, I'd see a small leaf shifting across the floor, the stem constantly slipping out of sight.

I pulled on my kameez[1], cursing myself. The long embroidered top drew attention with its sparkling gems. The slit sleeves billowed, while the crescent collar choked my neck. Every step I took caused the kameez to swish back and forth, drawing unwanted attention to it. I kept my hands straight at my side, trying to block the chounkeay[2]. The wind howled, scaring my kameez into a frenzy. It blew up and to the left while my back piece flew to the right. They spun in circles around my waist, fighting each other while I tried to keep moving forward. I pushed at them, hoping to straighten them but they fought back. They tangled and tossed against my hands, wrapping and tying them. As I walked, out of the corner of my eye, I'd see a lone leaf tumbling through the air, fighting itself.

I didn't dare look up from the ground, hanging my head low.

They bound my hands together, and forced my head low.

As I sat down, I could feel the strain of the muscles in my neck from my actions, but I let my head hang. I desperately searched through my luggage and finally found my savior. Hastily, I grabbed the green and white blanket from out of the luggage. Swirling green flowers and white vines clouded my vision.

My head hung low, watching the black tiles blur together. My neck begged to be brought back up but I refused. My body moved briskly while my hands clutched my luggage, while trying to smooth my rustling kameez. My legs moved mechanically as I grabbed the grey shawl from my mother's carry on, crinkling a lone leaf.

My hands trembled as I gracelessly spread my blanket across my quivering legs, trying to block them from the stares. The blanket billowed out

....

1 Traditional top worn in Pakistan

2 Slits on the side of the top separating it into a front and back piece

from time to time, revealing the dark grey denim underneath, teasing me.
Trembling, my hands constantly slid down to flatten the blanket and make
sure everything was concealed.

Hands shaking, I clumsily wrapped it against my tense shoulders,
trying to block my body from the stares. The shawl lazily swung back
and forth underneath my knees, barely covering the kameez. My
hands constantly slid down to make sure the shawl was doing its job of
concealing.

It was only once I had hidden that piece of me, that I raised my head
and faced the stares of Pakistan.

Only then, once I got assurance that it was still covered, would I
raise my head and look straight into the judgmental eyes of America.

As night fell, a hidden and crumpled leaf finally tore in half. The
two pieces drifted further and further away, for it could not exist as a
whole, as it was always somewhere in between.

Who Am I?

MADDIE KNOWLES

I played the violin for ten years. My parents made me play an instrument, and because they would not buy a harp for a six year old, I chose the violin instead. My abuelita loved the violin. I grew to love it, too. I remember when my tiny little violin came in its perfect case, and I took it out and began. The sounds were horrible. I was holding it wrong. My fingers were awkward. I didn't care. I was ecstatic. My first instructor was a college student called Danny. He lived in a little house covered in ivy, so thick it covered the windows. Inside was a cave and he taught me my first notes. Practicing was something I hated, and I was not that fond of Danny either. After about a year or two, he informed my mother that I was probably tone deaf. We looked for another teacher.

That was when I met Katrina. I came back from lessons with sore fingers and wrists. The sounds got better, the notes flowed more smoothly. She would make me improve, and she did it well. I wanted to get better, and I loved how when I got a pitch just right, it would ring out pure and light, and vibrate in my bones. Katrina thought I had pitch perfect hearing for a while. It turned out it was relative pitch, but that was a far cry from being pronounced tone deaf. Never have I possessed anything like a singing voice, but that violin became my vocal strings.

Years passed. I got better and better, not because I was particularly talented, but because lessons motivated me to keep going. Katrina tugged the music out of me, and occasionally it was perfection. Katrina became my friend. If I practiced, I did it for her. If I kept going, she was the reason. Lessons were a high point in my week. An hour of music, and improvement. An hour of dubious life advice and dirty jokes. Caramel syrup is an inside joke and it should stay that way. Katrina was a music teacher, an ex-oboe master, a dealer at a casino, a chess tournament winner, a dancer, and a true musician. Katrina is beautiful, and she will always be laughing in my memories.

My junior year of high school, and time was always running out. I had more school work than ever before, and I had the ACT to study for. I was taking art lessons and violin lessons. I was out with my friends during most of my free time. Something had to give. I could not give up art, it was my passion, my calling. The outlet for all the desperate hunger inside of me. So it was violin that I let go. I had known for years that the one reason I was still playing was Katrina. She was the best part of playing violin. I loved the instrument, but I loved her more. I made a decision. But I still miss her.

I see the violin case that her cat used to sleep in, resting in my closet, and a pang of regret rings through me. *I'll pick it up again,* I think to myself. *The muscle memory has to still be there, it'll all come back. This weekend, when I have time, I am going to play again.* But I know I won't. Not without her.

I prefer reading to writing. Obviously, the two exist in tandem, and neither one could exist without the other. But reading is receiving, and although receiving can be very much harder than giving, in this case it is not. Reading is not forcibly stuffed down the throat, unless you are unlucky enough to be a high schooler. Reading should be asked for, it should be hungered for, and then it is given with the most purpose. Reading is letting another person's thoughts into your brain, another person's questions that you sometimes have to answer. But writing is very different, at least it is for me.

Writing is never something I do in my free time, unless it is two in the morning and I am a gigantic cumulonimbus cloud, ready to let go. Writing is cathartic when it is like that. Sentences scratched violently onto innocent paper, words that only I will ever read. Aching poetry, stream of consciousness, letters that will never be sent. But I am finding out that I have more to say than I thought I did. And if

other people want to read my thoughts, then I may as well open the
door and let them in. I will always maintain that I am a good writer
only because I hunger for stories, for poetry. Poetry hums in my
bones, not the MLA format. But that's ok. I never meant for anyone
to read it anyways.

I A M F R O M

I am from a thousand places marked on no map
I am from the place beyond a Nebraska sunset
where the colors are born vivid and bleeding

I am from indigo mountains that are older than their names
The air is thin there and I think that's why I am in love
with the sky and hummingbirds

I am from a low green island that smells like rain
ancient trees secret gardens the mysterious Neolithic mounds
brooding silent atop Cleeve Hill

I am from a southern country I have only traveled to by word of
        mouth
a place of red flowers red flavors red stones
It breathes in the color of my eyes and the roll of my tongue

I am from a kingdom fantastic in a young hungry imagination
The adventures of forts running tree climbing breathless
suburban innocence sticks swords sunscreen smell

I am from my mother and father and aching whispered prayers
the second born but the first to grow up green alive
a void and no memories and blue eyes living just out of my grasp

I am from a tiny blue marble spinning in the dark
I am from a thousand moments and a tapestry of travelers
I am a girl ravenous and alive

and I am going somewhere new

I might have a great talent with writing. I doubt it. I think I write well because I read well. I do not read the newspaper. I do not read books about science or history. I read stories. Stories captivate me, in all the forms that they come in. Watching a good movie brings me just as much enjoyment as reading a good book. People are the best stories. Every action, every word, every twist of fate, leads a human along the tale of their life.

A girl named Lauren Patzke once told me that people come and go, and you never know when someone will appear and change everything. Because she never knows how long a person will stick around. She tries to appreciate them as much as she can, while she can.

I never forgot that. It boggles my brain to think every person I help at work, every person I talk to in class, every person I have ever touched, I have become part of their stories. However infinitesimal of a part I played, I still had a role, and they had a role in my story. It makes me think about the tiny actions that could be the monumental turning point for another person. Are we aware of how powerful we are? We can do *anything*. People say that we are the heroes of our own stories. I do not believe this. Our stories are not really our own. We are all connected in one infinite tapestry. I want to be the Fairy Godmother, the kind stranger, the seasoned traveler, the faithful traveler, the dangerous warrior, and the angel in disguise. What are you going to be?

Nothing Here for Me

ELIZABETH KOPETZKY

Take me beyond the sea
Somewhere we can make believe
There might be something more
On other shores, forgotten lore

I am a stowaway
And you are my ticket out (out of this dead end town)
A castaway, I am a throwaway
You are my anchor, don't let me drown, oh

I'm setting sail for other lands
Oh captain, hear my plea
There might be something left for you
But there's nothing here for me

So steer this ship toward no man's land
There's nothing left I haven't seen
All I need is you and all you need is me
Just us, the sun and the sea

I dream of going home
Of somewhere I may never know
But Wwhen I'm with you the ocean's ours
It's all I need, at least for now

I am abandoned words
A story that was never told
Lost pages, you found a pen
You made me your captain's log, oh

I'm setting sail for other lands
Oh captain, hear my plea
There might be something left for you
But there's nothing here for me

So steer this ship toward no man's land
There's nothing left I haven't seen
All I need is you and all you need is me
Just us, the sun and the sea
Just us, the sun and the sea

Raise the mast, our time has come
To set sail for our fate
Our lives begin at dawn

I'm setting sail for other lands
Oh captain, hear my plea
There might be something left for you
But there's nothing here for me

So steer this ship toward no man's land
There's nothing left I haven't seen
All I need is you and all you need is me
Just us, the sun and the sea
Just us, the sun and the sea
Just us, the sun and the sea.

Writing Is a Necessity

JACKIE LE

"Writing combats loneliness, creates a sense of self-worth, shows affections of the soul, and alleviates depressions." This line in particular stood out to me the most out of the entire chapter. I often hear my instructor talk about how being a good writer is writing from the bottom of a writer's heart, and being perfectly honest in the writing. In return, making a very productive skill, while coping with stress is how writing becomes rewarding. I often spend my leisure time playing video games, and tearing at my own self-esteem when I lose. I do not find that I have many other talents. Aside from writing and story-telling, I never found a hobby. The majority of the hobbies I had usually secluded myself from interacting with other people.

Writing to combat my depression when I was a teenager in high school seemed counter-productive at the time. When I wrote my thoughts and feelings on paper, it only further reminded me of how no one else would read what I wrote and share the same pain I was feeling: the pain of rejection, the pain of not having been loved by my biological parents, and the pain of not being able to do "teen things" at the age I was in. I wrote about how I hated every holiday. I wrote about how I dreaded every morning waking up for school, knowing exactly how each day was going to be. I dreaded believing that I could see the future, because I felt nothing good was ever going to happen, and I hated hearing how school therapists kept making false hope claims that things would get better. I knew that if anyone near my age would read my writing, they would judge. They would insult; they would not feel empathy, they would not want to associate themselves with me.

I have an indifferent opinion on how writing can combat loneliness, create a sense of self-worth, and alleviate depression. The effects writing had on me when I was a teenager did not seem to help as much as my providers said it would. However, I do realize that in times of distress, I can work on being a better writer, since I am writing my emotions out from the bottom of my heart. As I write more openly and honestly, I can both improve on a very important life skill and have a hobby that combats my mental health. In that essence, it can be a win-win situation, as it does help me cope along with allowing me to improve my skills as a writer. Writing is a necessity in my life, and using it to benefit myself is not something I should ever complain about.

"When 'whom' is correct, recast the sentence."

WILLIAM SAFIRE

I Know

CLAIRE LEONARD
Student at the University of Nebraska-Omaha

I am from a 60 square foot court
that raised me and taught me lessons
and shaped me into the person I am today
because I never quit
and stand up six times when I fall five

I am from late night practices
that drained me of all that I was
only to do it again the next day

I am from the pounding of volleyballs hitting the floor
and the gymnasium buzzing with excitement waiting for a game to start
fans heckling me, trying to pull my focus from the court

I am from the sacrifices that made my dream a reality
missing birthdays and parties and everything else
that made me tougher and more resilient

I am from the blood, sweat, and tears of being an athlete
the body aches and injuries that told me to stop

I am from the passion of volleyball
the grit of never giving up

When I am on the volleyball court
I know where I am from

R E N É E   L O C K S

The important thing is to keep the intention clear.

I don't have to do it the way I did it yesterday.

Cherish your vision, the music that stirs in your heart.

Right now my life is just one learning experience after another. By the end of the week I should be a genius.

Don't worry if the work is hard and your rewards are few. Remember the mighty oak was once a nut like you!

It's wonderful to get up in the morning knowing you're doing all you can do.

Go easy, and if you can't go easy, go as easy as you can.

We grow one petal at a time.

You can't tell the age of the heart by the gray of the hair.

Taking joy in life is a woman's best cosmetic.

Breathe, breathe, breathe, breathe, breathe, breathe.

Every Day I Bloom

BRENDA LOPEZ

When asked to describe myself, I silently panicked. It has always been easier for me to express thoughts about others than talk positively about me. It would help if I start by sharing one of the main factors that influenced the negative view I had of myself for a long time.

As a child, I excelled in academics and existential understandings. Many adults, such as my family and their close friends, believed that I was ahead of my years in terms of intellect and maturity. Though I was shy and quiet, I believed I could do anything and would surely succeed in adult life. Unfortunately, that mentality began to slowly crumble as I went through rough experiences. However, valuable lessons and new understandings rose within me that shed a new light on my self-perception.

One of the main factors that led me to have a negative view of myself was surrounding myself with people who would put me down by verbally, mentally, and emotionally abusing me. In one occasion, a so-called friend called me dumb for forgetting how to complete a task I was helping her with and for not being as knowledgeable as she was. I allowed those experiences to take over, emotionally and mentally. It worsened the self-image I had of myself. For years, I was under the impression that I was not smart or intelligent. I viewed myself as the complete opposite of how I viewed myself when I was a child, and it didn't help that I lacked constructive resources due to the upbringing I had.

The negative self-image hit a tipping point, and it was uphill from there. I asked myself, "Do I want to continue suffering or be happy?" I believed it was obvious and logical to choose happiness. Then it clicked. I thought, "What necessary steps do I have to take to be happier and grow as a person?" Before long, I began to smile more, meditate, and practice positive self-talk. I quit complaining, and I removed myself from toxic people and environments. I began to study the art and science of human behavior and read books on the ego. Eckhart Tolle has spoken about how the ego and negativity will eventually destroy itself through awareness. I found this to be true. I woke up and made the choice to change my mentality from a toxic one to a healthy state. I chose to love myself.

I remind myself that I am not what anyone told me I was. I do not have to remain in a negative state of being. I am better than I think I am. I am worth more. I affirm the following: I am ready to receive infinite opportunities that align with my desires. There is still time to reach my goals. I will show myself compassion, just as I have shown compassion to others. I will let my heart remind me that I deserve good things, even when my brain convinces me I don't. I am in control of where I focus my attention. I am in control of what I allow to remain in my mind. I am in control, and I am grateful. Within me lives health, creativity, and happiness.

I am important, not only to society, but to my family, friends, and myself. I will see through the chaos and listen to my heart. I forgive myself for making mistakes and will grow from them. Even though I stumble, at times, this is the process of human development. Every day I bloom.

Inspiration to Self

DESHAE LOTT

(I prefer being an essayist to a poet, but right now, poems fit into the crevices of time I have, and I'm learning to compose them in notes on my phone, which is a new way of writing for me. I recently re-read parts of an essay I drafted five+ years ago, and it's terrible, truly, but I have many other notes, more recent ideas. I just need the time to weave the threads. Here is what I recorded and shared in a reply to an impressive woman with severe physical disabilities; she emailed me about her current new health issues, so I shared some of mine, along with what I hope were compassionate and supportive comments regarding her situation.)

My speech therapist came again, today; still suggesting vocal rest and conservation. Dr. Koder now suspects laryngitis precursor to muscle loss that will take away my power to swallow and speak. It has led to interesting contemplations today, because writing by hand and using my laptop have become such a physical strain — painful and causing shortness of breath, high HR, and vent alarms. The reflections of today are about adaption, what we THINK defines us/empowers us, and our desire to connect with others.

In sum, the I AM of my soul connects to the I AM of God. Human life may be more or less pleasant for my I am, but my mind will be alive no matter what happens to me, as a human and no matter how I can or cannot convey that to others, which made me think of all kinds of situations in which souls lack a "voice." I have been blessed to have one.

Beethoven composed his last and most well-known symphony (9th) when he was completely deaf. There are so many dimensions to the open mind, even as the body closes off options. However, every week, multiple strangers email me, coming across my website, discussing their significant challenges in life. One was from a woman placed in human trafficking for many years and tortured, causing disability. In contrast, I had a wait in public and overheard a woman speaking of her seven cars and a Porsche she so disliked and wanted a new model and how she was going with friends to Dallas, Texas, again to shop, dine, and party.

Khoi, who cuts my nails, will go to Viet Nam to see family again soon. She will return, describing their lifestyle, how many family members live in a space smaller than my small kitchen, and how they lack medical care. It will remind me of my abundance, again, no doubt.

I would enjoy an easier life and fewer challenges others add that are avoidable, if mindfulness were in use. That said, my blessings have been manifold, and I would not prefer to appear completely oblivious to others' challenges and completely unaware of the abundance of my own blessings. I have held this sensibility since early childhood, and tried to appreciate and honor my blessings. However, each time I face another huge personal loss, I learn. It's humbling. We can honor our blessings but not really understand going without them, until we must, and that's okay.

In my twenties I said I didn't want to live, if health care consumed over 50 percent of my time, energy, and attention. Now, it's far above that. I also wrote a poem (below) about my voice showing love and connecting me to others, so my spirit doesn't die. It held truth but is ignorant. My spirit lives, even if it cannot communicate with any minds but mine and God's.

I am learning.

Inspiration to Self
no hands to paint the pictures
wrap the packages
prepare the repasts
placate the pained

no hands have I
no arms
no legs

but voice
not the breathtaking soloist's voice
but a lilting, living voice
have I

somehow the words
will tell my vision
show my love

the words
my legs
and arms
and hands
and fingers
connecting me to others
so my spirit
does not die

Did You Know that He (She) Had a Stroke?

PRESTON LOVE, JR.

Did you know that he (she) had a stroke? The aforementioned, menacing question is being asked in every city, every social circle, and every family, every day. Most recently, this haunting question has been asked about me, 76 years-old, 225 pounds, 6'4," and by all appearances in great health. I had a stroke on January 3, 2019, and I write this article to increase the awareness of my community to its dangers and provide facts and precautions. I am hoping that this article will increase the knowledge and the dialogue within our community about strokes and serve as an aid to prevention and give encouragement to others who may have suffered.

First of all, let me open by saying that since my stroke, I have been in intensive rehabilitation, with miraculous improvements and, God willing, hope to surface and return to my work in the first part of February. I surely want to give encouragement from my gained experience and knowledge. I am the beneficiary of prayer, and the expertise of a vast medical community. Strokes do not have to be totally debilitating, and your life is not over after a stroke.

Let me just share with you some facts about strokes:

- Stroke is the third leading cause of death in the United States.
- More than 140,000 people die each year from stroke in the United States
- Stroke is the leading cause of serious, long-term disability in the United States, causing more people to have to quit their jobs, and possibly need to have a full-time caretaker or live in a nursing home.

- Each year, approximately 795,000 people suffer a stroke

- Strokes can and do occur at ANY age. Nearly one fourth of strokes occur in people under the age of 65

- Average age in the state of Nebraska is 42

- Stroke death rates are higher for African-Americans than for whites, even at younger ages

- On average, someone in the United States has a stroke every 40 seconds

- The statistics are staggering — in fact, African-Americans are more impacted by stroke than any other racial groups within the American population. African-Americans are twice as likely to die from stroke as Caucasians, and their rate of first strokes is almost double that of Caucasians

- Strokes in this population tend to occur earlier in life. And as survivors, African-Americans are more likely to become disabled and experience difficulties with daily living and activities

- For men between the ages of 45 and 54, the risk of ischemic stroke — the most prevalent type of stroke, which is caused by a blood clot that blocks an artery — is three times higher in African-Americans than in Caucasians. I learned in speaking with several heath care providers, that in dealing with strokes, there is information that says African-American men need to be more trusting and conversational, and more aggressive, when dealing with medical professionals, with seeking information and preventing our own strokes

- For African-Americans between the ages of 20 and 44, the risk of stroke is nearly two-and-a-half times higher than it is for Caucasians

- According to the National Stroke Association, stroke or heart disease will claim the lives of half of all African-American women

- African-Americans have more severe strokes that are also more disabling

Here are some additional facts about strokes:

- Stroke happen to all ages; it is no longer an old person's disease
- 80% of all strokes can be prevented
- Stroke is the 5th leading cause of death and the leading cause of disability
- Over 800,000 occur each year

Below are some of the causes of strokes:

- High levels of bad cholesterol
- In the USA, 45% of Black males and 46% of Black females have high blood pressure. This is the number one risk factor for strokes in African-Americans
- Diabetes and lack of control of our sugar level
- Stress, lack of proper rest, alcohol, drug use, and any various combinations of all the above listed

The following are some myths about stroke:

Myth: Stroke cannot be prevented.
Fact: Up to 80 percent of strokes are preventable. With modification of risk factors: High blood pressure, diabetes, smoking, obesity, drug use, and high cholesterol.

Myth: There is no treatment for stroke.
Fact: At any sign of stroke call 9-1-1 immediately. Treatment may be available. Time is the most important thing when a stroke occurs. Every minute we wait we lose 1.9 million brain cells — we never gain these back.

Myth: Stroke only affects the elderly.
Fact: Stroke can happen to anyone at any time. Strokes are no longer an "old person" disease.

Myth: Stroke happens in the heart.

Fact: Stroke is a "brain attack." It affects your brain by either having a blood clot that doesn't allow the blood to flow throughout your vessels or a vessel that burst causing bleeding in the brain.

Myth: Stroke recovery only happens for the first few months after a stroke.
Fact: Stroke recovery is a lifelong process. Depending on where your stroke is located, how large the stroke is and how long you waited for treatment can affect your recovery.

Myth: Strokes are rare.
Fact: There are nearly 7 million stroke survivors in the U.S. Stroke is the 5th leading cause of death in the U.S.

Myth: Strokes are not hereditary.
Fact: Family history of stroke increases your chance for stroke.

Myth: If stroke symptoms go away, you don't have to see a doctor.
Fact: Temporary stroke symptoms are called transient ischemic attacks (TIA). They are warning signs prior to actual stroke and need to be taken seriously.

I am hoping that this article will provide information, education, maybe even prevention and understanding for our community, as it relates to strokes. My personal experience has been that we have vast expertise and support systems for strokes in and around north Omaha. Treatment may require at least Physical Therapy (PT), Occupational Therapy (OT) and Speech Therapy. I required all. My personal experience is with the Immanuel in-patient Rehabilitation Center, but I recommend that you carefully evaluate your options as to hospitals, rehab, and recovery services. I should also mention that Charles Drew Health Center has aggressive stroke programs, and I recommend that you consider them as a resource. For one, review their Fathers for a Lifetime Program," and website (https://

charlesdrew.com), and also be aware of "Together to End Stoke Ambassadors," President Theola Cooper. I also firmly want to commend Pastor Portia Cavitt, Clair United Methodist Church, who is an aggressive advocate for stroke information and prevention, who collaborated with me on this article. My final comment is that together we can increase awareness in our community about strokes, because we need all our people assets at 100%.

....

Statistics and facts are from the National Stroke Association.

Grapes

JENNIFER LUCZYNSKI

These round little things
So squishy, so juicy.

A big decision ahead,
Green or purpley-red?

Green is sour and tart
Purpley-red is sweet and plump.

Green is cheaper,
But purple-red has more grapes in their bag.

Though I guess people like the green most.
Since it's on sale now.

The green is seedless.
I wonder how many people have taken one from each.

I'm not prepared to make this decision just yet.
Maybe I should just get some oranges instead.

The Bookcase in Savannah

WENDY LUNDEEN

Written by women
Gifts to us from long ago
Reside in the mansion
Of Juliette Gordon Low

Their hearts and souls
Breathing each and every word
Leaping off the pages we turn
Emotions resolutely stirred

Each story shines a light
into other worlds
Each story written by
and for other girls

Each story dwells in us
And guides us to see
The magic authors bring
To you and me.

Colorful stories
Flooding in our veins like gold
Filling empty spaces with joy
Telling tales brave and bold

Whetting our appetites
Fueling every inch of our soul
Gripping with magnetic pull
These books make us whole

Each story shines a light
into other worlds
Each story written by
and for other girls

Each story dwells in us
And guides us to see
The magic authors bring
To you and me.

When I visited the Juliette Gordon Low Birthplace in Savannah in March 2019, I learned many things I didn't know when I was a Girl Scout in Atlantic, Iowa, years ago. She was an ardent believer in the potential of all girls and the importance of fostering their individual growth, character, and self-sufficiency. Juliette is credited with establishing and nurturing a global movement that changed the world. From a meeting in 1912 with the founder of Boy Scouts, Sir Robert Baden-Powell, she was inspired to establish Girl Scouts of the USA that same year. She was thrilled to announce to her cousin, "I've got something for the girls of Savannah, and all of America, and all the world, and we're going to start it tonight!"

From that first gathering of a small troop of 18 culturally and ethnically diverse girls, Juliette broke the conventions of the time — reaching across class, cultural, and ethnic boundaries to ensure all girls, including those with disabilities, had a place to grow and develop their leadership skills. She led Girl Scouts with passion and determination — ensuring it was, and always would be, an experience that was "girl led."

Juliette Gordon Low died January 17, 1927, at her home in Savannah, Georgia, after a long and private struggle with breast cancer. She was posthumously awarded the Presidential Medal of Freedom by President Barack Obama in 2012, the highest civilian award in the United States, for her "remarkable vision" and "her dedication to empowering girls everywhere."

According to our guide, the bookcase features books from a range of genres — memoirs, diaries, autobiographies, historical accounts, travel logs, scholarly works, novels, poems, journals, plays, children's books, graphic novels, comics, and beyond. Girl Scouts from around the world contributed books that they believe have the power to inspire girls of courage, confidence, and character. Our guide told us these books are written for women, about women, by women. It was truly inspirational! The visit dredged up memories of earning badges (the cooking badge was my first) and camping in the wilderness. We learned how to survive in the "wild." We built fires, made s'mores, hung our food in mesh bags in a tree, and sang songs. We hiked and explored nature, learning what to do if we discovered we were lost! We slept in tents and returned home exhausted but confident, courageous and proud, as young women should.

....

source: https://www.girlscouts.org/en/about-girl-scouts/our-history/juliette-gordon-low.html

Wendy Lundeen

MAIL

Dear Maddie Knowles,

I recently read your paper "Making Good Art: Talent, Grit, and Wonder," in the latest issue of Fine Lines. It is outstanding. You talk about how the phrase "Make Good Art" is a more "intimidating mandate." I loved that. I agree with it extremely. You ask the questions, "What does 'good art' even mean, and according to whose standards?" And, "What other kind of art is there?" It's hard to answer those questions sometimes. For some people, they only ever think of art as one thing. After reading your paper more and more, I came across your first experience as an artist. Your mom would set out paper and paints to let you explore with for hours. I thought this was a beautiful experience, and one similar to what I've experienced.

I've been an artist for as long as I can remember. When I was young, I would draw constantly, and I was always building and piecing different materials together to make weird formations. At a young age, I believe everything is art. Our imaginations run wild and free. It is not until we get older and truly experience art and the world that we start asking those questions of, "what does 'good art' even mean?" I think as we get older we limit ourselves to so many things, and I think we especially limit ourselves to the possibility of everything being art. Art is to create, and to understand the world. We create not for ourselves, but for everyone.

The last three pages of your paper truly gave me chills. As an artist, I found them profoundly inspiring and beautiful. You amazingly brought to paper the way I feel on a daily basis, both for the world and for art. When you talk about grit and talent, I find those sections especially well-written. In fact, your writing style is very similar to mine, so it is a joy to read your writing. I agreed immensely with what you had to say about grit and talent. Even though I have never seen your art,

I believe you are an amazing artist just by the way you write about it, and I believe you are an extremely gifted writer as well.

Sara Bradshaw

Dear *Fine Lines,*

(I emailed this letter to writing groups to inform them about this year's *Fine Lines* Creative Writing Summer Camp.)

I am a recently reborn writer. I had left that part of my dream behind for the sake of being a mother, breadwinner, and because of eldercare duties. It was through my exploration into re-entry options that I was invited to attend an editing session for the *Fine Lines Literary Journal*. I have contributed to that publication for almost every edition since 2016. Had *Fine Lines* not lived up to its motto, "Where Writers Grow," I would not be reaching out to you today. *Fine Lines* helps many hesitant dreamers become published writers. In the 28 years of its existence, the welcoming, motivating, and publishing the wannabes out there, *Fine Lines* never failed those of us who became dedicated to growing our skills. This publication has helped so many of us realize that we are writers at heart and capable of becoming published authors.

I attended the writers' camp and found, in crossing that threshold, by reading my work out loud, I shook off my fears and could LET myself be a writer. Now, I will MAKE myself work at being the best I can be.

It is with this in mind that I share the information about the June 24–28 summer writers' camp *Fine Lines* holds in Omaha. It is open to children, youth, and adults, which is an amazingly inspirational mix. I attached the registration flyer, hoping you will share it with your friends and writers.

If you have questions on the details of the Writing Camp, please go to www.finelines.org.

Sincerely,
Janet Bonet
Nebraska Supreme Court Certified, Spanish Interpreter

Dear *Fine Lines,*
My mother, Carolyn Feingold, was a poet, writer, and educator. She had work published in *Fine Lines.* She passed away on February 22, 2019. We asked for donations to *Fine Lines* in her memory.

Sincerely,
Katie Cameron

Dear Alex Cole,
Thank you for your kind words. I like this poem a lot, so I especially appreciate hearing from you. And I too live in the middle of town and would really love to live in the country.

As far as gender is concerned, "she" represents "summer in Nebraska," and she comes across to me as moody and temperamental, like a woman who's had it up to here. Why a woman? Seriously, no particular reason. That's just the image that entered my awareness when I was writing the poem.

I share your love of rural Nebraska ... nothing much going on, just summer afternoon sounds and motions ... crickets and grasshoppers, brown-eyed Susans growing by the road, old windmills lazily turning in a light breeze ... katydids in the evening in late summer ... alfalfa freshly cut ... I know that some people consider the cottonwood tree a nuisance (like milkweed, spreading cotton everywhere and clogging the air conditioning), but the cottonwood is my favorite tree. The undersides of the leaves are kind of a dull gray, but the tops are bright, shiny green, and when the wind blows the leaves rustle, and it's a sight to see when the colors change.

Why did I choose seasons? Well, I was writing specifically about August in Nebraska, which is temperamental and capricious. I have a love-hate relationship with August ... good memories of going back to school, but signals everywhere that winter is on the way, and I DO NOT LIKE winter!

Could you send me some of your poetry or tell me where to find it? Are you coming to Fine Lines camp in June? I hope so.

Keep in touch,
Mary Campbell

Dear *Fine Lines*,

Yay! Thank you, David! I will try to write something to send you for the next issue so I don't break my streak! Keep sending me submissions to edit, as I love helping out!

As a wildlife biologist for over a decade, my husband Geoff took many photos of wildlife and nature (owls, raptors, great blue herons, Sandhill cranes, moose, bear, deer, wolverines, pine martens, mountain goats, sheep, bison, and antelope). We've got lots of river, lake, and ocean shots. Would you be interested in any photos, if I sort through the best? They're from Montana, Yellowstone NP, Oregon, Idaho, Hawaii, and Washington. Geoff took a ton of photos for his hand drawings.

Yay! Thanks again David. I just so enjoy my *Fine Lines* connection. Take care!

Kristi FitzGerald
Hamilton, MT

Dear *Fine Lines*,

Hi, Lauren Rayner. I came across your writing, "The Sun, Stars, and Moon," in the *Fine Lines* 2018 Winter issue, and I loved the story so much that I had to reach out and let you know. I liked the colorful words you used. I could not stop reading your story until it was over. I went back and read the whole story again a couple of times, because I wanted to make sure I didn't miss a single detail. The writing was so vivid, and I was able to picture what you were describing. You tapped

into our sun, moon, and stars and gave them personalities and feelings. I wanted to share with you how those three objects we see in our
sky influence my life every day.

I am forever going to look at the sun, stars, and moon differently,
now. I thought your perspective on each was so unique, and it made
me realize that we all base our lives off them more than we think. I
hope that you continue to write, because the way you word things is
special. Your words make me think. I am glad I found your story, and I
will, without a doubt, remember it, always.

Elizabeth Greunke
UNO student

Dear *Fine Lines,*

I did receive the file to download the *Fine Lines* 2019 spring issue
and the PDF interactive copy. The hits keep coming! You have my
sincere congratulations to all the editors for another foray into the
world of encouraging and publishing such a diverse population of
writers, diverse in so very many ways.

I don't know whether you received my email of a few weeks ago
detailing my current disability status that has kept me from a fuller
participation in the quite amazing journey that is *Fine Lines*. Since
the January editors' meeting I have undergone two MRIs, one
reverse total shoulder replacement surgery, and will find out today,
most likely, whether I will need the same surgery for my other (left)
shoulder that is a source of chronic pain. I am 13 days out, as of today,
from my first surgery, living at home with Kay as my caretaker.

This disability set in during Christmas. When I saw you after that,
I had about 50% use of my right arm. Since surgery, I've had virtually
no use of the arm but can, to a degree, use my fingers. Weight-bearing
moves are taboo, as my body tries to grow bone around the artificial
new ball and socket. (Very cool surgery, from a scientific view!)

One of my challenges is to find ways to keep trying to write stuff. I
am experimenting with dictating my thoughts to my iPad and iPhone.
I composed a piece in memory of my hospice client who recently

died. I had visited him weekly for nearly 90 visits (in Nebraska City). It's frustrating not to be able to send you a "polished" piece, but I do think I will send it anyway since it is, to me, a poignant piece that explains one aspect of what it means to be a hospice volunteer.

I very much hope everyone at *Fine Lines* (and your Pomeranian guardian angels) are well, in spite of our very long winter. For Yolie, her kids at school, and all the teachers out there, I share this from Ralph W. Emerson: "Our chief want is someone who will inspire us to be what we know we could be." *Fine Lines* is so inspirational in this important way to countless others. Thanks for this wonderful work that makes a significant difference in the lives of so many.

Sincerely, and still writing on,
Vince McAndrew
Union, NE

Dear *Fine Lines,*

Each Sunday morning, I read "something." On my shelves are books such as *Meditations* (Marcus Aurelius), *Six Great Ideas* (Adler), *Honey from Stone* (Chet Raymo), *Time and the Art of Living* (Grudin), and *All I Really Know I Learned in Kindergarten* (Fulghum). I've been reading *All I Know* recently and have found much to laugh over, cry a little, and smile about. All *Fine Lines* readers will like it.

Barbara Oliver

Dear *Fine Lines,*

Your publication example is truly an inspiration. I received both the new *Fine Lines* PDF file and the printed book. These are much appreciated. They are incredible publishing achievements, exceeding all expectations.

Robert Runyon
Retired head librarian, University of Nebraska at Omaha

From Two Homes

SYDNEY MANN

I am from two homes
One with white picket fences, the other with weeds as high as your
    knees
I am from a father who hugs me tight, and a mother who hugs a bottle
Instead of her three children
I am from trying to be nothing like her, and be everything like my
    father
I am from alcoholism, and drug addiction
Becoming a mother at the age of four
So that my brothers never have to deal with all the demons like I do
I am from only seeing white on the weekends
Having to leave my children behind, hoping they will be fed and loved

I am from two homes
One with white picket fences, the other with weeds as high as your
    knees
I am from being forgotten outside
Waiting for someone to save us
I am from a father who will love me and a mother who tells me she
    does not like me
I am from escaping
Creating my own happiness, and making myself proud
I am from a happy home of my own
With no trace of her insight
I am from everything of my father, and nothing of my mother

Winding Roads

DAVID MARTIN

In 1829, the future President Martin Van Buren wrote to then President Andrew Jackson, asking him to slow down on his progressive moves to face the future in the young United States of America.

Dear President Jackson:

The canal system of this country is being threatened by the spread of a new form of transportation known as "railroads." The federal government MUST preserve the canals for the following reasons:

ONE: if canal boats are supplanted by these new "railroads," serious unemployment will result. Captains, docks, drivers and lock tenders will be left without means of livelihood, not to mention the numerous farmers now employed growing hay for horses.

TWO: Boat builders would suffer, and towline, whip and harness makers would be left destitute.

THREE: Canal boats are absolutely essential to the defense of the United States. In the event of the expected trouble with England, the Erie Canal would be the only means by which we could ever move the supplies so vital to waging modern war.

As you may well know, Mr. President, "railroad" carriages are pulled at the enormous speed of 15 miles per hour by "engines" which, in addition to endangering life and limb of passengers, roar and snort their way through the countryside, setting fire to crops, scaring the livestock,

and frightening women and children. The Almighty
certainly never intended that people should travel at such
breakneck speed.

Martin Van Buren,
Governor of New York

This letter, which was written three years after Thomas Jefferson
died, might be the ultimate example of conservative thinking. Really,
canal boats are better for the United States than railroads? Now, we
know those roaring and snorting engines that "endangered" passengers in 1829 are still vital to our country's economy, and fifteen miles
per hour is no longer "breakneck speed."

Mankind's journeys have come in many fashions: horses, bicycles,
boats, railroads, automobiles, airplanes, computers, cell phones, and
space travel. Whatever our mobility mode, look for the roads less trav-
elled. Life seldom follows a straight line from point A to Z, and our
personal journeys add clarity to the telling of our stories. They allow
us to have fun with the written word and build the creative corners
of our minds that we did not know existed. Each paragraph we write
acts like a railroad car of its own, carrying characters, messages, and a
cargo of ideas across vistas that complete the breakneck train ride of
our lives.

Some people think *Monte Walsh* was the best western novel
ever written (1963). Since the author also wrote *Shane* (1949), Jack
Schaefer captured the timely saga of a dying way of life, where the
lonely cowboy meets the changing modern way of living. It is ironic
that the *Monte Walsh* movie takes place in Harmony, Arizona.

My father always wanted to be a real cowboy, like Tom Mix, Lash
Larue, Hopalong Cassidy, Gene Autry, Roy Rogers, Shane, and Walsh,
but when he returned from WWII with three Purple Hearts, his legs
and feet were so damaged by bullets and shrapnel that they were
unable to do the hard riding and physical work a cowboy must do
every day. He only took his boots off to sleep, because he could hardly

walk without their firm, high arch support. I imagine him talking with one of these cowboys, and they are wearing their favorite pair of leather boots.

Dad's favorite companion was a beautiful Morgan mare named Gin. She ruled every pen and pasture she entered. Her eyes were alert. Her ears were always up. When I looked at her, I could see her thinking about how to survive in a world of animals and humans. Gin lived for thirty-three years, which is old for horses. From her, I learned it is a mistake to assume all animals will react identically to the same stimuli. Some need rewards at every turn. Some only want encouragement to achieve superior results. People are the same.

Every day, Mom suffered, because she hoped for an educated life, one that provided a better living, one where people graduated from college and became professionals. She flinched every time she heard the song "Don't Let Your Sons Grow Up to Be Cowboys." That ballad was not her friend. While she let me work with Dad during the day, she made sure I spent an equal amount of time with her in the town library, at piano practice, and doing homework for school. She smiled the most when we had late-night chats in the kitchen, puzzling over life's questions and the abstract ideas I found interesting in the books I read.

She let me find my own road in life. I wanted to be myself, but I had a hard time learning who that was. I searched for years to discover me. Many of my blue highways did not appear on maps. I rode horses in saddle club contests and learned cowboy lingo. I read Victor Hugo all night and loved the flow of his words. I coached young boys how to put basketballs into nets and took those skills into classrooms to score points with teachers who listened to me. I pumped gas and learned some of the oil business. I balanced a checkbook for the first time and took great pride in being thrifty. I drove grain trucks and felt the land's treasure riding in the back. I delivered newspapers and brought the world news to my customers' front doors. I wrote magazine articles, managed a church, studied philosophy, fed cattle, and learned how to adapt in life in order to survive.

I was frustrated with my imperfections. However, when I discovered "perfection" was just another word, and there were no perfect human beings, no perfect Standard English, no perfect religion, no perfect student, no perfect teacher, no perfect parent, no perfect planet, and no perfect god, I relaxed. I stopped looking for and expecting perfection in myself and others. The word "progress" became enough for me. If I improved a little each day, that was enough. This realization gave me reason to ride more trains and investigate more winding roads.

One day in my biology high school class, when I was dreaming out loud with friends, I said that I wanted to go to college and do something exciting, but I did not know what to study.

My teacher heard me and said, "Oh, you are just your father's son. You will be like him and run his gas station or one of his farms someday." I can still hear her tired, raspy voice say those words. They haunt me still.

She hardly ever talked to me, because she was my mother's and father's teacher, and she believed I was an average student, having known them. She did not see anything special about them or me, and I did not expect that she ever would. Still, this hurtful comment was not what I hoped to hear from any adult teacher. She was full of negativity, darkness, lack of hope, and I never felt inspired in her classroom. That day, I almost let her kill part of me, my dream of becoming the first person in my family to earn a college education.

After school was out for the summer that year, I was working with Dad, and one day we walked into his favorite saloon for lunch. He seemed so comfortable that a chill of premonition went down my spine. That bar represented his life and the status quo he liked. I just wanted to eat, get back on the tractor, finish my day's work, and in the evening go to the library. I wanted to live my life, not his. In high school, I knew that if I wanted to write, I needed to read more. I felt like a little bird with a broken wing, because I could not get off the ground. When healed, I imagined flying high, soaring with words beneath my wings. Mom would like that.

I had plans to read, write about topics that were fun to investigate, and discover substantial information that would pull me into my future adult life. My pearls of joy were those books resting on the rows of shelves. Each volume was a treasure of its own, and I dreamed that one day my name would have a place on a shelf, too.

That night, a librarian asked me, "Are you a writer?"

She caught me off guard, and I blushed. "Well, I want to be one, someday, but I don't know if I have what it takes to get started."

She said with a smile, "You won't know until you try."

Winding roads have curves, and some have bridges. Forgiveness is a bridge between leaving the past and improving tomorrow. I learned to face difficult times, when I found chaos is where creativity is born. The more I read, the more I changed, and the toughest times taught me the most. Those books led me over rough waters, where I learned to forgive myself. When I opened the books, I imagined light erupting from the pages, and I walked forward into their light. One of the earliest self-affirmation bridges I experienced was when my passion for reading helped me through my toughest year. I read 150 books in 12 months. I felt more confident about a lot of things when that year ended. Those bridges taught me to not let my limitations define me.

Once, Dad looked at me, and without speaking, he asked, "Why do you want to be different?"

I responded in the same way, "Some of me is you. Some of me is Mom. I just want to be me. That is who I want to be."

He did not know what to say, so he said nothing.

Years later, I heard Bob Marley sing what I felt: "One love, one heart, let's get together and feel all right."

With these lessons, I grew page by page. I dug deeper. I thought harder. I saw further.

When I was lonely, I found puppies that took me in. Every dog needed a boy or a girl. Children liked their dogs, and dogs liked their boys and girls. Puppies helped me make the best of the way things turned out. They taught me to be humble enough to be coached, and I learned even the youngest and smallest in a litter can learn. The most stubborn puppy changed his attitude, when motivated to do so. When my furry friends were stubborn, I got down on the floor with them, let them lick my face, looked them in both eyes, told them what they had to do, and never let them do otherwise. They did not forget the look in my eyes, the tone of my voice, what I told them, and how much I cared for them. If they didn't follow my commands, I did not care enough.

Grandfather was a positive role model for me in many ways, and I felt lucky to be around him on the weekends, when Mother and I came for visits on Saturday and Sunday afternoons. When I was a little boy, maybe eight-years-old, reading did not come easily for me, and opening a book required much planning and effort.

One day, I walked into Grandfather's library, and there was a half-cut apple on the card-table next to his comfortable reading chair, a steaming cup of coffee, three open books lying next to each other, Beethoven's "Moonlight Sonata" playing on the big radio, and hand-written notes on a large, yellow tablet. As I sat down, the breeze outside ruffled the shades in the open window.

He was the smartest man I knew, and his interests included agriculture, human evolution, politics, and the St. Louis Cardinals. There was no question I ever asked him that he could not answer. At that age, all I had to do was listen. When he talked, he kept me at the end of his outstretched arms, and when he felt an important point in the conversation was about to arrive, he squeezed my shoulders for emphasis, so I would know to remember what he said.

We lived in a small town, and as far as I knew, no one important lived there. To most of the townsfolk, Grandfather seemed like any ordinary 60-year-old man, but he felt special to me. Although he farmed every day, I never saw him sweat. How is that possible? I asked my mother that same question. She said she did not know, so I watched him closely. After a few weeks of diligent observation, I could see that he never hurried. He never pushed. He smiled all the time, and he talked to all the animals on the farm. It seemed as if he had the best job in the world. What did this mean?

Grandfather was an organizer, a planner, and he never did anything or spoke a word unless he thought about his actions ahead of time. He always got up early, before the sun rose, and when it was the coolest part of the day, he did eight hours of work before noon. Then he would eat lunch and take a nap. When he worked in the afternoon, he was in the shade, if possible, took ten minutes out of every hour for a cool drink, put his feet up, and rested awhile. His smile always showed up, because he enjoyed what he did. His love for farming was contagious, and we all wanted to help him.

One day, after lunch, he and I sat on the shady front porch. His eyes were closed, as he rested, before he went back to the field to work. I was listening to a train going down the tracks in the distance, blowing its whistle.

I asked him a question. "Grandpa, will I grow up to be like you?"

He opened his eyes slowly. "What did you say?"

"Well, you seem so happy all the time, and you like what you do every day. I don't know anybody else who likes what they do so much. I want to be like that."

His eyes got bigger, and he laughed. "If I help other people and do a good job at it, that is a good thing, right?"

"Yes."

"We are a family, and we are supposed to help each other in as many ways as possible. Well, being a conscientious farmer is doing God's work. Feeding people healthy food is one man's way of praying. I often feel like an artist of the soil, when I drive my tractor during planting season. I plow, disc, till, plant, weed the rows, and harvest the crops. When I take care of the Earth, it takes care of me. Our heaven might just be below our feet."

"I'm not sure I understand all of that. Last week, my teacher tried to tell us what a metaphor was. Did you do one of those just now?"

"Maybe."

"It would be nice if more people worked with those goals in mind, right?

He stood up to go back to work, arranged his hat, placed his hands on my shoulders, and squeezed them.

Then he smiled and said, "In the future, instead of planting soybeans, wheat, and corn every spring, wouldn't it be great to have a tractor that could plant truth, justice, and freedom for all? In the fall, we'd harvest knowledge, intelligence, and wisdom. Those different crops in the barn would come in pretty handy when we needed them. We must never limit ourselves. We will never know what we can achieve until we try."

I replied, "I want a job like that."

He hugged me, and I saw his eyes twinkle.

"Don't over-think it, sonny," he said. "Just begin."

Unafraid

VINCE McANDREW

So common an event
we don't see it as a brave letting go,
a capitulating to gravity's pull
a bird falling from a tree
only to catch itself mid-plunge
with a flap of wings
lest it crash into the ground
arresting its free-fall swiftly, gracefully
so routinely we groundlings
take it for granted
because that's just the way it is between
gravity and winged
incarnations of evolved stardust:
Holy Matter taking flight
lifting into the air
above Earth, above gravity
unafraid of letting go.

The Power of My Hands

ROBERTO MENJIVAR

My hands are unique. I use them daily because they have multipur-
poses. They help me to write, brush my teeth, grab things, cook, do
gardening, sense hot and cold surfaces. My hands are an important
part of my body, and without my hands, life would have been hard.
There are five fingers in each of my hands. Every finger is necessary
because each and every one of them forms a part of the hand and has a
specific purpose.

The color of my hands is brown, and it represents my Latino inheri-
tance. Every scar on my hand has left a memory on my life. When I
was a kid, I fainted a couple of times, because I was afraid every time I
saw my own blood coming out of my hand when I accidentally made
a cut. One day, I was peeling coconuts using a machete, and I accidentally made a cut on my left thumb. I remember how warm I felt the
blood was coming out of my finger, and after that, I do not remember
anything because I lost consciousness. When I recovered, my grandparents were there. It was scary and painful for me, but I overcame it,
because I made a couple of cuts on my fingers accidentally, again, and
nothing happened.

My hands are unique and beautiful. They are very special, and I
would not perform the same if I would not have even one of them. I
am grateful to have both of my hands, because I can use them to create
and perform different actions: to write my school papers, to do the
oil change on my mother's car, and to clean the house. There are a lot
of things that our hands help us do. It would be hard to describe my
hands in just a word, but if I were to describe them in a single word, it
would be "utilitarian."

A Personal Affirmation

ABDIRIZAK MOHAMUD

I was born in 1996 in the middle of the long Somali civil war. I received most of my education in Somalia before I came to the United States in 2015. My life's journey has impacted me. It gave me a picture of who I am, today. I was all about curiosity, as I grew up. Curiosity is a sign of a scientist, and that is why my major is pre-med.

As a child, I liked to go to the mountains, climb trees, and chase deer all day long, because I did not like to play with other children. The only game they played was soccer, which was boring to me. I could not kick a piece of leather all day. I asked my grandmother to take me to the wilderness, introduce me to the trees, and learn which crops we could eat. Every Thursday and Friday, my grandmother would take me to the wilderness and let me explore. I learned a lot, but my friends did not.

They begged me to let them go along, which I always liked. It was exciting and a way to sense freedom, instead of staying home all day. We ran and chased each other. We played a game called *Isbaacsi* in Somali, but in English it can be the chasing game, tag. We made a circle and two groups. Half of the first group was going to stay and guard the circle, while the others chased the other group. If you get caught, you will stay in the circle until the end of the game, unless someone from your group gets in the circle and taps you. Other than that, we swam in the sea or at the lake.

We fished and ate wild crops in the country. Among those crops was gob, hohob, dhafarur, murcod, and murcayo. They were delicious, and I get homesick thinking about these good times. When my friends and I saw a herd of goats, cattle, or camels, we ran to them to see if we could get milk. The country families did not hesitate to give us milk, water, and meat, because it is our culture to provide care for others. They treated us like their boys, because we spoke one language, and we were a homogeneous society, except they called us "the city boys."

On the other hand, I was a curious man. While I was in the wild, I liked to question a lot of things that my grandmother taught me. One of the things I questioned was why ropes can be made out of certain trees and not others? Why do some animals stay in groups and protect each other, and some do not? I did not get answers for everything. Those questions remain in my head. I believed that every tree has a purpose. I was also curious about why some animals dry up (get out of milk) faster than others. I asked one lady, "Why does this goat dry faster than the others?" She told me that her mother was like this. I realized that it has to do with their genetics, and sometimes this is passed down to offspring, just like humans.

One of the things I liked to do was to sit within the gatherings of elders. They were a source of wisdom for me. Those men talked about history, poetry, and stories of those ahead of us. I liked how they talked; it was pure and mature thinking combined with wisdom. We were young men who listened to them every morning after the "Fajr" prayer at a restaurant across the street from the mosque. Each one in the restaurant ordered a cup of tea and enjoyed the beautiful stories our grandparents offered.

I miss those days.

Lost Horse Beargrass
Photo by Kristi FitzGerald

The Invitation

ORIAH MOUNTAIN DREAMER
Indian Elder, 1994

It doesn't interest me what you do for a living. I want to know what you ache for, and if you dare to dream of meeting your heart's longing. It doesn't interest me how old you are. I want to know if you will risk looking like a fool for love, for your dreams, for the adventure of being alive.

It doesn't interest me what planets are squaring your moon. I want to know if you have touched the center of your own sorrow, if you have been opened by life's betrayals or have become shriveled and closed from fear of further pain.

I want to know if you can sit with pain, mine or your own, without moving to hide it or fade it or fix it.

I want to know if you can be with joy, mine or your own, if you can dance with wildness and let the ecstasy fill you to the tips of your fingers and toes without cautioning us to be careful, be realistic, or to remember the limitations of being human.

It doesn't interest me if the story you're telling me is true. I want to know if you can be true to yourself, if you can bear the accusation of betrayal and not betray your own soul.

I want to know if you can see beauty even when it is not pretty every day, and if you can source your life from God's presence.

I want to know if you can live with failure and still stand on the edge of the lake and shout to the silver of the full moon, "Yes!"

It doesn't interest me who you are, how you came to be here. I want to know if you will stand in the center of the fire with me and not shrink back.

It doesn't interest me where or what or with whom you have studied. I want to know what sustains you from the inside when all else falls away.

I want to know if you can be alone with yourself, and if you truly like the company you keep in the empty moments.

Spring Chickadee
Photo by Kristi FitzGerald

NATIVE SPIRITS

"We are part of the Earth, and it is part of us. This we know. The earth does not belong to us. We belong to the Earth." — *Chief Seattle*

"It does not require many words to speak the truth." — *Chief Joseph*

"Children must early learn the beauty of generosity. They are taught to give what they prize most, that they may taste the happiness of giving." — *Ohiyesa*

"Even as you desire good treatment, so render it." — *Handsome Lake*

"What is life? It is the flash of a firefly in the night. It is the little shadow which runs across the grass and loses itself in the Sunset." — *Crowfoot*

"You must speak straight so that your words may go as sunlight into our hearts." — *Chief Cochise*

"O great Spirit, help me never judge another until I have walked two weeks in their moccasins." — *Edwin Laughing Fox*

"All things are connected like the blood that unites us. We did not weave the web of life, we are merely a strand in it. Whatever we do to the web, we do to ourselves." — *Chief Seattle*

"My hand is not the same color as yours, but if you pierce it, I shall feel the pain. The blood will be the same color. We are men, the same God made us. All I ask is what is mine, my land, my freedom, my dignity as a man." — *Luther Standing Bear, Ponca chief, stood against the US Government in 1879, and established for the first time that "an Indian is a person within the meaning of the law"*

One Weekend in Omaha

STEVEN NORDEEN

News of newly-minted hips and knees
sprinkle the conversations, Dickie Metzger's
trio of transplants tops them all.

The girls still envy the homecoming queen
and rightfully so, until they know the tragedies
that has them hug their grandchildren
just a little tighter when they visit next.

There are successes and failures,
surprises and the expected;
two suicides are both and neither.

Spouses in the stands tell of teen perplexity
at the halt and grey that shuffle up the sidelines
for our halftime introduction, caring not
that Dickie led their beloved Bulldogs
to homecoming glory 50 years before.

I haven't thought of you in half a century,
so, no, I don't remember you.

What I really say pours oil
upon the awkward waters
our unspoken accord: ignore
the acrid ghosts of teenage angst,
the vapors that still sting,
still keeping cool at all cost. We bury
the aftertaste, pass judgment
on the bitterness of our beer.

Go Deeper

KRISTEN G. NORMAN

It's a New Year
never a new slate.

It's a time to gently tweak
softly tinker, what

weighs you down
What lifts you up

Do what makes your soul sing!
slow…to enjoy the journey

More.
really listen.

catch the glints
Lend a hand

Extend a smile
just be.

Stroke

JOANNA O'KEEFE

I walked out the door
of the old country inn
into the slanting light of day.
Suddenly

I could not see;
I could not stand;
I could not speak.

Collapsed
into the strong arms of my husband,
everything seemed surreal —
like a slow motion movie or a dream
where I am the detached observer.

Above the sirens
my beloved's anguished cry —
"Don't leave me! Don't leave me!"
pierced as a sharp arrow
straight through my heart.

Lying in healing sunlight,
I later became aware
of a profound gratitude
welling up from deep within.

Birdsong was sweeter;
grass greener, and the daffodils,
bursting forth in buttercup yellow
lovelier than ever.

Lifting my eyes to the heavens,
I wondered, what should I do
with my blessed second chance?

Mother Teresa's Prayer

ANDY PAPPAS

O, God we pray for those
Who suffer from injustice
Because of their race
Color or religion
For those imprisoned
For those who fight oppression
O, God we pray
chain to chain

Lord we're all broken, but we're not alone
We're chained together, all the way home
Someday you'll free us, wash clean all our pain
Broken together, chain to chain

O, God we pray
For those who are hounded
For those who speak their truth
For those tempted to violence
For those who are hungry
Who can't help themselves
O, God we pray
chain to chain

Lord we're all broken, but we're not alone
We're chained together, all the way home
Someday you'll free us, wash clean all our pain
Broken together, chain to chain
Broken together, chain to chain

Power in a Pen Stroke

RHONDA PARSONS

Power in a pen stroke
Power in ink and paint
Power, power to create
The uncreated consciousness of the human race
The artist, yes, has powers sublime
the chisel and stone awaken the mind
angels are set free, humanity flies
Oh, the power of Michelangelo to carve the Divine
Triangles, circles, and squares called *Mrs. Jones's Many Faces*
The beauty of abstract thinking she enables
And tangled up in patterns, Zen becomes me
Oh, the power of pen stroke to ignite the Divine
Starry, starry night
And Kinkade's works of light
transform this dark, dreary world into a clear moonlit night
melodious melodies make the sun rise
splendors on the horizon I see
in the inmost corners of my mind
colors of light and love, colors of the Divine
Oh, the power of the music note to "tune me "into the Divine
I sparkle like diamonds to learn the story of a jeweler
And pattern myself to perfection at mosaic and tile
The grittiness of Eastwood and Hallmark tearjerkers
Avatar, Hidden Figures and other true stories
Take me to another world, make me part of their story
Human we are, though we come in different colors, sizes
Human we are, warmed by One Light Divine
Oh, the power of the cinema to make a shining "star"
The beauty the eyes behold, the vibrations that please the ear

The brush impressing on the canvas soul
What power, what power, what power
Do they have to break off these nether world shackles
And spark the Divine inside?
Side by side, dark and light
Send signals up the spine
Soul "sees," Soul "hears," and strives for the light inside
Every color, every note, mosaic tile and movie
Makes a glimmer, makes a gleam on the jewels of virtue inside
What a glorious way to become the angels Michelangelo set free
Power in a pen stroke
Power in ink and paint
Power, power to create
The uncreated consciousness of the human race

//

"The road to hell is paved with adverbs."

STEPHEN KING

//

The Clock

TORI PEDERSEN

I am steadfast,
My rhythm unchangeable.
My face stares into hers, but she rarely sees me.
No, instead, she sees memories, dreams.

She remembers where she was the last time she saw me.
She remembers what she was hoping for.
She remembers the pit of anxiety in her stomach.
She remembers the boredom that seemed to drag on.

She looks at me now, and still doesn't see me.
She doesn't look at the beauty of all the pieces that make one whole.
A whole that she relies on more than anything else,
For I am the keeper of her life.

No, she looks at me now and wishes for me to change,
To break my rhythm,
Release my hold.
But I cannot,
For I am her keeper.

She wishes for me to change to fit her needs, her wants.
She rarely looks at me with a smile.
I look into her face and see anticipation, sometimes dread.
She looks into mine and sees restraint.

My rhythm upsets her,
But she accepts that she cannot change it.
For I am the keeper of her life.
Her hopes, fears, and dreams all rely on me,
Though my existence is a creation of her own mind.
For I am the keeper of her life,
For as long as she is the keeper of mine.

The Snake and the Hummingbird

CHARLENE PIERCE

Remarkable for nothing,
but the art of enticing
by the power of its eyes.
I admire it much.

The rattle is loud and distinct when angry.
When pleased, a distant trepidation.
Wherever they are met
open war is declared.

His eyes filled with madness and rage,
He thrust out his tongue as snakes do,
hissed through his teeth with inconceivable strength,
an object of terror to all bystanders.

When they have fixed their eyes
on an animal, it becomes immovable.
The victim, arrested by some invincible power,
rushes to the jaw of the snake and is swallowed.

Wild blossoms attract the attention
of birds, their flight so rapid
You cannot distinguish the motion
of their wings.

Nature has lavished her most splendid colors
on this little bird. Eyes like diamonds,
reflecting light on all sides. Taught
to find those mellifluous particles that serve

for food. Yet leaves them untouched, underprized
of anything our eyes can distinguish.

Sometimes they will tear and lacerate
the flowers into a hundred pieces.
They often fight with the fury
of lions until one combatant falls a sacrifice and dies.
Where do passions find room in so diminutive a body?

And I, deprived of fangs
sitting solitary and pensive
incapable of further resistance
abandon to the current.

....

A Found Poem from Chapter 10 "On Snakes; and on the Humming-Bird" in
Letters from an American Farmer by J. Hector St. John de Crevecoeur 1980.

The Hiding Spot

NINA PODARIU

Student at Omaha Westside High School

My grandfather was scarcely found without a book in hand. After
retiring, he made himself a permanent home on an old, stained
champagne armchair, where he'd sit and read for hours. The wrinkles
lining his old face grew even deeper when he'd furrow his woolly black
brows in concentration. Despite his age, he still had most of his hair,
though he seemed not to take pride in the fact and kept it short. One
could never quite tell whether or not he cared about his appearance.
He wore a white dress shirt with grey slacks every day, regardless
of whether or not anyone outside of family would see him that day.
Though his wife would walk the streets of Bucharest for hours with
her grandchildren, he rarely exercised. His thin frame could only be
attributed to his fast metabolism. The only thing you could tell for
sure about him was his passion for literature, though he'd been an
engineer by trade.

Despite the small size of the apartment he shared with his wife, one
wall was covered with shelves brimming with books. Some were old,
others new, and the differences in their textures and colors created
a mosaic along the wall of the otherwise bland room. I'd always
assumed that all the books were his, though it was a rather presump-
tuous assumption, because I'd never once seen my grandmother reach
for anything but a photo frame or tv remote from those shelves. While
she seemed to have little interest in the bookshelves that pulled the
entire room together, grandfather regarded them with a sort of reverence. He knew exactly where each book belonged, and could recall
what was hidden between its pages.

I felt most loved and trusted by him when he'd call for me to
retrieve a book off the shelves. First, he'd tell me which of the

bookcases it was in, then which shelf it was on, and then the title. His request was preceded by my grandmother asking him for some cash before she headed to the market. The book grandfather asked for always depended on how much money she needed. Once I found the requested book and offered it to him, he'd flip through the pages with purpose, until he reached several neat, crisp bills tucked between the pages. After pulling out the required sum, he'd close the book gently, allow his hands to linger on the cover for a moment or two, before handing it back to me. Grandmother would collect the money, and I'd turn back to the wall of shelves. Oftentimes, I couldn't quite remember where the book belonged. I was younger then, my attention span would only stretch long enough for one pursuit at a time.

Upon seeing my struggle, grandfather would unfold himself from his worn out armchair and straighten his long-limbed body to its full height. He rarely moved about unless it was to use the restroom or stand on the balcony for a smoke, but every time he did, a bone somewhere in his body would crack. He'd make his way toward me with deliberate steps, take his thick black rimmed glasses off his head where they rested (like sunglasses), and balance them on his nose before returning the book to its rightful spot. And then, he'd fold himself onto the arm chair once more and continue his reading.

His retired life was surrounded by those books, and when he died, pieces of him remained tucked between their pages.

Parking Lots

CATHY PORTER

spread news
as the tribes gather and scrape
the cement

while the day pours rain
or sunlight on the well-lubricated

the global meeting place
of the bored and restless

drinks and smokes get passed
secret handshakes

lies spread faster
than the latest disease
nobody has a home
until words are depleted

and people go
their separate ways
act as if they don't remember
the voices they slept with

Remembering the Embrace

FABRICE B. POUSSIN

What does it take for the child
to receive the embrace of a frigid day?

He looks up to the sky for comfort
the giant sees to a horizon so distant
forgetful of the offspring who needs a hand.

What does it take for a touch
stolen in the midst of mere dreams?

He knows a crowd of strangers surrounds
the days he lets unravel as the clock runs
unaware that tomorrow will steal their breaths.

What does it take for a breast
to be cupped in the palms of another?

He waits roaming, almost invisible
as his infinite hopes continue to slowly beat
pleading at the rhythm of a lost beginning.

What does it take for that passion
to become free in the prison of fear?

He shivers in a shell crushed by the multitude
bruised by the punches of unknown foes
begging that the ache would give way to joy.

But what does it take to be seen
and received as a gift to the one in ashes?

Grooves upon a smile multiply to tell the tale
of a gentle soul who dies under the anvil
his chest to brittles at last he goes to sleep.

Tea with a Man

KEVIN RAMSDEN
Student at Oregon State University-Cascades

I drank tea with a man today.
The tea was black and loose leaf.
He put honey on the table.
We sat and drank in silence.
The man watched me.

I drank tea with a man today.
His face was white,
And it blinded me from the
Shadows dancing across his canvas.

I drank tea with a man today.
She sipped from a mug of many faces.
A tear fell.
The man licked the falling drop, and
Consumed what was left.

I drank tea with a man today.
There was whole milk,
She poured it into her cup.
The leaf muddled with the cow.

I drank tea with a man today.
They knew man meant nothing.
No gender, no race, no face.
I screamed, "WOAH-MAN!" — Woman.
Think it's something different?

I drank tea with a man today.
They cried be a man:

He/Him/His:
Cultural Predator.

I drank tea with a man today.
He said nothing.

I drank tea with a man today.
She said you are wrong.

I drank tea with a man today.
They said one day you'll see,

Man's honey crusted lips,
Milk bleeding from wrists.

I drank tea with a man today.

I drank tea with a man today.

Anti-Semitism: Prevalence in My Life

CHLOE RAY

Acceptance is a key concept learned in the Jewish faith. Yet, 1.09 billion people in the world today harbor hatred towards Jews (*ADL Global 100*). This statistic was produced by the Anti-Defamation League by surveying about 55,000 people worldwide in 2015. It is not uncommon for Jewish people to be discriminated against due to their beliefs, and as a Jewish person myself, I know firsthand how humankind can retain Anti-Semitic tendencies. Like most of the Jewish community, Anti-Semitism has been an unfortunate component of my life. Anti-Semitism has revealed itself through its impacts on my religious pride and my relationship with victims of the Holocaust.

Anti-Semitism is not a modern concept that rears its ugly head only in the 21st Century. The term "Anti-Semitism" was started by German, Wilhelm Marr, to explain the anti-Jewish campaigns in Central Europe in 1879. The viewpoint is much more ancient than when the term was coined. Anti-Semitism has been around since the Abrahamic faiths split, due to differentiating beliefs. During the Hellenistic Age in the first century, Jews who left Palestine were socially segregated by pagans due to being monotheistic (Berenbaum). After Jesus was crucified, Christian Anti-Semitism became prominent because of the idea that the Jewish people were to blame. Jews were perceived as "Christ Killers" and "Devils" ("Anti-Semitism"). This belief followed to 70 CE after the destruction of the Temple of Jerusalem and the banishment of Jews. During the Roman Empire, laws by Roman emperors were created in order to segregate and diminish the Jewish population. Jews all over medieval Europe were stripped of their rights, citizenship, and ability to get jobs. Since then, Jewish people have been persecuted from Russia, Spain, Egypt, Germany, Poland, and a plethora of other countries from all around the globe (Berenbaum). A prime example of discrimination to the religious group is the Holocaust, in World War II. The rise of the "Aryans" in Europe caused strengthened hostility towards Jews which was expressed through official government policy. Jews were forced into ghettos and transported into concentration and death camps. This eventually resulted in Hitler's "final solution," the gruesome goal to exterminate all Jews through genocide. Six million Jews, two-thirds of the Jewish population were brutally murdered simply due to their beliefs ("Essential Facts about the Holocaust"). Thus, Jews have been persecuted throughout history, and this continues today.

Growing up, I was ashamed to be Jewish. At first, I only felt excluded, because a man with a beard never came through my chimney to deliver presents, and a bunny never left plastic eggs filled with candy in my yard. Around fourth grade, a newfound embarrassment for my religious differences boiled inside me. I remember clearly the day a fifth grader inscribed a swastika in my brother's notebook. In that same year, I was told by a fellow classmate my first joke about the Holocaust. I finally realized that Santa and the Easter Bunny were not the only things that divided people's opinions on my faith. It resulted in hiding my identity. The end of every year became a nerve-racking time for me in elementary school. I pretended that I also received iPods and Silly Bands for Christmas and that Judaism was never a piece of me. Middle school started, and I wanted to start fresh. My mother had given me a delicate Star of David necklace that I decided to wear during my first week of junior high. On the first day of school, a classmate noticed the pendant around my neck. He loudly told the class as he made direct eye contact with me, "Jews killed Jesus. They deserved to die in the Holocaust." I felt the same wave of embarrassment that I experienced too often in elementary school. During passing period, I sped to the bathroom to rip off my necklace and throw it in the depths of my backpack. Later that day, when I arrived home, the Star of David was shoved in the back of a drawer not to be seen for years.

During my sophomore year of high school, I was offered an internship at the Anti-Defamation League in Omaha. I interviewed half-heartedly, because I was worried about what connotations someone would receive upon reading that organization's name on my resume. Would they know I was Jewish and not want to hire me? Something in me knew that I needed to partake in the internship, so I became their summer intern. Through the internship, I heard my colleagues' own stories of Anti-Semitic comments and actions they experienced. I viewed pictures of Jewish graves in the Midwest destroyed or littered with swastikas. A new feeling washed over me. I realized that I should not be ashamed of being Jewish, because I would be giving in to these Anti-Semitic people. I would be giving them what they wanted. I started to wear my Star of David necklace to high school daily, although it still brought consequences. Holocaust jokes, discriminatory acts, and stereotypical comments were still blurted out in class and plastered on social media. Instead of hiding my necklace and my religion, I was open about it and even occasionally attempted to educate the ignorant people who threw hateful comments out. Unfortunately, but not unexpectedly, I did not change these people's minds.

My experiences with Anti-Semitism are minuscule compared to my family that was hit by Hitler's wrath in World War II. My great-grandmother was one of nine children, and only six of them made it out of Poland alive. The three older siblings settled down with children and spouses in Sherishow, so they concluded to wait out the possible consequences. This was not uncommon. It is hard for a person of any religion to believe that humankind can commit the act of genocide to anyone. The Jews in Sherishow were murdered by being rounded up and shot in the town square. The Nazis purposefully forced all children to go first, and they made the parents view the wrongful death of their loved ones. The parents were then killed. Two of the children, my great-grandma's nephews, were sent to Auschwitz instead. One of the children worked as a blacksmith with his father, so he was visibly strong when he stepped off the cattle cars to be sorted. He was chosen by the Nazis to be a Sonderkommando, a worker at the crematoriums in the death camp. He was ordered to haul the deceased bodies from the gas chambers to be cremated, in a forced attempt to hide all evidence of cruelty at Auschwitz. Sonderkommandos had a higher chance of survival in Auschwitz because the dead bodies provided warmth in the freezing winters. Only 100 of the approximately 2,000 Sonderkommandos in Auschwitz remained upon liberation (Shields). The Sonderkommando lived, but his brother died unrecorded in the death camp. The former blacksmith was able to migrate to the United States and settle in Brooklyn, New York City. He married a woman he met at Auschwitz and they had three children. When the couple reached their old age, their daughter moved them to Jerusalem. My great-grandmother's nephew developed dementia, and he believed he was reliving his horrific experiences in Auschwitz until his death in Israel.

World War II did not mark the end of Anti-Semitism. Almost two weeks ago in Pittsburgh, Pennsylvania, Robert D. Bowers open fired into a synagogue, brutally murdering eleven innocent people because of their religion (Campbell). Over a year ago, white nationalists took to the streets and rallied in Charlottesville, Virginia, chanting sayings from early Nazi propaganda (Wagner). In 2003, two suicide bombers in Turkey attacked a synagogue during services. In France, synagogues have been set on fire. The amount of Holocaust deniers continues to rise (Rifkin). Anti-Semitism has no end in sight and will remain not only a part of my life but of Jews globally.

REFERENCES

ADL Global 100. Anti-Defamation League, 2015, http://global100.adl.org/

"Anti-Semitism." *Anti-Defamation League,* https://www.adl.org/anti-semitism

Berenbaum, Michael. "Anti-Semitism." *Encyclopedia Britannica,* 13 September 2018, https://www.britannica.com/topic/anti-Semitism/Introduction

"Essential Facts About the Holocaust." *Thought Co,* https://www.thoughtco.com/holocaust-facts-1779663

Robertson, Campbell. "11 Killed in Synagogue Massacre; Suspect Charged With 29 Counts." *New York Times,* https://www.nytimes.com/2018/10/27/us/active-shooter-pittsburgh- synagogue-shooting.html

Rifkin, Ira. "Anti-Semitism in the 21st Century." *My Jewish Learning,* https://www.myjewishlearning.com/article/anti-semitism-in-the-21st-century/

Shields, Jacqueline. "Concentration Camps: The Sonderkommando." *Jewish Virtual Library,* https://www.jewishvirtuallibrary.org/the-sonderkommando

Wagner, Meg. "Blood and Soil: Protestors Chant Nazi slogan in Charlottesville." *CNN,* 12 August 2017, *https://www.cnn.com/2017/08/12/us/charlottesville-unite-the-right- rally/index.html*

Frightening Lightning
Photo by Derek Burdeny
derekburdenyphotography.com

Eggheads Can Be Creative: A Personal Essay on Weird Mechanics

THOMAS REDINGTON

Student at the University of Nebraska at Omaha

According to dictionary.com, the word "funky" is defined as "stylish and exciting; cool." This is how I would describe many pioneers and imbeciles in the fields of mechanics and engineering and the way they went about solving issues they faced, whether it was how to make a car run faster and longer or how to give one soldier the firepower of many. Learning about these quirky, funky, and downright idiotic feats of ingenuity has always intrigued me. Since the industrial revolution, man has been able to take invention and innovation to the extremes, from watches on the wrist with hundreds of small, precisely made parts to hundred-thousand-ton warships capable of wiping out small towns with a few volleys of their guns. It seems our only limit is our imagination. I love learning about these inventions, and why they have shaped my life.

Guns were invented to kill. There is no way around it; their main purpose is to propel a projectile at rapid speed to make dead that which was once alive. I will not get into the politics of firearms, because this is not a persuasive argument for or against them. I am only going to illustrate some firearms that are more than meets the eye. First is the Howell Automatic Rifle, spawned from the trenches of the Great War. In WWI, all major combatants used single-shot rifles, which were made for long range combat. In theory, it was a good idea, but in practice, not so much. In fact, on many sectors of the Western Front, the opposing sides were barely one-hundred yards apart.

The bolt-action rifle was made obsolete by the time the first trench was dug. Enter the Howell Automatic rifle, which did all the work, and one only had to pull the trigger. This was an ingenious conversion of the British Army's standard issue rifle. A piston was added to the side of the rifle that used the expanding gases from the explosion of the bullet to cycle the action for the soldier, allowing him to fire rapidly. The trigger was also modified, and a vertical grip was added, resulting in a rifle straight from a steampunk novel. This was wonderful in concept, but a long hunk of metal shooting backwards faster than the blink of an eye proved to be rather unpleasant to have only a fraction of an inch from one's face. Firing full-sized rifle ammunition at a rapid rate was hell for the soldier's shoulder. These factors along with manufacturing costs caused the Howell to be removed from contention. The sub-machinegun was made to answer the same problem as the Howell. It gave one soldier the firepower of many.

John Thompson's submachinegun initially nicknamed "The Annihilator" and "The Trench Broom," for obvious reasons, is infamous. The Tommy-gun, as it was most widely known, became a staple of twentieth century America and ended its career with over half a century of service. This longevity owes itself to the Thompson's robust, effective design. That is not to say it was perfect; in fact, the Thompson was far from it. It fired on an open-bolt system, meaning the bolt stayed open until the gun was fired. In the forward position, the bolt would stay locked in place under the Blish Principle of Metal Adhesion, a theory of physics that two different metals have a different frictional resistance. This is not a physical law and is completely bogus. In fact, the man who coined the idea, a naval officer named John Blish, had no formal experience in the world of physics or engineering. As it turned out, the Thompson was using a simple mechanical disadvantage; wherein, the locks that held the bolt in place would slide upward before allowing the rest of the bolt to travel. The "Blish lock" was omitted from the gun in favor of a simpler, cheaper, single-piece bolt that used its weight to stay closed when firing.

The Russian AN-94 was a gun straight from a science-fiction novel, designed to allow a soldier to penetrate most body armor. The boys in the lab went a little overboard with this one. The AN-94 had a special "burst" mode, which fired two rounds at a blistering speed, while the user only felt the recoil of one. To achieve this, there was a special "elevator" in the gun that put a bullet half way between the magazine and the chamber, halving the cycle time and bringing the cyclic rate to nearly 2000 rpm. While innovative, it was a very expensive rifle and was only used by Special Forces and police units.

The automobile is one of man's greatest inventions. Ever since its inception, man has been trying to improve the automobile, make it faster, safer, and more efficient. The BMW "Brutus" is none of these things. The BMW "Brutus" is a testament to man's arrogance and an abomination in the eyes of God. If I were to meet the men who built this and ask them "Why did you build this?" I guess they would respond with, "We built it because we were bored, and we could." The Brutus is special, because it uses the 47 Liter (2868 cubic inch) BMW V12 putting out over 500 horse power, the same engine used in some German WWII bomber aircraft. As British auto-journalist and imbecile-extraordinaire, Jeremy Clarkson, put it: "This car is actively trying to kill you, the noise is literally deafening, the steering wheel doesn't work, and you need the legs of an Olympic weight lifter to use the clutch, and despite all that, it's bloody brilliant. You see, there's no fun in a car that steers, brakes, and changes gears for you, in this car... you'll break a sweat just turning the starter."

The last of the unorthodox mechanical adventures will be a dive into military tanks. They combine the mobility and complexity of cars with the explosive intricacy of firearms. The tank is called a "tank" because the British tried to keep this new armored behemoth a secret during the First World War. All official records of the first tank described it as a new vehicle to bring water and other liquids to the front lines. By World War II, tanks pretty much looked the same as they do today, engine in the rear, a few men in the armored crew area, and a BFG (Big Freaking Gun) in a fully rotating turret on top.

One of the most complex of these was the German Panzer, a
heavily armed war machine capable of beating just about anything
it faced, except for its arch-nemesis, general use and abuse. The
engineers spent so much time creating tight seams and near perfect
welds, they didn't think it would be necessary to make the transmission easy to access. This is fine in a Honda Accord, but it is not in a
thirty-ton machine that needs to go cross country for most of its life.
The Panther's transmission was horrendously under-powered for the
work load it needed to perform, which led to near constant break-
downs. The tank would have to be brought back to a garage, the
turret would be removed, the crew compartment would be gutted,
the transmission would be heaved backward on a set of rails and
removed from the gaping hole in the roof, a process which could
take many days not factoring in the scarcity of replacement parts.
American tankers with similar problems would usually walk back to
base and wait for a new tank, and be on their merry way, a process
which would take a day, at most.

While humdrum and boring to many, mechanics and engineering
have helped me to think critically and solve problems in unconven-
tional ways. Since my early childhood, one of my favorite pastimes has
been playing with Lego bricks. With just a handful of pieces, one can
create an infinite number of things that perform an infinite number
of tasks. In my seventh-grade science fair project, I researched the
lowly gear and how integral it is to our lives from making our cars
stay on the road with differential steering to keeping our clocks timed
correctly. I helped the Nebraska State Science Bowl finalists from
my school build a robotic car to go to nationals with them, because I
knew so much about mechanics and related fields. My love of ooky,
kooky, and spooky mechanics led me to the University of Nebraska's
Construction Management Program. Here I am.

The men and women who had the idea to put pistons, springs,
gears, and wheels together and create something that runs perfectly
deserve respect; however, it is that special group of people who tried

to make something radical, who ventured into the unknown and either created something awesome or something that goes horribly wrong, that I admire. They had no idea what could happen, but they forged on, pushing the barriers of science and science fiction to change the world.

I love quirky, goofy, funky engineering and mechanics, because they illustrate the blending of egg-head engineering and the limitless bounds of mankind's quest to invent and create. Machines can be art just as much as music, painting, and writing. One only needs to look for it. To quote Confucius: "Everything has beauty, but not everyone sees it."

///

"Tears are words that need to be written."

PAUL COELHO

///

Grounded

DAVID H. REINARZ

He had to ground himself before he kissed her.
I don't mean he had to steady himself,
plant his feet firmly on the ground,
although that would be an appropriate preparation
for what was about to happen.

He had to ground himself before he kissed her,
because sparks were going to fly.
He wasn't sure if the flow of energy was coming from the sky
and channeling through her
or coming from the earth in some eruption via him.
Maybe it was both.
Maybe it was the concatenation of circumstances
that brought them together.
Maybe the power present in the close proximity of their lips
was more than the cosmos could keep under control,
and it just burst out in an act of spontaneous combustion.

Whatever.
No one should be harmed.
He touched the lamp at the bedside.
The light flickered briefly then extinguished.
As he leaned in, a blue and gold finger of electricity
arced from her finger to the metal bed frame.

Their lips touched.
The cosmos sighed
then smiled.

Dark and Light of Night and Day

MERCEDES J. RENKEN

The dazzling stars gleam within the night sky.
No such light could be as brilliant and bright.

Across the display comets shoot by.
In the imperfect silence of the night.

Far below lies cities stretched far and wide.
With their own glowing lights filling the dark.

The moon's great force upon the ocean's tide.
The moon and stars, too, seen from a small park.

In the far away great distance, gleaming
a sphere so big and bold is seen in air.

Other stars' view began disappearing.
All that was left was one intertwined pair.

Until one remains, which is not final.
It is the sun's, moon's, stars', and sky's cycle.

Fear

JOSHUA REUTING
Student at Millard South High School, Omaha

A pungent aroma filled the air, as I cautiously proceeded through the corn maze. What was this? Where was it coming from? I refused to believe evil forces were at play, but I had to keep an open mind.

Left, right, right, left. I navigated my way through the maze. Left, right, left, left. Where am I? I'd definitely seen that scarecrow before. I had the map to solve it; how could I be lost? The smell was growing stronger, I decided to go with my wits instead of the map. I crumpled it up, tossed it near the scarecrow, and headed through the walls of corn. It was surprisingly sharp, as I emerged from the wall full of new cuts. I looked around, disgusted. The smell was even more prevalent, and I was unable to locate where to go except ahead.

I charged through the next wall. Fewer scratches this time; however, the smell was now assaulting my nostrils. It was so close that I could taste it. I looked around, and to my dismay, there was nowhere to go. Corn surrounded the 3-foot wide square I was in. Why was this here? Why was it not marked on the map? I wearily looked ahead and marched through the wall of corn.

The vile stench filled the air in this section, one that nearly brought me to my knees. It was a smell that can only be related to death that had gone unnoticed for the entirety of a teenager's summer vacation and had been left in a shed to rot. I covered my mouth with my hands, only to receive an unimaginable result. Vomit filtered through the cracks of my fingers, and the chunks that were too large to squeeze through were forced back into my mouth, which forced another round of throwing up, this time without the hand to cover my mouth. There was only one thing left to do.

I gathered myself, brushed my hands off in the dirt, and charged with everything I had through the wall of corn. I was hit by stalks, tumbled, and eventually crashed down into the bone dry dirt with a heavy thud and was met by complete silence. I held my breath, as I stood up, attempting to keep the dirt out of my eyes. Before I could open them, I was slammed into by a smell sent straight from hell by the Devil himself. This aroma could penetrate any gas mask and turn the strongest man into an infant, or a child crying for his mommy at 2:39 AM because his closet door opened itself. Monsters are real. I figured this out today, because in the middle of this maze stood a scarecrow, rotting away to his bones with a map of the corn maze crumpled up, lying next to him.

I approached the scarecrow, fingers covering my nose, pinching out any smells. Left foot, right foot, left foot, right. I almost had to teach myself how to walk again. The stench was swarming every opening in my body, and the scratches from the razor blade corn stalks began to secrete a diluted white liquid. I instinctively removed my hand from my nose to brush the liquid off myself, and without even breathing through my nose, I went through the all-too familiar cycle of encountering the smell, only this time it was closer, seeing as I had taken a mere four steps towards the scarecrow. This had to be the source of the smell, and there was nothing else in sight.

The liquid burned. Badly. Not only did it scorch me while coming out of the openings in my skin, but upon contact with my fingertips, it felt as if I was inching too closely to an open flame. I plugged my nose and slowly approached the scarecrow. Left foot, right foot, left, right, left, right, left. I was now a few feet from the scarecrow, and the smell radiating from it was now knocking on my closed lips, begging to have me taste it.

"Hello?" I called out to nobody, "What's going on here? Who did this?" I don't know why, nobody was even close to me except this damn scarecrow.

"You'll find out," a chilling breath muttered out onto the back of my neck. I felt every hair emerge from its relaxed position on my body into a completely erect pose, as if they were screaming to me, "Danger! Danger!" I didn't dare move. I don't know why, maybe it was for the same reason a 5-year-old assumes his blankets will save him from the boogeyman. They won't. If the boogeyman wanted to harm the child, he would thrust himself from the closet and viciously rip the blanket off the child with the inhuman strength he possessed, but he didn't.

These beings don't get pleasure from the result. They do it for the buildup. The experience, the sheer thrill of stalking and striking fear into their prey for as long as they possibly can is why this child is able to stare at a shapeshifting demon from across his dark room, only to have his father bravely check this exact area and find a jacket hanging in the "danger zone."

"But dad! He was there, I promise!"

"You're just imagining things, go back to bed. You're fine." Isolation. Fear. Mental instability. Am I really seeing this ghost, or am I just imagining? Of course, I'm imagining, there's no such thing as the paranormal.

If the monster is able to provoke these feelings in its target, it's already game over. There's no escaping. Which is why I assume I was brought to the middle of this maze. We all have a purpose, everything happens for a reason. I know it does. I was the 5-year-old who was told by my dad that everything was going to be all right. I saw the shape-shifting demon prance from wall to wall, taunting me.

This was my boogeyman. I knew it.

I turned around, only to see myself facing another scarecrow. I know this wasn't here before. I walked in a straight line. I was imagining things. Turn back around. I'll be fine, Dad promised.

I darted back to look at the original scarecrow, but he wasn't there. I must have been going insane. I turned back to look at the second scarecrow, but he wasn't there either. I was panicking. I didn't know what to think. I turned back around, again, only to see both scarecrows, arms locked, violently staring into my soul. They knew. They knew all of my secrets. My chest crippled in pain, and I almost dropped to the ground, as tears began to well up behind my frightened eyeballs. I didn't want to wait anymore. The monsters were real, Dad.

I broke through their locked arms and ran. I didn't know where I was running—I was just running. It seemed like the right thing to do. I ran until I was away from the scarecrows, the stench, the boogeyman, and everything. I couldn't stop myself. I ran until each step brought the pain of a dozen rusty needles to every inch of my body.

It didn't matter how far I ran, the smell followed. It seemed to grow closer to me, the farther I ran. I couldn't take it anymore. My entire body seized up and the pain was unbearable. I had to face this monster. It was the only option. When I turned around, there was no corn maze. There were no scarecrows. There was only a shadow.

"What do you want?" I shouted and received a garbled answer of what sounded like someone mashed their hands into a keyboard until they lost feeling. My heart sank, but I didn't let it show. Any fear I let surface was an open target.

I took a step toward the shadow and another. Right, left, right, left. The shadow mimicked me, and took an equal amount of steps toward me. We stared back at each other, only for him to break the silence.

"Michael!" And before I knew it, he lunged at me, and I was hit with complete darkness.

I struggled to unclench my eyelids from their shut position. I rose to my feet and brushed dirt off the back of my head. Where am I? Why is there corn? And dear Lord, what is that smell?

Driving on the Flight Line

ROBERT RICKER

I was in the United States Air Force from June 1992 to June 1996. For all four years I was stationed at Offutt Air Force Base in Nebraska, serving in the 55th Supply Squadron. As a member of the Supply Squadron, each airman/airwoman is issued a flight line badge. This badge allows you entry to the flight line where the planes are parked and maintained. Offutt Air Force Base houses the RC-135s, KC-135s, and Boeing 747s, otherwise known as the E-4s, or "President's Planes." The following is an account of the layout of the flight line during this time and my experiences of learning how to drive on the flight line.

I arrived at Offutt at the end of July 1992. Prior to the Air Force, I had never been on a plane until the beginning of June 1992, when I flew from Pittsburgh to San Antonio for basic training. I was one month shy of my twenty-second birthday. Needless to say, the idea of driving around planes was intimidating. My first time on flight line, my boss drove me out to show me the ropes and the protocol to follow when a plane was preparing to taxi to the runway. Again, I was intimidated. To add a twist to the story, my line badge, which I was issued by the Air Force, had the letter E on it by my name. The E stood for "escort." This meant I could escort people who did not have a line badge onto the flight line, with the understanding he/she had to stay with me at all times.

The main entrance to the flight line was off from the maintenance facility. The maintenance facility is where the mechanics work on the planes if the situation requires an extended period of time. Otherwise, the maintenance crews work out on the flight line. At the entrance to the flight line, one encountered an MP (short for military police). Two forms of identification were required: your standard military ID, which everyone was issued in basic training, and your line badge.

As you entered the flight line, the KCs and RCs were parked in two rows, one on the left and one on the right, facing each other. The middle space was for traffic and when a plane would taxi to the runway. In terms of the number of planes, 5 to 6 planes, sitting next to each other comprised one row. The E-4s were at the end of the flight line facing the entrance sitting in front of their own special hangar. There were two spots for these planes in front of the hangar.

Upon entering the flight line, one looked immediately to the middle of the line to see if a person in a fluorescent vest was standing with two rods, one in each hand. This meant a plane was about to taxi to the runway. An individual driving on the flight line had to pull over, basically anywhere, although not too close to the parked planes, with the assurance they were not in the path of the departing plane.

Now, when I first started to go to the flight line, which was primarily to the E-4 hangar, there were times I would not wear my line badge. I cannot remember if I was advised to wear my line badge at all times on the flight line, but if I was, it did not register. If a 747 was in the hangar for maintenance, an MP would be stationed near the plane, machine gun in hand. I would stroll through the hangar without my line badge, oblivious to the violation I was committing. This went on for at least my first 4 months travelling on the flight line.

One day in the warehouse, I overheard a conversation between my co-workers, "Screech," and another patron.

"Did you hear what happened to Mark?" asked "Screech."

"He got jacked up" replied Screech, when the other person said he had not heard.

Naturally, this caught my attention. "Screech," I asked, "what happened to Mark?"

My friend informed me how our co-worker, Mark, forgot to clip his line badge on, was in the E-4 hangar, was spotted by one of the MPs, and two military policemen literally jacked him up against a wall, machine gun pointed at him the whole time, and searched him from head to toe.

I tried to remain calm the whole time, hearing this while adding at least 10 years to my age. I asked Screech what happened next.

He said the MPs take you to a designated spot, call your supervisor, and you cannot go anywhere until your supervisor comes out to the line to get you. The MPs create their own file on you, not to mention whatever disciplinary action your own supervisor may take.

I quickly learned that by not wearing your line badge, the military police viewed you as a threat to the operations of the flight line and the ever so important mission of the "President's planes." Keep in mind, I am one of a handful of people in the warehouse with escort on my line badge.

After hearing all of this, "Screech" asked me a rhetorical question of what was Mark thinking.

Yes, what was Mark thinking?

To this day I still am amazed at what could have happened within my first 4 months of learning how to perform duties on the flight line.

Leaving the parking area of the E-4 hangar one drove near the runway and entered a spot where the planes would exit to get on the runway. I was leaving the E-4 hangar one winter day, both windows up, radio on. As I was making the turn to enter back onto the flight line, a plane was about to exit. I quickly pulled over to a spot where I could not alter its path. I remember looking into the cockpit of the plane and seeing the look of fear on the pilot's face when I happened to look up and notice how I was heading straight into the plane.

You are issued your military identification in basic training. When you arrived at Offutt, it took roughly one month to receive your line badge. My first unit in the warehouse was Pickup and Delivery. With escort on my line badge, this meant I was responsible for taking new people in our unit out to the flight line to show them the ropes. My first year of doing this, I hope I was able to hide my nerves and the fact that, in showing the new person the protocol, a plane would not be ready for take-off. We got a lot of new people that first year, and needless to say, I was a basket case at times.

One morning in April 1994 (I will get to how I remember this) I was making a delivery with a co-worker with my friend doing the driving. Our first stop was the E-4 hangar. Upon entering the runway my friend immediately became awestruck. "Robert I don't believe it!" Not really paying attention (I figured my friend became smitten with a female mechanic), he kept repeating, "I don't believe it!"

It was not until we were half way through the runway that I realized, in one of the spots designated for the 747's, was Air Force One. I was not as awestruck as my friend, but was impressed with the number of military policemen around it, all with machine guns. As soon as we got to the parking area of the hangar, my friend said we are going back around. My instincts told me what would happen next. We drove back around slowly, just as the first time, only this time we were stopped by an MP. With machine gun in hand, he asked for our identification. My friend was having an out of body experience the whole time at the sight of Air Force One. He had many questions for the MP. The MP hardly revealed anything other than it was Vice President Gore who did the travelling to Offutt.

I proceeded to tell the MP, "Tell him Duke should have won last night." The MP laughed as he gave us our identification back and told us we could go. Why do I remember this occurring in April 1994? It was two days after Arkansas defeated Duke for the NCAA men's basketball championship.

I worked in Pickup and Delivery for two years. After my first year, I was able to navigate driving on the flight line with ease. I made it a point to always have my line badge on at all times on the line. I was never able to solve the mystery of the mission of the "President's planes." At the time, I was told by someone in the maintenance squadron how the inside of the E-4s, in terms of electrical set-ups, was identical to Air Force One. Whenever the President was flying on Air Force One, an E-4 would simultaneously fly in the air. If an evil element wanted to do harm to Air Force One, their radar would show two planes with the same radar mechanisms in the air at the same time, thus throwing off the trail of the sinister element. Over the years, I have asked other people from Offutt about the mission of the E-4s, and almost inevitably, they would not know. From what I understood about the RCs and KCs is they were reconnaissance planes. When I was in Saudi Arabia during the spring of 1995, I was the supply person for RCs and KCs stationed there from Offutt. I was in a reconnaissance squadron during that trip.

My recollections of my time in the Air Force were a great deal of trial and error and learning by doing. Naturally, advanced weapons systems and working with and on the numerous fleet of planes in the Air Force inventory requires a great deal of training; however, I went from living in a two room apartment in Cumberland, MD, having never been on a plane before at the beginning of the summer of 1992, to having experienced four trips on an airplane and driving around planes on a flight line, in a manner of months. A great deal of growth occurred within me during this time, all the while, saving money and earning the GI Bill for my education after my enlistment in the Air Force. The Air Force is an environment of pin your ears back and go forward. For those who choose this path, remember, wear your line badge.

A School Shooting: Sensory Overload's Worst Nightmare

ELENA ROBINSON

Imagine, for a moment, being me. I am standing in a hotel room with some friends. We are having a discussion about our plans for the day. One of my friends says something the others do not agree with, and they all begin loudly talking over each other. I feel my eye twitch, but I try to convince myself it is nothing. Then, like dousing a person in gasoline and lighting him on fire, all hell broke loose inside my mind. Sensory overload is a sensory processing disorder that is common in people with autism. It occurs when one or more of a person's senses are overstimulated, causing the person intense discomfort and anxiety. This is the story of how I found out I have sensory overload, how I told some of the people closest to me, and the worst sensory experience I have ever had. Sensory overload is real, and it is ruining my life.

When I was fourteen, my therapist told me I have sensory overload. I never liked that woman. She did not seem to care about me, and she never told me anything I thought was relevant to my life. I was telling her about a specific instance in which I was hanging out with some friends, we were listening to loud music, and all of a sudden, I felt like I was dying. I could hear the blood pounding in my ears, and the sound of my friends singing was no longer at the forefront of my hearing, but it was still there, driving me off the edge. I closed my eyes. It was the first time several of those people had seen me cry. I was not expecting much from telling her about this, but she was my therapist after all, and though I had experienced things similar to this before, I

always assumed it was a mild panic attack and moved on with my life.
I was afraid of how this made me feel. For the first time in months, she
surprised me. Of course, in an attempt to make a joke, she started the
conversation with, "What, are you autistic or something?" Needless to
say, I did not think it was funny.

I have had sensory overload triggered by everything from concerts
to someone tapping a pen on a table while I am trying to concentrate.
Things that have triggered me in the past will not always trigger me
in the future, and I am always discovering new things that send me
hurtling over the edge. This was something that was difficult to explain
to the people who matter the most to me. Renn is my best friend,
and maybe, that is why I was afraid to tell him. He is afraid to tell me
things for the same reason. We do not want to lose each other, so we
keep things from each other that we believe will make the other leave
us. I told Nikki first. For a while they were very cautious around me,
apologizing any time they made a single loud noise, shushing people
for me when we were in groups, trying their best to be helpful to me.
Eventually I made myself clearer. Not everything causes this. It is
obvious if something is bothering me. When I told Renn, he acted in
a similar way for a couple days, but then he researched it himself. He
has become my biggest support system. He can tell when I am having
trouble with a certain situation, and he gets me out of it when I cannot
rescue myself.

I remember my worst sensory overload experience like it was
yesterday. It was a surprisingly warm December 13. I had already
had a panic attack earlier that day, so I was on edge. The sucker my
second-hour teacher gave me, when I finally rejoined class, shifted to
the bottom of my backpack. I had first lunch, so, when the intercom
came on after less than ten minutes of English, many students were off
campus for second lunch. Even more were in the cafeteria. We went
into lockdown. We were told there were police in the building, and
they had been called by a student claiming there was a school shooter.
We all shoved into a corner, every student frantically texting their

friends and family members, quietly asking the teacher if he had any idea what was going on. He told us he was supposed to discourage us from using social media or contacting friends, but as long as we turned our sound off, he wanted to know what was going on as much as we did.

I would not say I am afraid to die. Sitting next to Renn in the farthest corner of the room, having heard from only a few of the people I had messaged, I was afraid the people I loved were going to die. Our class was one of the eight to be escorted out of the building. Everyone with a car wanted to leave, even if it meant taking as many underclassmen as could fit in their cars home first. We were not allowed within twenty feet of the parking lot. As kids started to come back from second lunch, we explained to them what little we knew about the situation. A friend of mine's sister was not answering her phone. It was his birthday. Watching men with bulletproof vests and guns bigger than I am run into the building, I had my second panic attack of the day.

Less than an hour later, we were sent back to class. The principal came over the intercom and told us it was a false alarm. Someone had called the police and told them we were all going to die, as a prank. School was not canceled for the rest of the day, but students were called to the office in groups of thirty as their parents came to pick them up or called them out. We were sent to our last class to ride out the day. I had psychology with one of my favorite teachers, and I thought, if I could just learn *something* in that class, everything would be okay. Despite half of the school going home, for the first time since it started, everyone in that class was present. They were all very excited to see who could scream the loudest to get their thoughts over the noise. Who they thought called, why the principal was lying to us about there not actually being a shooter and who it was, and their tragic story of being forced to sit next to that kid who does not wear deodorant. Maybe, it was the stress of the situation. Maybe, it was leaving the dead silent environment of my English class and entering what I assumed would be a similar situation, but instead being greeted with the emotional equivalent of a jet taking off. I can usually tell when something is going to be too much before it gets to that point. This time, the door closed behind me, and I was in tears. I could hear the slight break in the voice of the girl next to me, I could hear my lungs expanding and contracting. The sound of the room closed around me like a boa constrictor squeezing the life out of its prey. I did not hear myself ask to go out in the hallway. I do not remember hearing my teacher telling me to sit in the Social Studies Office, but I must have, because that is where I went.

I sat underneath a table in the corner. The sudden silence of the office was nearly as deafening as the room I had just left, and the ringing in my ears had never had such a negative impact on my mental health, but at least it was finally quiet. Someone came in to grab some papers from the printer. She did not see me. One of my friends texted me back to say said friend was in the bathroom listening to music, when the announcement happened. The police took them to the office. I stole a juice box from the refrigerator. The teacher who had given me the sucker came into the office and sat down at the conference table. When he sighed, it was like a gunshot. I did not realize I had stopped crying, until I felt new tears start streaming down my cheeks. He heard me sniff. He did not mean to be rude, but he started asking me questions. What was I doing in there? Why was I crying? Did I feel safe at home? I did not hate the sound of his voice, but in my sensitive state, it was like nails scraped on a chalkboard. When I could respond, I only brought myself to say two words, "Too loud." He left the room. He got my psychology teacher out of his class, and they discussed what I was doing out of class. It had been over an hour; school was going to end soon, and I was still unable to hear anything louder than a pencil scratching paper without crying again. I felt completely useless. I could not have moved my body if an actual shooter had shown up and tried to kill me. I was still in that room almost two hours after school ended, and as soon as I got home, I locked myself in my room for the rest of the night.

I have had other moments since then that have lasted much longer, but I was able to go on with my life. Sensory overload is real, and it is ruining my life. This was the story of the worst sensory experience I have ever had, as well as, how I found out I have sensory overload, and how I told my two closest friends. This story is my truth. Being able to write about this without having several panic attacks was a blessing. Sensory overload is possible for most people to experience during intense sensory experiences, but it is most common in people with autism and anxiety disorders. It is hard to listen when noise makes me cry.

///

"To write is to worship."

KRISTEN WETHERELL

///

The Dance Practice

JOHN TIMOTHY ROBINSON

The way she moved across this wooden floor
was like a dancer leaping high in bounds
with grace, a soaring gesture up and more
than once was caught in fleeting eyes, her gown.

Of all the days I watched her dance, not once
was someone ever there to smile or stare,
as I had often stopped or stooped so much
in keep with my lone task of clean and care.

Though I would not intrude upon her time,
and only often watched in just a musing way.
I never saw her in these halls, the shine
and gold in glare of footlights gleamed, held her sway.

So many faces fill the walks, unknown.
That twirling figure, I will not forget, has grown.

Major League Baseball Ballparks: Los Angeles to Boston and All Those In-Between

HUNTER RUD

Baseball is simple, and it's hard to believe that such an experience would evolve into the multi-billion-dollar business it is today. Yet, when someone digs deeper and explores the intricacies of the game, its complexion is unmistakable, and even after a century of existence, it is expanding. Just like the game itself, the venues in which the battles are fought have blossomed extensively over time, and although they may appear to be similar, each ballpark is unique in its own way. From the classic Wrigley Field in Chicago to the modern and high-tech Sun-Trust Park, the towering pillars of concrete and fresh-cut grass have their own stories to tell and their own ranking among the competition. Having seen the thirty parks myself, exploring the concourses and climbing the towering reaches of the upper decks, I pride myself on being able to break these palaces down into a few select categories. Ranging from worn-out and replaceable to mediocre, knowing they are a blend of inexplicable beauty, both new and old, every team has earned a ranking one way or another.

Unlike men, not all ballparks are created equal, and for a few unfortunate tenants who reside in the depths of the baseball world, the case for replacement could not be more obvious. With the days of the cookie-cutter stadium long gone and the need to share a field with a football team in the rear-view mirror, only a few souls remain on these distant reaches. The few poor souls of MLB reside thousands of miles away from one another, yet the dislike for them creates a bridge sturdy enough to hoist them simultaneously. Catwalks soaring above the playing surface in St. Petersburg, the extensive foul ground creating oceans of grass and dirt beyond the white lines in Oakland, and a cavernous fan experience north of the border in Toronto are but a few of the aspects that drag these locations to the bottom of the pit.

In these three venues, we find some of the worst attendance figures in the league, as well as, consistent backlash from the league and fans for improvements or replacements to be made. Tampa Bay suffers from being an out of date enclosed facility. Oakland shares the same ordeals while continuing to be the only stadium hosting two sporting teams. Toronto leaves much to be desired and could use some much-needed updates. The individual inconveniences of each park create a fan group who would rather not go and a player base expecting more than what they are receiving. These lower tier structures are the true doldrums of the major leagues, and the separation between those three and the remaining twenty-seven is impressively insurmountable.

In stark contrast to the previous category, there are ballparks that excel at delivering some of the key aspects needed with the experience, while falling short of a few others. These certain pros and cons can differ immensely from one another just as many of these ballparks do, but in their own ways, these stadiums fall just a hair short of being magnificent. One perfect way of noting this would be to compare Marlins Park and Yankee Stadium, two fields that land in this intermediary category for different reasons. Marlins Park, for instance, is a beautiful and modern arena that provides every necessary amenity for the fans and players but falls short because the Miami fan base fails to support the team due to losing records, resulting in embarrassingly low attendance figures, and a lifeless game-time atmosphere. On the contrary, Yankee Stadium in New York packs the house on a nightly basis and is known to have ruthless and rowdy fans spread throughout, due to past history, the ballpark fails to captivate the audience at all, being bland and barebones in many areas. For all the venues within this specific category, the blame can almost always be pinned on one of these two specific areas, or possibly both. Miami is joined by the likes of Cincinnati, Seattle, Cleveland, Anaheim, and Texas in the fan base does not fill the seats due to weather and a slacking team. In cities such as Chicago (White Sox), Houston, and Milwaukee, the stadiums themselves lack the overall good feel. These are still incredible places to view a game, and the sport of baseball is alive and well within each of them.

The final category is a compilation of the best ballparks in the game, but I feel that to really do them all the justice, it should be further split into two subdivisions. The first branch is the modern palace group, an elite squadron of stadiums built within recent memory that hit all the right notes creating an enjoyable place to watch a game and are hastily and superbly serviceable to every fan who steps through the turnstiles that evening. From Camden Yards in Baltimore where the Baltimore and Ohio Warehouse rises above the right field pavilion, serenading Eutaw Street, as the Oriole fans walk the hallowed concourse. Pittsburgh is where the skyline view of the city paints a picture in the background as the players create art on the field. Stadiums that combine the home city and the sport of baseball to deliver to each fan an experience are those that have earned the honor of being the best in the world. Denver, Minnesota, New York (Mets), Philadelphia, and Detroit have stadiums that instill lifelong memories that are truly unmatched by any other venue in the sport. These are the cities that when the construction broke ground and the metal beams began to be vaulted up, the fans were the biggest influence just as they should be. In their own ways, these are modern monuments, museums of the sport, and castles of the region that grace the cityscape along with the skyscrapers.

There are three stadiums that are true ancient marvels of the sports world. From the crammed streets of Boston, to the north side of windy Chicago, and the humid hills of Los Angeles lie the final three coliseums. These venues embody what baseball is all about, bringing

an American pastime into the modern age. Fenway Park, the oldest
stadium in baseball, has all the charm of 1912, and through a tumul-
tuous life where demolition crews waited on standby, it has managed
to scratch a path out, and now, it's an irreplaceable relic of the New
England region. With quirks like the Green Monster and Pesky's
Pole, the stadium by all standards shouldn't exist, but it is loved for its
crammed concourses and skinny wooden seats because it is a prime
example of the sport and the city in which it lies. In a similar fashion,
Wrigley Field embodies the gritty city of Chicago, the bricks encapsu-
lating the rich history, and the iconic ivy under the baskets on the outfield wall. Lastly, Dodger Stadium rises from the West Coast skyline,
sporting a sleek modern feel, while remaining true to the fifty-year-old
legacy that it boasts. From the atrocious traffic to the rigged design
on the outfield canopy representing the Hollywood Hills, and the
color of the seats meant to mimic the washing of the waves, Dodger
Stadium is renowned and idolized with a legacy and city to go along
with it. Ballparks like these keep the integrity of baseball grounded in
the past, while showing that a sport so enriched with history can still
flourish in the modern day.

Watching a Major League Baseball game in person is unlike any
other experience someone could ever have. Hearing the boisterous
crowd erupt after a fabulous play or an individual finally securing
that first autograph from an iconic hero on the field, the first-hand
thrill is a treasure just like the structure it is played in. Coast-to-coast,
nosebleed section or first row, the game itself is a different animal
in person, and the stadium in which the game is played matters just
as much. As fans, it is our home away from home, a place where we
can be around people just like ourselves, enjoying the sport that we
cherish more than anything else. All the cities and their stadiums hold
their own secrets and individual identities. For most that goes unseen,
but if individuals search long enough and go far enough, people will
know exactly why it's a joy to be in Section 113, Row 17, Seat 8, rather
than watching the game on a couch at home.

One Fine Day

ROBERT RUNYON

It's spring in Omaha! There's a bright, warm sun splashing balmy shades of light across the landscape. This is a refreshing change from the freezing weather that had us hunkering down, scurrying for shelter from the wintery blasts of a polar vortex dipping down from Canada.

It's 8:30 AM and a garage door repairman, Kal Holmes, a Kenny Rogers look-alike, comes ambling out of his van up my driveway where I'm waiting in the garage at the appointed hour. He's tall, with squinty eyes that twinkle in his animated, bearded face and talkative with a practiced gift of gab that's both professional and surprisingly personal. His head is canted slightly to one side, projecting kindness and confidentiality to our conversation. Within a couple of minutes, I know his wife died of leukemia in January. He's weathering that shock and loss, and he's fifty-nine years old. He seems like an old friend from the get-go, rather than a technician making his required rounds in the game of commerce.

We walk around the garage together, and he expounds upon the broken spring on one of the double doors, the reason for his visit. He shares engaging stories of homeowners' surprise when a spring suddenly breaks. It releases its stored energy with a thunderous bang; unwinding and smashing violently into cars, doors, or windows that may be nearby.

"People get scared when they hear that loud bang," he says. "They're so unnerved they call 911. They think someone's been shot."

I'm absorbed in his expert explanation and glad I wasn't in the garage when that spring let loose. I'm still sizing him up on this early morning walk about my cluttered garage. He studies the loose and broken spring closely.

"We'll fix that for sure," he comments.

"Wow, you've got big hands," I remark.

"Yeah my feet are even bigger — size fifteen shoes," he admits, sounding a bit like a sideshow freak!

"The shoe store doesn't keep them in stock," he said. "I have to order them for mail delivery. I hope nobody gets a hernia from carrying them up on my porch," was his witty aside.

"I like your attitude," I said.

"I like to have fun. I love what I do, mainly. But sometimes, depending on the weather, I might have a bad attitude. When that happens, I don't like myself. You start talking with yourself. You do something wrong. You're arguing with yourself. Then you got troubles."

He recalled one of his regular customers who called for an annual checkup of his garage doors. After a quick look, he told him, "Everything's fine; you don't need me this time." In response, his customer confided, "Yeah, but I like my Kal time."

Kal has a mellow, resonant voice; natural pauses and precise intonation, revealing a deliberate and reflective manner: a natural storyteller. It was easy to see why his customers enjoyed chewing the fat with him. I reveled in his charming, disarming way of doing business. The cut-throat competition and challenges of the marketplace were far away.

Later that day, I wend my way over to UNO's Criss Library, to check out the latest acquisitions on the new book shelves near the door. It is there I spotted two recently published books which caught my fancy.

> *Sapiens: A Brief History of Humankind,* by Yuval Noah Harari.

> *Play: How It Shapes the Brain, Opens the Imagination, and Invigorates the Soul,* by Stuart Brown.

Stumbling upon these particular titles rekindles a joyful serendipity that I often feel in a fresh discovery upon a library shelf. It's probably no more than the self-indulging tickle of a dilettante, but it's nevertheless a treasured experience. It also presents its challenges, however.

On reflection, these books pose a quandary in this reader's mind. How might I ever find time to read the first; a heavy-duty, 464-page tome of colossal scope, by an Oxford trained historian now teaching in Israel? A bold endorsement by Jared Diamond (a back-cover blurb), has my salivary juices running. *But I should stay focused on my own writing project.* Perhaps my reading choices should relate more to personal experiences rather than abstract reveries about the origins of humankind. My curiosity follows the scent of personal remembrance, but it is easily distracted. Avoid something so vast and universal as the roots of our collective humanity. Through imagination, I strive to dig back into my own earlier life; sorting out what happened, how, when, where, and why. If I am to be the writer I claim to be, I must build from that ground up.

I opt for play at writing.

Take some notes. Here, on this lovely spring day, I need to pursue a deeper joy, a sense of presence in and beyond the moment. *Seize the Day* (Saul Bellow). Now is the time to dig and plough, to plant and reap some chosen words and phrases in the sunshine of my eighties.

As I approach home around 3:00 PM, I spy an unfamiliar car in my driveway. I know immediately that it must belong to the graduate student assigned to prepare a short biographical profile of my wife for the UNO Women's Archives Project. I'm very excited about this recognition that is being accorded her. Sheila has a strong personal story to tell, about growing up in Scotland, coming to America, our getting married in a wee country kirk in her home town of Dumfries, her various jobs, and her singular contributions to the same university where I served in the library.

It had come to my attention that her biographer had discovered a population spike of women receiving computer science degrees, in the mid-1980s. Sheila received her B.S., Magna Cum Laud, in 1984. She was within a unique coterie of women entering the new field of information technology at that time. It would shortly become heavily dominated by male recruits. Her technical acumen, confirmed by membership in Mensa, was to make a big difference in our family fortune. Without her second income as a computer programmer, we would never have been able to travel to seven continents or to live in a style much beyond that of our own parents.

I purposely drove by the house, not wanting to interrupt her interview by showing up too early. Finally, I decided to enter the garage and slip quietly into my downstairs office. I forgot I had scheduled a salesman for a visit on this afternoon regarding the replacement of our hot water heater. I was feeling quite high throughout this day, beginning with the weather, the repaired garage door spring, and followed by Sheila's archive profile finally getting underway.

The garage doorbell rang. There stood George, a home appliance salesman. This was certainly not the best time to discuss water heaters. Most people would choose to avoid that conversation at any time. Water heaters do not inspire excitement of any kind. They might qualify as the most forgotten and forgettable piece of home infrastructure. But they do wear out and also require maintenance, like everything else in a family home. It would become a sit-down conversation, but nowhere near as engaging as the garage door repairman in the morning. It appears that my fifteen-year old water heater is past the average life span for such equipment. There is also a new federal regulation taking effect in six weeks to require a new heater design that will raise the standard price by $500. There can be a significant financial saving through purchase of last year's model now rather than the updated model later after the new regulation takes effect.

This is about shifting emotional gears, from a joyful welcoming of developing events, to a requirement for dispassionate rational scrutiny of technical details and a cost/benefit analysis. I have found that I no longer make such mental gymnastic exercises, quickly. It calls for skepticism, probing questions, and a suspension of trust and belief. This conflicts with my attitude (I'll call it euphoria) in the earlier hours of my day. Do I wish at this point to drill down deeply into the life and comparative merits of *water heaters*? You get my drift.

I ponder. I question. I scope out the topic. I delay. I yearn for a break in this sales pitch. Another opinion is needed, but my wife is still being interviewed upstairs. *How can she have a three-hour interview?* It must be going well. I will certainly not interrupt that.

So, after some consternation, I decide to decide. I'll say, "Yes," now, because I don't wish to readdress this squishy topic down the road. The bottom line is a commitment to install a new water heater in two weeks for $1,600. I sign on the dotted line.

Later that evening, I have second thoughts, buyer's remorse. It was that self-questioning which friendly Kal, the overhead door guy, talked about in the morning. I should have waited. Kal would have told me not to cave in to an artificial power play and phony deadline proposed by a stranger. He would just shrug off the urgency of a pressure pitch about water heaters. This is life in the fast lane. Slow down. Perhaps, my son was right about selling this old house and moving into an apartment.

But all is not lost. This could be the makings of a story about the ups and downs of a day in the life of a retiree. Meager stuff like this might reawaken creative juices in the joy of writing.

Midge of Midge's Cafe

MARJORIE SAISER

She could have been a dancer
and once in a while
she looks back

while carrying a tray of dirty dishes
to the kitchen. She runs the cafe,
her name in red letters on the window.

Friday mornings she
rolls out pie crust,
has to stop for a customer,

wipe the flour off her hands,
pour coffee, make small-town
small-talk. Saturday night

the tails of her white blouse are
knotted over her flat belly,
she's at the cash register, at the booth,

she's at the grill, turn the burger,
lay on a slice of cheddar,

hair pulled back
into a black foxtail, swinging,
step here and here, quick quick slow

one back, two forward,
cross behind, pivot,

the finer points of getting
where you aim to go.

The Bird Sings

JIMMY SALHANY

(Christine Salhany asked her husband, Jimmy, to help her write an auto-biographical statement. This is what he created, while they were sitting on the porch.)

Waking in the morning involves more than opening our eyes, for it is the mind that interprets the eyes. Then, I realize how I need to connect to the secret, as it is undoubtedly part of me. Is it the smell of the flowers or the dominance of the color green? I plant because it calls me more than for nourishment, but for love, that plants may provide the essence in our blood. And I, like the plants, participate in emotional cycles of thought and love. This is the critical step to identify my existence. It is not who I am. It is that I am. Be it the plant or the mind.

The bird sings.

Sonnet for the Lost Woods

SALLY SANDLER

Who pauses to pay homage to the trees
buried in a concrete cemetery —
those that were a leafy sanctuary
brought by civilization to its knees?

Where were the mourners, when the forests died
the noble warriors mankind didn't save?
No flags or flowers placed upon their graves,
no one recited last rites; no one cried.

Departed souls, and we can only mourn
for all the soldiers prematurely downed...
for every tree that fell without a sound
was guardian of a time when we were born.

A house we can rebuild, a bridge, a road...
but trees will leave us pathless when they go.

Broken Records

STUART SEDLAK

When I was in high school, it was my dream to play baseball. I had a very strong arm, but all other facets of my game were lacking. I worked hard on my batting and fielding, but looking back, I just didn't have that much talent. I tried out for the baseball team my freshman and sophomore years, but did not make the team. I was heartbroken each time I was cut. That heartbreak fueled my determination to make the team the following year.

My junior year, I was determined to make the team. I prepared all winter to improve my game. When it was time for tryouts in February, I was ready. It was a blustery cold evening the first night of tryouts. Naturally, the cold Nebraska winters were not conducive to playing baseball out of doors, so tryouts were held in the high school gymnasium. When I arrived at the gym, I was ready to make a statement.

At the beginning of tryouts, I selected a partner to play catch with and warm up. After about five minutes of warming up, my arm felt better than ever. Coaches were roaming around the gym, covertly taking notes on their clipboards. I wanted to show off my arm right away. I reared up and fired the ball to my partner as hard as I could. The ball sailed like a Frisbee caught in the wind. The trajectory was much too high. A tenth of a second later, a loud crash was audible throughout the gym. Instantly, there was absolute silence. Broken glass and plastic letters were strewn all over the hard maple basketball court. I had broken the school sports record display.

At that moment, the coach's whistle blew. "Boys, gather 'round me right now!" he said sternly.

Eighty young men gathered around the coach.

"Who threw that baseball?" he asked.

I looked around, for what it seemed like a minute, and sheepishly raised my hand.

"Come see me tomorrow morning before school."

My high school had a glass display case with a letter board enclosed. In the glass case, many of the sports records were displayed. Among the sports records displayed were track and field, swimming, and basketball. I was responsible for ruining this case, which obviously someone spent a great deal of time putting together.

The next morning I arrived at school early. I was sick to my stomach. There was a lump in my stomach the size of a regulation baseball. I did not want to go talk to the baseball coach. I put off my meeting with him as long as I could. I finally mustered up enough courage to go into the homeroom he was assigned. He made me apologize to each coach that had a sport represented on the record board. This was a true test of my bravery. Reluctantly, I visited each coach and vehemently apologized for my errant throw. I expected the worst. The basketball coach was especially intimidating to talk to. Luckily, all the coaches were understanding. Apologizing was not nearly as bad as I expected.

I learned a lesson that day. I learned to face my fears and not run away. Running away from things you are scared of only makes things worse in the long run. I felt tremendous relief after my visits with the coaches. Most of them commended me for owning up to my mistake. I did not make the baseball team that year, but I *did* do something that nobody else can say they accomplished in the storied history of my high school. I broke all the records.

Lace Curtains

SUE SHELBURNE

I remember at the top of the stairs in the springtime how
I could smell the fresh air drifting in through the open
bedroom window I shared with my sister and how the
white lace curtains danced and swayed at the open
window in the morning light.

I remember how the scent of fresh air was familiar
and comforting to my little girl senses, coupled with
the same scent of freshly turned soil my father carried
into the house with him after a day of tilling the ground
to plant his crops.

In the mornings, through the open window, when
I was waking up, I remember how I could hear the
squeaking of the sturdy chain that held my tire swing
from a branch of the oak tree on the front lawn, moving
back and forth, as if gently pushed by an unseen hand.

I remember when fully awake, the first thing I could
see through the lace curtains was the far reaching
branches at the very top of that ancient tree and how in
the winter its icy branches scraped against the window,
even as it sheltered me.

Sometimes, now at night, when I go to bed, weary from the day,
I long to go to sleep on crisp white sheets, perfumed with the
scent of fresh air and sunshine, washed by my mother in an
old ringer washing machine and hung out to dry, all day on a
clothes line in the side yard.

It doesn't matter how many years pass or how old I become,
it is always the memory of the senses that make me want to go
back to that house, even though it's no longer there, the house
that cradled my childhood, and still speaks to me
so poignantly of home.

A Bird in the...
Photo by Katie Cameron

I Am in Paris —

D. N. SIMMERS

Your grandfather is here, as
one day you will come back
with friends and
spend time in the City of Lights.

Go to the famous tower of steel that overlooks the city.
See the city through your own eyes.

But tonight,
let me hold your hand,
let me tell you
about the warm people here —

about the old hotel with staff helping to give the city a good name.

The restaurants —

busy waiters and the bookstores, owners, and clerks.

The old streets with cobblestones
worn down by millions of shoes
going over them through the centuries.

You will look out,
one day into the sky, breathe the air
and fall in love with this place,
like I have.

....

*Note: Written by d. n. simmers on September 30, 2018, in the old city in Paris
for his granddaughter Isla's upcoming birthday*

ER

KALPNA SINGH-CHITNIS

My case wasn't serious,
so I waited in the lobby of the ER
for my turn to come.

Patients needed to have patience.
Except those, who showed severe symptoms
like fever, nausea, and fits.

But I didn't vomit. My temperature remained stable.
And I was able to hold the ground,
like a tree standing in a storm.

I did not show any cuts and bruises.
I did not bleed or collapse,
like many others did,

and were rushed into a room, without any delay,
where the doctors were ready to diagnose
and treat them immediately.

I just had some internal injuries, no one knew.
I bled inside. I died in front of everyone,
Without anyone noticing me.

Reverberations & the Magnitude

LAURA STREETER

Feels like I've been standin' in here for days
& I'm starin' right into the hungry crowd
& I wish that I could just hear your voice
Blurry faces starin' back at me
A hint of smoke that lingers in the air....

> I wish that I was somewhere else
> (Can't get over what you said)
> I wish that I was somewhere else
> (The last words that you said)
> Wish I was somewhere else
> Wish I was somewhere else

& I don't think you'll ever, ever
never, never, no you'll never, ever, ever see it my way
& the last words that you said
(the very last words that you said)
are still stuck in my head
& these feelings amplify
like white noise through this room

& then I'm stuck in this big 'ol box with
reverberations & the magnitude
All I can think is that I really need some air
& that I'm cursed like Echo's allegory of despair

> & I can barely breathe
> I can barely breathe
> I can barely breathe
> Wear my heart on my sleeve

Lucky for me, I can see the lines on the highway
(Been drivin' all night)
But the truth is no matter how far I drive
Still can't clear my mind
& I can't find a place to crash
& every road sign that I pass
just reminds me that I'm moving further
(and further and further and further and further) away

& that I'm halfway to nowhere
(Already gone)
I'm halfway to nowhere
(Like nothing is wrong)
Halfway to nowhere
Halfway to nowhere

Rose Bud

GARY TAYLOR

the flower grows in the sidewalk crack
it thrives, for where it's at
it lives even though it lacks
it's got a few petals
that broke off and fell
and the stem has healed scratches
and bends as well
with no one that tends to it
people even stepped on it
yet it continues to grow
few people notice the beautiful rose
it's perfectly imperfect
and how it exists;
no one knows
except God I suppose
it is special
unlike the hundreds that grow in gardens
as it grows between concrete slabs in dirt
instead of soil
it got treated as a weed
as the others were treated like royals
it went against all odds
and that;
that makes it the most beautiful of them all
long live the rose
that continues to grow
in the sidewalk crack

Untrustworthy Narrator

JAMES TILLOTSON

It doesn't sound like a train, at least, not when it hits. The wind becomes a hard quiet, filling your ears, your mouth, your nose, your lungs with grey white liquid air. You empty out as it fills you up, rushing in to replace the last unheard prayer you scream out. The atmospheric vortex pressing down upon you is all there is, and there is no rush of wind to mimic a passing freight car. You are alone in the tornado's belly, as it replaces your world, your senses, and you.

That is how I remember it. What memory I possess of that day has become pigeonholed. Once crystal-clear remembrances clouded by brain damage or carved away to be repressed in the unfinished basement of my mind. I have debated the merits of researching this moment; it would not be difficult. The internet could fill the holes of my memory with other people's words, allowing me to recount the events in detail. But these would not be my words and that would not be my truth.

A cabin collapsed around and on top of me, torn away by an earth-bound tempest. I saw a man ripped through a flimsy door by invisible fingers, lifeless forms of children as others screamed in confused fear. I cried more that day than the entirety of my life. I should remember every detail in perfect clarity. Yet the day, the year, nearly every inter-action and moment of those days prior I have no memory of. What I am left with is fragments, blurry images and the vague notion of a story as though I only observed it from the outside instead of taking part. I have become the untrustworthy narrator of my own life.

The day was either Wednesday or Thursday, and the Dunkin' had run out. Inside the staff cabin, I drank milk from a Styrofoam cup, while the metal folding chair under me, somehow freezing in summer,

served in coffee's stead to wake me up. Rain drummed on the roof
of the small building like fat fingers on a desk distracting me from
the red, three-ringed binder in front of me. For months, I neglected
this, the thirty-page lesson plan that was my duty to teach that night.
My goal was to read through it twice and pray I could skate through
the presentation without making a fool of myself. Outside, the sky
hung low, fat clouds falling lower, as they became tinged with green,
disgorging lightning like a bloated corpse belches flies. I hadn't seen
the sunrise, and with the sheet of atmospheric mist obscuring the sky,
I can't be sure it ever did that day, as no glowing orb of scalding light
could be seen through the clouds. It became like a second sun, those
constant pale flashes lighting up the three-day-old mud and trees,
hypnotizing me every time I stepped outside.

I can never forget those three images; they have stuck deep within
me while the rest fell away. My eyes never left the boiling pot of
clouds that stretched as far as I could see, obscuring the summer
blue. The sky had never hung so low. I'm sure I could have climbed
to the top of one of the cottonwoods and run my fingers along its
electric surface, but I had chalked it up to nothing more than the
second ill omen of the day. The empty coffee pot and my caffeine
withdrawal, the first as the knot of worry in my stomach grew with
each passing second, the red binder in my hands mocked me as
I watched other staff give their presentations. All but those three
images are lost to me, all but the last hour.

We sat where we always sat for dinner, the staff building, resting
paper plates of an unremembered dinner next to tall, fat plastic bottles
of cold water. We may have joked, we may have sat in silence as the toll
of wading through ankle deep mud wore on us. Or it might have been
the old radio in the corner being watched by the adult staff as though
it were the danger and not the storm they had warned us about prior
to serving up the meal. They watched the bulky wood box as the
words "A tornado watch is in effect for...until" repeated over and over
in an uncaring computerized voice; in turn we watched them. The

siren came to life without warning. It was a monster waking up on top
of us like some sort of dying giant bird letting out one final angry cry
as we ran through the door.

Our group diverted, two packs of boys sprinting across the wet
earth, spurred on by the sound of the siren and the knowledge that
beyond the thicket of wind-swept leaves one group of young campers
sat in a valley. We didn't know it was behind us, following at the edge
of the valley as we rushed the campers inside the tiny cabin that sat
inside the valley. Inside, the panicked, wet campers milled about,
murmuring to each other against the still-screaming siren whose
shrill voice could still be heard in the distance. We sat them down
at their small, chipped, cheap, reject schoolhouse tables and hushed
them with the three-finger hand sign of the scouts. The projector was
brought out to play a movie as the storm passed, but as the slim DVD
slid into the player, it struck.

I can never forget the tension. This span of minutes has been fixed,
nailed there by the twin nails of lonely horror and cold pain. When I
think back to these moments, I feel myself there, housed in the fussy
moments of a failing memory as my senses are taken by the tornado.
My sight replaced by blinding mist, the sound of the klaxon gone, it
took away the four walls of the cabin. The steepled wood roof and
creaky metal door became my reality in its stead.

We pushed the young scouts under their tables hoping the flimsy
shelter would save them with the same logic of "duck and cover." I
pressed close against them, my arm and back spread across two as
I held them down. The door blew off its hinges, sucked back as the
tornado touched the cabin. For a moment, the grey-haired form of a
senior counselor was lit by the outside light; then he was plucked from
the concrete floor by invisible fingers and pulled back to wherever
the door had flown. My eyes stung, as the wind stepped across the
threshold, particles of dust rode the wind, and water filled my eyes,
as thousands of wind-driven needles sewing my eyes shut against
the pain. I held the two bodies beneath me until they were gone. I

stretched my body, as I sought something solid to grasp. All I felt was confusion washing over me, unmooring all coherent thought I had, until all I had was fear. Fearful of dying inside that lonely quiet gray space with my lungs full of fog and my ears so full of sound, I could hear nothing.

I prayed in that moment for God to save me from harm. Instead, I was struck in the head by debris. Whether it was a brick from the collapsing chimney, a chair, a table, I do not know, but I do know where it struck. It hit the back of my head with a hollow thud, jarring my teeth together with a snap and plunging me into a black void of unconscious.

I woke up under a pile of rubble, my legs pinned by something I couldn't see. The sky was clear and dark, as the sun set beyond the hills. I stared up at it, wondering what happened to the roof and the walls. Boys walked about, mouths agape, as they stared down at the dissolved building. They pulled me from the rubble, letting me rest on the ground, the pain in my back and legs a throbbing fire that hinted at a deep breakage in a bone. Someone threw the sopping projector screen across my body, telling me it would keep me warm, keep me awake. I tried to explain to them it only made me colder, but my tired tongue could barely manage a groan. The paramedics arrived, as two boys tried to convince me to sing a song to keep awake, fearing if I slept I would drift across the Styx.

Later, I met one of the boys who had covered me with the wet projector screen, forcing me to recall the puddles of cold water it dropped onto me and the pop song they tried to get me to hum. He told me he saved my life with that action, remembering some frail dying form on the floor needing the comfort of a tarp flung across his aching body.

The paramedics tended to those they could reach, as people moved behind me digging others from the rubble; four did not make it. The heavy stone chimney that may have weighed more than all the time-worn lumber and rusty nails of the cabin put together had fallen like so many trees beneath the onslaught. Hundreds of the okra orange clay bricks that had risen above the faded black roof's siding fell with more force than those hollow winds around me to crush children.

I read tarot, and the sixteenth card of the major arcana is the tower. A straight stone stack struck by lightning, breaking apart under the impact of a storm as people fall from its top. Destruction, on the small darkly-colored card means old ideas swept away in that moment. The broken tower means death.

Gloved hands pulled the tarp from me asking where I felt, or if I felt, pain as they poked and prodded my sides and stomach. His fingers felt oddly warm against my wet stone skin, and I winced in affirmation, grumbling about the ache in my knees and the throbbing ball of pain in my back. In a moment that will embarrass me until I die, my shoes and pants were cut off, as he inspected my pasty, white, cold thighs for injuries. I lay in my rain-damp boxers against concrete, as a stranger jabbed me unceremoniously with his fingers searching for breaks, abrasions, and impaled detritus before setting me on a stretcher to be carried away to an ambulance. The rain beginning to fall anew.

My body stiffened, as I reached the hospital, my muscles knotting themselves into bundles of stress once the adrenaline left my system. Scans were done of my back and legs, finding a fracture on my lumbar. My father soon arrived. I wept openly asking to know if the few Scouts I knew were alive, the number who died, and demanded information on the other cabin. He watched, phone in hand, not replying with anything other than "I don't know" in a monotone. He left soon after, not coming back, until the next day to bring me home.

My mother heard about the incident that night on the news. She spent hours calling every contact she had in the Red Cross for information on me, as the news played in the background reporting information as quickly as it came. My father neglected to call her, and he did not pick up when she called, until the next day.

Into the Maze

CYNTHIA CARTER

Fifth grade at Logan View Elementary School

I followed the librarian
Into the maze,
For fear if I went without
I would freeze in a trance.

As I followed her in,
She told a scary tale,
Of ghosts and goblins.
I eyed the graveyard on the roof.

Suddenly the Ghost of Death was
Knocking at the window,
I let out a mere meep,
Scared she would take me.

When I trailed out I was
Quite rattled for the jump
Scare at the end,
I got in line once more.

The volunteers were pounding at
The walls. Though I knew it
Was all fake, I squeezed
Tight my hands.

When we left that night,
I asked my dad
If I could become a
Volunteer next year.

He said "You sure can!"
Into the maze ...

....

This and the following seven poems were written by students in Sheryl
Uehling's fifth grade class at Logan View Elementary School, Hooper,
Nebraska.

The Wig at School

HANNAH JENSEN
Fifth grade at Logan View Elementary School

There once was a wig,
Which was SUPER big.
It was at school,
And it was super cool.
And the pig wore the wig.

Starbucks Coffee

RYLIE PEKAREK
Fifth grade at Logan View Elementary School

Starbucks

Hot, liquid

Steaming, chugging, drinking

Take it to Mrs. Uehling

Coffee

Sun and Moon

HARLEE STEELE
Fifth grade at Logan View Elementary School

Sun

Bright, Shiny
Shining, Floating, Spinning
Gas, Hawaii, Lunar, Space
Moving, Turning, Glimmering
Dark, Glimmer

Moon

Weather Feelings

JAYDEN STILLMAN
Fifth grade at Logan View Elementary School

The weather is nice
It seems to be bright
I feel joyful
It's so wonderful

Now it seems to snow
It's so cold
The wind doesn't help
I wish it will go

Now it started to rain
I'm feeling depressed
This isn't fun
It's also cold
The sun went back home
I wish it could be sunny

Christmas By

AUBREY UHING
Fifth grade at Logan View Elementary School

Sleigh bells ring. Jingles jing. Carols sing.
Lights and decor. Snow is falling. Getting ready for the holidays.

Gifts under the tree soon to be opened. Giving away presents.

School canceled. Late starts. Christmas break.

Get coats on and more because it's gonna snow.
Let it snow. Let it snow. Let it snow!

Sitting by the fire with a blanket. Hot chocolate in one hand.
In my onesie and my fluffy socks.
In the other hand, my phone checking the weather.

Power is off. Get the flashlights.
Here we come batteries and generators.

Wake up on the 25th.
Santa came last night!
Time that the holidays are over.

Music to My Ears

JLYNN VOLLMER
Fifth grade at Logan View Elementary School

Flute
Smooth, squeaky
tweet, twitter, toot
Ask where music shop
Silver

Softball

MARYN WRAGGE
Fifth grade at Logan View Elementary School

Fast pitch and toss,
Pitching, Throwing, Sliding
Softball is the best sport EVER

YOU DON'T KNOW
EVERYTHING!

More than half of the coastline of the entire United States is in Alaska.

The Amazon rainforest produces more than 20% of the world's oxygen supply. The Amazon River pushes so much water into the Atlantic Ocean that, more than one hundred miles at sea off the mouth of the river, one can dip fresh water out of the ocean. The volume of water in the Amazon River is greater than the next eight largest rivers in the world combined and three times the flow of all rivers in the United States.

Antarctica is the only land on our planet that is not owned by any country. Ninety percent of the world's ice covers Antarctica. This ice also represents seventy percent of all the fresh water in the world. As strange as it sounds, however, Antarctica is essentially a desert. The average yearly total precipitation is about two inches. Antarctica is the driest place on the planet, with an absolute humidity lower than the Gobi Desert.

Brazil got its name from the nut, not the other way around.

(Can you top that? Tell us what you know that no one else does.)

Missing the Monsters

DAVID WALLER

"Daddy, please look! There's a monster under there!" Charlie pleaded.

"Charlie, you're seven years old," his dad sighed, irritation creeping into his voice. "You need to grow up a little bit. There are no monsters under your bed, there's no evil clown in your closet, and the tree outside your window is not going to get you. Now stop this silliness and go to bed."

"O-okay," Charlie whimpered, as his dad walked out the door.

"I love you, kiddo."

"I love you, too, Daddy."

Click

The door shut, and the room grew dark. Charlie watched, eyes wide open, as the shadows grew longer and larger, reaching out for him, closing in on him. Something snarled at the foot of his bed, and the boy could feel the bedsprings shift and creak beneath him. A gnarled hand reached out from under the bed, clawing at his mattress as it pulled itself up with its long, hairy arms. Another hand joined it, and a rotten smell permeated the air. As Charlie watched, a face emerged from the darkness. It had putrid, grey skin and was surrounded by matted, mangy fur. Its yellow eyes glowed in the darkness, and what looked like blood curdled around its fanged mouth.

It bared its teeth and snarled, "Aren't you gonna hide under the covers, Charlie?"

"My daddy says you're not real, and I need to grow up and stop being scared of you," Charlie whispered, more ashamed and sad than frightened.

The monster winced. "Oh," it said, no longer snarling. "He said that, huh?"

Charlie nodded.

"Hoo boy," the monster sighed. "Wasn't ready for this kind of talk tonight." It shuffled out from under the bed and sat on the end of the mattress, its hands in its lap. It took a deep breath and sighed again.

"Look, Charlie," it said, fidgeting. "I'm sure your dad didn't mean to be so brusque about it."

"Brusque?" Charlie interrupted.

"It means, like, rough," the monster continued. "He's just got a lot on his mind. You see, when you get older, you stop being afraid of monsters under the bed, and you start getting scared of a lot of other things. Different things."

"Like what?"

"Well, like money."

"Money's not scary."

"No, but running out of it is. Your dad has to worry about keeping his job, paying his bills, and feeding you guys. He also worries about sending you to the right school, about bullying, tests, and other things that might happen to you. Then there's the stuff he sees on the news, and that'd scare the *bejeezus* out of anyone. Not to mention he's a single dad, so he's scared he's gonna mess up and not raise you and your brother Tom right. Heck, Tom just came out of the closet, and he's not sure how to handle that."

"Closet?"

"I've been in his closet," another voice added. "He just stuffs it with things he doesn't want to put away. How's he supposed to fit in there in the first place? I don't think you know what you're talking about, Gargrok."

"That's not what I'm talking about, Chuckles," the monster growled, turning towards Charlie's closet. "Clowns, I swear," it said, shaking its head.

"So, what am I supposed to do?" Charlie asked.

"Nothing," the monster said, in a very matter-of-fact tone. "For now, just be a kid. Draw weird things on the walls and color outside the lines. Play a ton of video games, eat ice cream, run around outside, fall off your bike and chip a tooth. Just enjoy the time you have right now. You'll look back and fondly remember the time when all you had to be afraid of was monsters, but that stuff will worry about itself when the time comes. For now, forget about it and enjoy life. That's your only job, now. And maybe cut your dad some slack, you know?"

"Okay, I'll do that," Charlie said, smiling up at the monster.

The monster gave him a toothy smile of its own and patted him on the head with its gaunt, clawed hand.

"Now, you get back under those covers," it said. "I wouldn't want to have to bite your toes off after this little talk."

"Okay."

"Good night, kiddo."

"Good night, monster."

With that, the monster shuffled off the bed and crawled underneath it, back into the shadows. Charlie pulled his blanket over himself, taking extra effort to make sure no body parts poked out for the monsters to find, and went to sleep.

"I'm gonna miss that kid," the tree outside the window sighed.

"Yeah, I know," the monster replied.

FINE LINES

We encourage submissions to *Fine Lines*. We have printed writing by an eight-year-old third grader, a ninety-four-year-old great, great grandmother, students, teachers, professors, janitors, doctors, lawyers, ministers, truck drivers, nurses, and scientists. If you want to read interesting ideas, *Fine Lines* is for you. Send us a submission, and you could become a published writer, too.

What to submit: We welcome articles on topics of interest to our readers about interesting life experiences. Our editors encourage a variety of styles. We accept articles and practical submissions that describe innovative views of life's challenges. We are glad to receive work encouraging stimulating dialog that crosses traditional rhetorical and disciplinary boundaries, forms, and roles. We provide a forum for writers of all ability levels. We reserve the right to reject submissions that use profanity, abusive violence in all forms, alcohol, and drugs.

What we disclaim: The views expressed in *Fine Lines* are solely those of the authors. Therefore, *Fine Lines* is not intended to represent any author's political or religious point of view. Our purpose is to be a capable writing vehicle for all serious, intelligent, and compassionate thinkers.

What we require: Submissions must be sent via email file-attachments or laser-quality hard copies. If replies are requested, include a self-addressed, stamped envelope, or mention this in the submission. Use the MLA format with all submissions. To complete your submission, include a one paragraph autobiographical statement and a digital, head-shoulder photo. When sending submissions via email, submit all work in Microsoft Word (.doc) or in Adobe Portable Document Format (.pdf). Send correspondence to Fine Lines, PO Box 241713, Omaha, NE 68124. Send your questions, comments, concerns, and letters to the editor at fine-lines@cox.net.

Fine Lines Summer Writing Camps: Our week-long "campers" range in age from third grade to senior adults, and every session is filled with comedy, art, dance, music, history, and writing. These week-long workshops are filled with inspiration. They motivate authors to tackle their writing projects. Check our website for more details.

Remember, if it is not written down, it did not happen. Improved literacy adds clarity and passion to our lives. Composition is hard work, and it brings order to chaos, beauty to existence, and celebration to the mysterious.

Scarlet Flax: Summer Wildflower Beauty
Photo by Ron Boerner

Lessons My Younger Brother Taught Me

BRIANNA WARNER

"Do good to others and every man can be a Superman," a quote from the *Superman* comic books fits my younger brother perfectly in the way he lived his life. He never cared about someone's race, nor what they had done in their past. He was a friend to everyone and anyone who needed it. Brothers truly are a blessing in disguise whether we are willing to admit it or not. For me, my brother was my superhero. I may have never realized it, but I was learning life lessons as I grew up next to him.

All younger brothers are weird. They do those silly little things that can make it hard to be seen with them in public sometimes. Every time we would go to the grocery store, he would dance down the aisles. He never cared who was watching him. He embraced his inner weirdness. Even if I would just roll my eyes and turn beet red whenever he did it, I knew in my heart that was him just being himself. It was okay to be weird. My brother was never afraid to show who he truly was to me, to our family, or to the rest of the world. He had a "Take me as I am or not at all" mentality. The weekend before my brother got sick, we went to a football game with our dad, and our two other siblings. He was in his total element: loud music, sports, and food. That was the weirdest he ever was. At halftime, they were playing music, and my brother stood up from his seat and started to dance. He did not think twice about it. He started dancing and singing and laughing without a care in the world. His weirdness was one of the things that would always manage to cheer me up. I could be bawling my eyes out, and he would come up to me and make a weird face and start talking about something incredibly random. He would make me forget why I was crying in the first place. Being able to be weird is truly the most liberating feeling in the world. He taught me that being myself is acceptable, and anyone who does not accept that is not worth my time. As the youngest sibling of the five of us, he was the brunt of all of our jokes, and he was happy with that. He knew it was okay to laugh at himself, and almost always he would join in and make fun of himself with the rest of us.

My brother taught me to never give up on anything. He would tell me that I have yet to experience my hardest battle. When I was eight years old, my mother told us she was pregnant with the new addition to our family, a baby boy. My parents were overjoyed and filled with pure excitement as they always wanted to have a large family. My brother was so loved before he was even born, and in January of 2009 my family welcomed the newest and final member of our family. He was very early and faced health complications from the start, but he was loved. My mother did not get to bring my brother home from the hospital this time around, as she had her own post-delivery complications to tend to, so, I stepped in. I played the role as a proud big sister and helped take care of my brother for the first two months of his life. When he was three months old, he developed a respiratory infection, and the doctors told us that it would bring hardships into his life until the day he died, not knowing when that would be. My brother fought the odds and got over his infection quickly and would go on to live out a practically normal life. He never developed asthma as the doctors predicted he would and he very rarely got sick. My brother was an absolute champion when it came to beating the odds. My brother was my superhero. When he was diagnosed with leukemia in March of this year, he fought it with every breath he took. My brother beat leukemia, which is something I know he would be proud of. What he could never beat was the everlasting effects it had on his body. My brother passed away exactly one month after being diagnosed, and he fought for all of that month. He never gave up, and he was right, I have yet to experience my hardest battle. Even struggling with addiction, I thought that would end up being the hardest thing I would ever have to go through in my life. I never thought I would lose someone I was so close to, who was the perfect representation of a good person.

My brother was a true inspiration to so many people, including me. I never gave up when it came to suffering through the pains of withdrawal, and I definitely never gave up when it came to the pain of losing him. Grief takes a lot from a person, including the will to live, but knowing that my brother was able to go through something so painful, I knew that I could go through this pain. My brother is my motivation for going through a hard situation, and my life was never easy. He taught me that giving up was never the answer, and if I were to do that, I was weak. Losing him was only a speed bump in this story, because I know he would never want me to give up.

There are so few people on this planet who know how to love someone unconditionally. Everyone is capable of love, as well as deserving of it, but rarely does anyone truly understand what it means to unconditionally love someone. My brother never needed a reason to love someone. He just did it, and he did it with such raw passion. He was the person who would want to be anyone, and everyone's friend, whether they liked it or not. My brother was the shoulder to lean on when times get hard, and better yet, he was a living example of a good friend. At my brother's funeral, we had around five-hundred people in attendance ranging from kids from the neighborhood, his bus driver, teachers from his school. Anyone who had my brother in his life came to say their goodbyes. My brother loved every single one of them in his own special way. It is still hard to believe he is gone, but I know his unconditional love still manages to rain down from above. I still find myself talking to him about my hard days, and people may look at me like I am crazy, but he was my shoulder to lean on through everything.

My brother taught me that it is completely normal to miss someone. I miss my brother every second of the day. I would give anything to pick up the phone and call him, just to hear his voice one more time. My brother is my entire world, and that will never change. He was a gift given to my family when we never thought it would be possible, and we loved him for the entire nine years and three months of his life. Days are hard without his laugh, and his smile, but it is okay to miss him, because I am a human who was given the gift of an amazing younger brother. I often sit and wonder what his life could have been if he had never been sick. Would he have been a doctor, or maybe even a musician? One thing I do know is that he is my superhero.

People often think of their siblings as an annoyance, but that is something I will refuse to do. Siblings were given to us for a reason, to teach us something in our lives. My brother taught me so many things in his short life, and he was wise beyond his years. He taught me patience and kindness. He taught me how to laugh at my own mistakes. He taught me that it is one-hundred-percent okay to cry when a sad commercial comes on the television. My brother is the real reason I have become the person I am, and I often envy the person he was. I know that no one on this planet is perfect, and I know that even more now that my brother is gone, because I know that my brother was truly a perfect person. My only hope in this life is to be the person he was, and I will continue to share his story of hope and positivity. My brother taught me so many things in his nine short years of life, and I am forever grateful for every lesson.

WRITING UNITES US!

"I don't care where I am.
I compose."

ANDRE PREVIN

"May you be at peace.
May your heart remain open.
May you awaken to the light of your own true nature.
May you be healed.
May you be a source of healing for all beings."

TIBETAN BUDDHIST PRAYER

"There are four things in this life that will change you.
Love, music, art, and loss.
The first three will keep you wild and full of passion.
May you allow the last to make you brave."

ERIN VAN BUREN

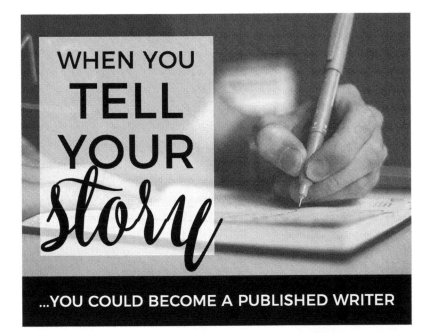

CONTRIBUTORS

TESSA ADAMS: "Life is beautiful! I am a creative writing teacher and an English 9 teacher at Millard South High School, Omaha, NE. I love what I do. When I'm not at school, I am with my husband playing with our three children. I enjoy running, playing with my dogs, reading, and writing."

LUCY ADKINS received her bachelor's degree at Auburn University in Alabama. Her poetry has been published in *Nebraska Territory, Plainsongs*, and the anthologies *Woven on the Wind, Times of Sorrow-Times of Grace, The Poets Against the War,* and *Crazy Woman Creek*. She leads several writers' workshops.

TRACY AHRENS lives in Illinois, has been a journalist/writer for over 25 years and has published seven books, including two books of poetry. As of January 2018, she had earned 60 writing awards locally, statewide, and nationally. She is a member of the Illinois Woman's Press Association, National Federation of Press Women, Dog Writers Association of America, and the Cat Writers' Association. Her author statement reads: "Poetry is an escape for me from journalistic writing. It's a time to play with words as life moves me. It's the ultimate brevity — a pen stroke — a signature that etches lasting impressions."

DUANE ANDERSON is currently living in La Vista, NE. He graduated from Augustana College in Rock Island, IL, and worked at the Union Pacific Railroad for 37 years. After his retirement in 2013, he started writing poetry. He had his poems published in *Saga, Poetry Now, Telephone, Lunch, Touchstone, Pastiche: Poems of Place,* and the *Omaha World-Herald* in the late 1970s and '80s.

STEVE BARBER is an old guy living in Portland, Oregon, who spends his time reading, writing, and hiking with his dog and other friends. He has had numerous stories published in various journals.

GARY BECK has spent most of his adult life as a theater director, and as an art dealer when he couldn't make a living in theater. He has eleven published chapbooks and three more accepted for publication. His original plays and translations of Moliere, Aristophanes and Sophocles have been produced Off Broadway. His poetry, fiction and essays have appeared in hundreds of literary magazines. He currently lives in New York City.

JOSEPH S. BENSON is a veteran, retired educator, and writes from Hiawatha, Kansas.

ALLISSANDRA BEQUETTE is a senior in high school, dual-enrolled in several foreign language and literature university courses. She has worked at independent, non-profit art organizations as a classroom assistant and for several publications which contribute to the promotion of culture around the world. These experiences have given her a wide societal perspective and the wish to apply that perspective to fiction and poetry. She is most interested in reating a space where people of all genders, nationalities, and more can feel understood through their universal emotions.

RON BOERNER is a native Nebraskan, born in Nebraska City and now living in North Platte, where he moved in 1969 to take a teaching job at North Platte High School. That is also where he met his wife-to-be, Sheila, an English teacher there at the time.

KRISTI BOLLING: "My story is, well, stories. I have been writing them for as long I can remember. I'm always going on adventures with my writing. I'll never forget the first work of mine that was published. I was so excited that I couldn't stop talking about it. Later in high school, I was told to make a portfolio for English class. I wrote the first two chapters of a book that other kids would finish for me. I'm still writing stories. There's just something about writing that opens up a secret part that I never knew I had in me."

JANET BONET writes fiction as J Eleanor Bonet to honor her Aunt Eleanor, who encouraged her to "just be as crazy as you want to be and don't give a hoot about what others think." She writes non-fiction as Janet E. Bonet, for academic and community activism purposes. Her educational background reaches to the "all but thesis" level in anthropology/sociology, and she has a BA minor in Spanish. She is a freelance professional translator and interpreter, because she loves words and is dedicated to social and environmental justice. She resides in the house she was raised in on the edge of South Omaha's Spring Lake Park. She is happily letting her yard revert back to the wildwood it was meant to be. In her mind, nature should be natural.

SUSAN GRADY BRISTOL is a member of the National League of American Pen Women, Omaha Branch.

LIN BRUMMELS is a Nebraska licensed mental health practitioner and certified professional counselor. She earned a bachelor's degree in psychology from the University of Nebraska-Lincoln and a master's degree In Rehabilitation Counseling from Syracuse University. She has published poetry in *Paddlefish,* the *San Pedro River Review, Plainsongs,* Nebraska *Life Magazine,* and several anthologies. Her essay "Civilization" was published in *Ankle High and Knee Deep,* a collection of women's reflections on western rural life. Her poetry chapbook, *Hard Times,* was published by *Finishing Line Press* in 2015 and won the 2016 Nebraska Book Award for chapbooks. *Cottonwood Strong,* also from *Finishing Line Press,* was published in 2019.

DEREK BURDENY is an award winning, internationally recognized photographer from Omaha, Nebraska. Derek's main photographic passions are chasing severe weather through tornado alley in the central USA, to chasing solar storms and the aurora borealis in far northern Norway. See more of his photos at www.derekburdenyphotography.com.

JAYME BUSSING graduated from Yutan, NE, High School and Metropolitan Community College, Omaha, with a major in Creative Writing. She is now working on a Bachelor's Degree in English Literature (major) and Creative Writing (minor) at Purdue University.

AMANDA CAILLAU is past President of the National Art Educators Association, University of Nebraska at Omaha student chapter, a graduate of UNO, and teaches art in the Omaha area.

MARY CAMPBELL, a native of Omaha, NE, is a writer, musician, writing coach, and certified meditation instructor whose award-winning poetry has appeared in scores of periodicals, including publications of the Kansas Poetry Society and the Arizona Poetry Society. A longtime writer and editor at the University of Arizona, Mary is the author, coauthor, or ghostwriter of more than twenty books. She has written or co-written hundreds of songs, poems, stories, essays, news and magazine features, blog posts, and podcasts. Mary has composed for and directed children's and adults' choirs; has led church-school, preschool, and meditation classes; has taught in a nationwide children's ballroom-dance program; and has produced three children and, indirectly, nine grandchildren.

KATIE CAMERON is a mom and wife, theatre enthusiast, amateur photographer and occasional quilter. She volunteers at many arts organizations in and around Omaha, and works as a school counselor at Benson High School.

BUD CASSIDAY is an artist and English teacher. He works at Metropolitan Community College in Elkhorn, NE. Some of his artwork and writing may be found at artbycassiday.blogspot.com.

YUAN CHANGMING lives in Vancouver, British Columbia, Canada, where he edits *Poetry Pacific.* He was nominated ten times for Pushcart awards, has been published over 1,000 times across 43 countries, and won the 2018 Naji Naaman's Literary Prize.

GENEVIEVE CHEREK-GARCIA: "I love life and do things-from the heart. My life has been diversified. I went to business school, ran a childcare business, studied piano and voice, have written music, like to sing, write poetry, create art, and at one time was a professional dance teacher in New York, Chicago, Atlanta, Missouri, and Virginia. I have gained all my knowledge from reading and doing research. I especially like ancient history. I have four adult children and was married for 52 years.

ED CONNOLLY is a retired business executive, lives in Hawaii and Omaha, and enjoys writing memoir articles.

GEOFF FITZGERALD is an artist, photographer, and Wolverine Watch Biologist in Montana.

KRISTI FITZGERALD had her first poem, "The Great Big Lion from Nastle," and accompanying illustration published in the local newspaper when she was nine years old. She has bachelor's degrees in English and theater with graduate work in costume design. She is a member of Willamette Writers, is a finisher of NaNoWriMo for two years running, and belongs to two writer's groups. She has had two articles and two poems published in *Renaissance Magazine* and several stories in *Chicken Soup for the Soul*. She's currently editing her first novel, a young adult fantasy, with dreams of publication. She lives in Hamilton, Montana.

MARCIA CALHOUN FORECKI lives in Council Bluffs, IA. Her academic background is in the Spanish language. She earned a Master of Arts Degree from the University of Wisconsin-Milwaukee. Her first book, *Speak to Me*, about her son's deafness, was published by Gallaudet University Press and earned a national book award. Her story "The Gift of the Spanish Lady" was published in the *Bellevue Literary Journal* and nominated for a Pushcart Prize.

NANCY GENEVIEVE is a Special Editor for *Fine Lines* and an Emerita Associate Professor of English at the University of Illinois at Springfield (UIS). She taught creative writing for ten years at Eureka College (IL) before teaching creative writing for ten years at UIS; she retired in 2010, and she and her husband live in Massachusetts.

ELIZABETH GRAHAM is from Gallup, NM, and a sophomore at the University of Nebraska in Lincoln. Ever since she was little, she has loved to write.

LEILONNI HAGLER: "Writing has been my passion since I was a little girl. I was published in a young writer's anthology when I was in high school and have been dreaming of being a writer ever since! I am currently taking online courses for my bachelor's degree in English at the University of Phoenix, working towards my goal to teach creative writing. You can follow my writing at leilonnihagler@weebly.com."

MOLLY HALLIGAN is a stay-at-home mom who lives in Ralston, NE, and writes poetry.

AMANDA B. HANSEN-WEIGNER is proud to call herself a recent graduate of the University of Nebraska at Omaha. She holds her Bachelor's in General Studies and is certified in English Literature, Music, and Creative Writing. She is a recent addition to the *Fine Lines* Journal Editorial staff and posts for their Social Media sites, where she feels she is part of a team. She is a stay-at-home mom who owns an Etsy shop called Stitchery Poetry, where she cross-stitches her own poetry. She resides in Omaha with her husband, newborn son, and their family dog, Max. Her poetry can be found in countless issues of *Fine Lines*, as well as *13th Floor Magazine*. You can find more about Amanda at her website, www.amandabeatricehansen.com.

PATRICIA HARRIS is a teacher at Monroe Middle School in the Omaha Public Schools.

KATHIE HASKINS lives in Papillion, Nebraska, with her husband, Joel, and son Jay. She enjoys writing poems and reflections about nature, everyday life, and is grateful to be a special editor of *Fine Lines*. Her hobbies include gardening, backyard bird watching, and reading.

NIA KARMANN: "Having the opportunity to share my outlook on life and the amazing beauty and wonder that God has given us is my passion. I receive great pleasure in capturing a fraction of God's awe-inspiring canvas while taking photos, and, in doing so, it allows me to express my freedom while escaping the box that Spina Bifida creates. Shooting from a wheelchair gives my work a unique perspective of unusual angles, shapes, and scenes, and I am very willing to do whatever it takes to capture the right angle. I am an award winning photographer and have been published in magazines and hope my work inspires every reader of *Fine Lines*."

NEHA KHALID "I attend Westside High School and am currently a senior. I will be attending college in the fall but have not decided where. I love to write because it helps me deal with the stress that I experience in school. Expressing myself is important because no one can understand me without hearing my thoughts and beliefs, items that can be expressed through writing. I express myself so people can understand what it is truly like being a child of immigrants. I want people to understand the everyday struggles that we go through. I want people to see us as humans, too."

DESHAE LOTT: From 1993–2017, she taught English courses at one of these universities: Louisiana State University in Shreveport, Texas A&M University, and the University of Illinois at Springfield. Spirituality and living with a disability both infuse her professional scholarship, essays, and poetry. In 2011, Lott received for one of her essays an EXCEL Gold Medal from Association Media and Publishing. She has served as a co-editor of the American Religion and Literature Society Newsletter and has published on a variety of nineteenth-and twentieth-century Americans including Margaret Fuller, George Moses Horton, Mary Mann, Julia Smith, Walt Whitman, Jack Kerouac, George Oppen, Maya Angelou, and Annie Dillard. A mixture of syncretism and individualism appears in mysticism, and Lott's teaching and publishing primarily highlight mystics who concurrently endeavor to and model how to contribute constructively to their communities.

PRESTON LOVE, JR. has a Bachelor of Science Degree from the University of Nebraska, Lincoln; a Master's Degree from Bellevue University, Omaha, in Professional Studies; and many career accomplishments. A few are listed here: former UNL (Husker) football player and Detroit Lions draftee; IBM pioneer marketing executive (1966–1980); opened Atlanta's first retail computer store in 1980; organized and ran Jesse Jackson's presidential candidacy in 1984; wrote and performs: *Adam Clayton Powell*, a one-man performance; award-winning newspaper columnist (*Omaha Star* column "Black Votes Matter"; national lecturer: Nashville Film Festival (on urban voting and the documentary film, *One Vote)*; UNO Adjunct Professor (teaches African-American Experience in Politics); author: *Economic Cataracts, The Jackson Papers*, and *"Bridge to Your History"*; originator of the Black Votes Matter Initiative; Nebraska Black Sports Hall of Fame Inductee; Commendation for Excellence from Nebraska Secretary of State for *Omaha Star* Newspaper Column; NAACP Presidents Award (2018); presented the Distinguished Citizen Award by the West Point Society of Nebraska and Western Iowa on March 30, 2019, at its annual West Point Founders Day in Omaha, Nebraska.

WENDY LUNDEEN retired from teaching in the Omaha Public School District, where she taught Spanish at Central High School and at Alice Buffett Middle School. Señora Lundeen is a "Yaya" to six grandchildren and is writing a book about her two grandsons' struggles with Duchenne Muscular Dystrophy, a terminal illness. Her passions include writing poetry, singing in the church choir, traveling, acting, and dancing every year as "Oma" in *Nutcracker Delights*. For more than a decade, she has led a group of young writers every year at the *Fine Lines* Summer Creative Writing Camp.

DAVID MARTIN is the founder and managing editor of *Fine Lines*, a non-profit quarterly journal that has published creative writing by "young authors of all ages" since 1992. All writers are welcome to submit their poetry, prose, photography, and artwork. This publication has printed work by authors from all fifty states and forty other countries. The website (www.finelines.org) has more information about submission guidelines and a sample journal to view. He has published two books of essays and poetry (*Facing the Blank Page* and *Little Birds with Broken Wings*), which may be found at Boutique of Quality Books, www.bqbpublishing.com.

VINCE MCANDREW is retired from the Omaha Public Schools, where he was a teacher, counselor, and administrator. He is now giving full attention to his grandchildren and his poetry.

BARB MOTES: "As a retired educator, I plan to spend time exploring the life and environment around me. Being a Colorado native, I have always had an appreciation for nature and its beauty. The use of photography enables me to express that passion for nature."

DR. STEVEN NORDEEN is Professor Emeritus, Department of Pathology, at the University of Colorado Denver School of Medicine, Anschutz Medical Campus, Aurora, CO. "In my semi-retirement, I have picked up writing again, trying to hone my craft. Hopefully, as an attendee at one of Bill Kloefkorn's readings said to him afterwards, 'I liked your poems, even though I understood them.'"

KRISTEN NORMAN is a poet who writes in Edgartown, MA.

ANNE OBRADOVICH works as a lab technician at Creighton University, Omaha, NE, researching zebra fish inner ear development. She completed her B.S. in biology and French at Creighton. In her free time, Anne enjoys writing poetry, playing the trombone, knitting, and scuba diving.

JOANNA O'KEEFE, a graduate of Syracuse University in New York, is the author of five books of poetry. Her classic poem, "Come to the Garden" was read at the 51 National Prayer Breakfast in Washington, D.C. "Writing, I found was a bridge to wholeness — a way to get in touch with my feelings, hopes, and dreams, a way to listen to the Spirit's voice within." One of her most recent accomplishments is her poem turned into song, "America at the Crossroads," released in 2014. JoAnna has been offering presentations integrating her poetry with spirituality since 1991. She lives in Omaha, Nebraska, with her husband Jack. To learn more about JoAnna visit her website at www.joannaokeefe.com.

ANDY PAPPAS is a manager at Valentino's Pizza in Lincoln, NE. His passions are many. Primarily, he writes song lyrics, plays the piano, and sings with his band, Normal Blvd. He likes to make people get up out of their chairs and dance.

RHONDA PARSONS is a member of the Rockford, Illinois, Writer's Guild. Her first book, *If a Picture Is Worth a Thousand Words,* won the Rockford Writer's Guild Award. She draws her inspiration from nature and sees it as source of spiritual wisdom. Her dogs are her joy.

TORI PEDERSEN is a freshman at the University of Nebraska-Lincoln from Omaha, Nebraska. She is studying Hospitality and dreams of one day planning concerts and also working with some non-profits. In her free time, she loves to write poetry, play the ukulele, and spend time outside.

CHARLENE PIERCE is a local sales manager of the *Omaha World Herald* newspaper.

CATHY PORTER: her poetry has appeared in *Plainsongs, Chaffin Journal, Kentucky Review, Hubbub, Homestead Review,* and various other journals in the US and UK. She has two chapbooks available from Finishing Line Press: *A Life in the Day* and *Dust and Angels.* Her most recent collection, *Exit Songs,* was released in 2016 from Dancing Girl Press in Chicago. She is a two-time Pushcart Prize nominee. She works at Iowa Western Community College and lives in Omaha, NE, with her husband, Lenny, their golden retriever, Lucky, and the king and queen cats, Cody and Mini. Feel free to contact her at clcon@q.com.

FABRICE POUSSIN: "I'm the advisor for *The Chimes,* the Shorter University award winning poetry and arts publication in Rome, GA. My writing and photography have been published in print, including *Kestrel, Symposium, La Pensee Universelle, Paris,* and other art and literature magazines in the United States and abroad."

DAVID REINARZ has been writing fiction short stories and poetry since 2015, when he participated in the "7 Doctors Writers Workshop" sponsored by the University of Nebraska Medical Center and The Nebraska Writers Collective. He continues to participate in a "7 Doctors" Alumni Group. He lives in Omaha with the love of his life, Lynne. He graduated from Benson High School, attended the University of Nebraska at Omaha, and graduated with a BA in Philosophy and Religious Studies. He is retired from a thirty year career of managing professional retail bicycle shops.

ROBERT RICKER has a Bachelor's Degree in History from UNO. He served four years in the U.S. Air Force, is a voracious reader, and likes politics, economics, and Tolstoy.

JOHN TIMOTHY ROBINSON is a graduate of the Marshall University Creative Writing Program in Huntington, West Virginia. He has an interest in critical theory of poetry and American formalism. He is an educator for Mason County Schools, WV, and is working on a creative dissertation in contemporary poetry.

ROBERT RUNYON grew up in Summit, New Jersey. At Wesleyan University, he studied philosophy, psychology, and the French language. He later received a Master's Degree in Library Science from Rutgers University. For over thirty years, he served as an academic library administrator. Sometime after retirement from the University of Nebraska at Omaha's Criss Library in 2001, he returned to UNO to take courses in Creative Nonfiction. Now an octogenarian, he is working on a memoir of travel, family, nature, and aging.

MARJORIE SAISER lives in Lincoln, NE, and is the author of six books of poetry and co-editor of two anthologies. Her work has been published in *American Life in Poetry, Nimrod, Rattle.com, PoetryMagazine.com, RHINO, Chattahoochee Review, Poetry East, Poet Lore,* and other journals. She has received the WILLA Award and nominations for the Pushcart Prize.

JAMES M. SALHANY is a retired professor of internal medicine and biochemistry at the University of Nebraska Medical Center, where he taught and performed research in molecular biophysics. He did his graduate studies at the University of Chicago, where he obtained his Master's and PhD degrees. His poems attempt to present scientific concepts in humanistic terms. Now, he spends most of his time writing and producing song recordings. He has 110 original songs on Reverb Nation, where his songs are ranked #1 in the nation. He is on the *Fine Lines* Board of Directors.

SALLY SANDLER: At once transcendent and accessible, Sandler's writing gives voice to her generation of Baby Boomers and their elders. She illuminates their shared concerns over the passage of time and fading idealism, the death of parents, and loss of the environment, while maintaining hope for wisdom yet to come. Sandler writes in classic forms to honor poetry's roots while also addressing contemporary issues. She is a graduate of the University of Michigan and lives in San Diego, California.

STUART SEDLAK is a student at Metropolitan Community College in Omaha, NE. There's no place he would rather be than at a ballpark. A huge baseball fan, he enjoys attending Kansas City Royals and Omaha Storm Chasers games. He looks forward to taking his new son, Carson, to future contests.

SUE SHELBURNE is originally from Kentucky but now lives in Omaha, NE. She enjoys decorating, photography, acrylics, and writing, which has been a constant companion in her life for as long as she can remember. Writing is her therapist, her friend through lonely times, and her mirror that reflects best. Putting words together has never been a laborious thing for her, because she writes the words that want to be written and in the way they want to be expressed. It is her responsibility not to censor them. When she honors that responsibility, they read back to her with a light of their own truth.

D. N. SIMMERS lives in British Columbia, Canada, and writes poetry. He is an on-line *Fine Lines* editor. Widely published in the USA, he has also been published in England, Wales, and New Zealand.

KALPNA SINGH-CHITNIS: Born and raised in the land of the Buddha, Gaya, Bihar, India, she began to write poetry at the age of fourteen. She moved to the United States in 1994, leaving behind her promising career as a Lecturer of Political Science, Actor, and a Fashion Model in Mumbai. She lived in Chicagoland for nine years, before coming to Los Angeles, and pursuing a degree in Film Directing at the New York Film Academy, at the Universal Studios in Hollywood, from where she graduated in 2004. Known for her directorial debut feature *Goodbye My Friend* and *Girl with an Accent*, she is also the founder and director of the Silent River Film and Literary Society" and the festival director of the Silent River Film Festival in the USA. "I opened my eyes to find poetry before me. I turned my back on it to face reality. Ever since I'm transformed into a river of songs."

KIM MCNEALY SOSIN was a professor and department chair of economics at the University of Nebraska at Omaha, until her retirement a few years ago. She published numerous articles in economics journals and created and continues to maintain several websites. She enjoys photography and writing and has been focused on reading and writing poetry. She also collects vintage fountain pens.

LAURA STREETER is an Omaha, NE, native who has enjoyed writing most of her life. She enjoys writing poetry, essays, and song lyrics. She is a musician and singer and performs with the band Bazile Mills, an alternative indie folk rock band, who write their own original songs. Laura is a contributing writer and composer for the band, sings, plays keyboard, guitar, and ukulele. You can hear Bazile Mill's songs on Spotify, Sound Cloud, iTunes, and CDBaby. Laura was inspired by her late Aunt, "Rosie" Weskirchen Maher, a former English and Drama teacher.

JAMES TILLOTSON is a student in Omaha, Nebraska, currently working on a degree in English literature and creative writing. He is working on writing and publishing his short stories. His preferred genres are horror and romance.

DAVID WALLER joined *Fine Lines* as an intern in the fall of 2014 and has since become a permanent member of the journal's staff. He regularly submits essays and short stories, the latter which he hopes to collect into a book after he's written enough of them. He has had numerous pieces published in *Fine Lines,* and his favorite thing about writing is character creation.

PLEASE SUPPORT OUR SPONSORS

Now Available:

In *Come with Me,* Kate finds herself in a dream, walking through a secret door in her closet and into the outdoors. Kate takes flight, soaring with white doves, riding silky swans, weaving through the branches of trees and catching pink flower petals floating in the wind. She is wrapped in lullaby breezes under the moon and stars.

"As the author herself battled cancer, Tracy Ahrens was inspired by the strength and tenderness that young Kate had as she too fought this terrible disease. Come With Me gently carries the reader through the beauty and wonder of life, even if it is only a dream."

ANNA GROB, AUTHOR OF THE WILD ANIMAL SURVIVAL SERIES

Available at Amazon.com

Now Available:

Print Edition at Amazon.com
Full-Color PDF Edition at FineLines.org

Silver Departures

Kathy Hastings

Traditional paintings and photography
www.kathyhastings.com • email: dkstudios@aol.com
(360) 920-6634

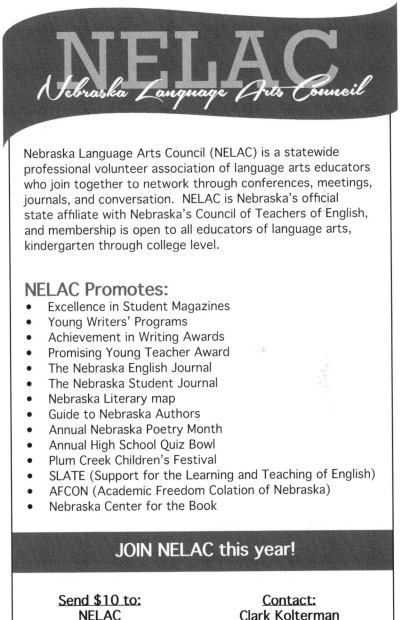

Nebraska Language Arts Council (NELAC) is a statewide professional volunteer association of language arts educators who join together to network through conferences, meetings, journals, and conversation. NELAC is Nebraska's official state affiliate with Nebraska's Council of Teachers of English, and membership is open to all educators of language arts, kindergarten through college level.

NELAC Promotes:

- Excellence in Student Magazines
- Young Writers' Programs
- Achievement in Writing Awards
- Promising Young Teacher Award
- The Nebraska English Journal
- The Nebraska Student Journal
- Nebraska Literary map
- Guide to Nebraska Authors
- Annual Nebraska Poetry Month
- Annual High School Quiz Bowl
- Plum Creek Children's Festival
- SLATE (Support for the Learning and Teaching of English)
- AFCON (Academic Freedom Colation of Nebraska)
- Nebraska Center for the Book

JOIN NELAC this year!

Send $10 to:
NELAC
PO Box 83944
Lincoln, NE 68501-3944

Contact:
Clark Kolterman
Ckolte00@connectseward.org

AFCON
Academic Freedom Coalition of Nebraska

Academic Freedom Coalition of Nebraska promotes academic freedom in education and research contexts. This includes freedoms of belief and expression and access to information and ideas.

As a Member, you can help us:

- Support applications of the First Amendment in academic contexts, including elementary and secondary schools, colleges, universities, and libraries.

- Educate Nebraskans about the meaning and value of intellectual freedom, intellectual diversity, mutual respect, open communication, and uninhibited pursuit of knowledge, including the role of these ideas in academic contexts and in democratic self-government.

- Assist students, teachers, librarians, and researchers confronted with censorship, indoctrination, or suppression of ideas.

- Act as a liason among groups in Nebraska that support academic freedom issues.

To become a member:

Send dues, organization or individual name, address and phone number to:
Cathi McCurtry
15 N. Thomas Avenue
Oakland, Nebraska 68045

AFCONebr.org

2019 Summer Camp for Creative Writers
Grades 4-12, College, and Adults

Dream   Reflect   Journey
Imagine Explore
Create   Discover
Travel

Write On!   The road less traveled...

This is our 20th year of creating *Fine Lines* writing summer camps for students of all ages. Join writers who add clarity and passion to their lives with the written word. We have fun with sentences, learn to play while developing poems, stories, essays, and discover creative corners of our minds that we did not know existed.

Where: Beveridge Magnet Middle School
1616 S 120th St, Omaha, NE 68144
When: June 24-28, 8:30 a.m. – 12:00 p.m.

Use PayPal or make checks out to *Fine Lines* ($150/person). The registration fee includes a camp T-shirt, snacks, guest speakers, editing help, and possible publication in the *Fine Lines* quarterly journal.

- -

Name _____ Age/Grade (next Sept.) _____

Address _____ City/St _____ Zip Code _____

Phone _____ Email _____

School _____ T-shirt size: (circle) Adult: S M L XL 2X Youth: S M L XL

During *Fine Lines'* camps, photos for publicity are taken. When attending this event, we may include your image. Release Signature: Parent-Guardian-Camper _____.

This camper has read and agrees to the 2019 Participation Waiver and Release agreement.
Signature: Parent-Guardian-Camper _____.

Camp Director: David Martin, fine-lines@cox.net, 402-871-3682
Fine Lines is a 501(c) (3) non-profit organization (www.finelines.org).
Send checks to *Fine Lines*, PO Box 241713, Omaha, NE 68124.
PayPal is available (www.paypal.com).

www.finelines.org

Made in the USA
Columbia, SC
11 June 2019